Ethnic Diasporas & Great Power Strategies in Asia

Robert Wirsing
&
Rouben Azizian

India Research Press
&
Asia-Pacific Center for Security Studies
Honolulu, Hawaii

Ethnic Diasporas &
Great Power Strategies in Asia
Robert Wirsing & Rouben Azizian

India Research Press
Flat No.6, Khan Market, New Delhi - 110 003
Ph.: 24694610; Fax : 24618637
www.indiaresearchpress.com
contact@indiaresearchpress.com; bahrisons@vsnl.com

2007

ISBN thirteen: 978-81-8386-032-1
ISBN ten: 81-8386-032-X

Cataloguing data
includes Bibliography & Index
1. Ethnicity : India /China /Russia 2. Diaspora : India /China /Russia
3. Migration : India /China /Russia
4. Socio-Economy : India /China /Russia
5. Strategic Alliance : India /China /Russia
I. Title II. Author

Printed for *India Research Press* at Focus Impressions, New Delhi.

Preface

A significant portion of the world's population consists of ethnic diasporas. These are the dispersed, migrant, or (in some cases) "overseas" communities which, because they may claim a national homeland not currently the one in which they are domiciled, enjoy a status in the newer homeland distinct from other "indigenous" ethnic minorities. Varying in size, socio-economic standing, and also in the degree of surviving cultural identity and group cohesion, they differ enormously amongst themselves in terms of both the character and the importance of the roles they now occupy in their adopted homelands. They have been in the crosshairs of academic, journalistic, and policy-maker inquiry for a long time, and in many countries not just because they are large in number, but also because they have sometimes generated baffling, even tragic, problems of social and political integration. Widely, even if often erroneously, believed to harbor bifurcated cultural and political loyalties, they have at times been central elements in national and global controversy. In some lands, the loyalty issue has placed them under great suspicion—in a few cases also under grave threat of physical harm. The present era's fascination with the terrorist threat and the potential for its spread around the world via disaffected diasporic communities seems certain to keep this issue very much alive.

This volume's focus on the strategic links between three Asian great powers (China, Russia, and India) and their respective ethnic diasporas inevitably brings the matter of political loyalty to center stage. Russians worry, of course, about the political leanings of the ethnic Chinese settled in the Russian Far East; Indians naturally seek to build and maintain ties with their prosperous migrant co-ethnics in the United States, the United Kingdom, and elsewhere; and the many countries on China's periphery in which ethnic Chinese have settled inescapably give thought, in this age of China's momentous rise to global power, to the long-term loyalties of these settlers. Along with the matter of loyalty, however, the contributions to this volume enable us to examine in detail a whole range of issues that figure in the calculations of great power strategists when it comes to the ethnic diasporas—from disputes over the actual size of the diaspora communities to disputes over their cultural cohesion and political influence.

Underway for two years or so, this project has acquired many debts. The editors owe the largest thanks of all to the authors of the chapters that fill the book's pages. It is to their seasoned professionalism, meticulous research, and sound judgment that the book owes most of its merit. To the Asia-Pacific Center for Security Studies (APCSS), which has been not only the editors' employer but also the sponsor of the conference that provided the initial impetus for the book, the project owes both its origin and its evolution to publication. The editors want to express particular thanks to the Center's Director, Lt Gen Edwin P. Smith, U.S. Army (rtd), whose commitment to serious research—and commitment as well of generous funds to support it—played a significant role in bringing the book to completion in its final stages.

Unsung heroes in this venture, without whose professional skills and dogged perseverance the book might never have seen light of day, were Lt. Commander Angela Torres, Chief Procurement Officer, APCSS; Dottie Kaneshiro, Administrative Support, APCSS; and Steven Cyncewicz, our New York-based copy-editor, whose keen eye and sound judgment saved all of us from the jaws of grammatical and syntactical error.

The editors express their deep gratitude, too, to Anuj Bahri Malhotra, CEO and Head of Academic Division, India Research Press and Tara Press Publishers, for overseeing the putting of essential final touches to the project, and for maintaining extraordinary patience and good humor even when deadlines passed us by. For her kindness in putting us in touch with the IRP, we want to thank Binalakshmi Nepram, faithful friend and activist extraordinaire of New Delhi.

To our wives Irina and Nancy, of course, we owe not just the traditional benediction for their unswerving support of our professional labors, but also a loving caress for being the reason and the inspiration for it all.

Rouben Azizian and Robert Wirsing
Honolulu
October 2006

Authors' Biographies

DR. ROBERT G. WIRSING. Dr. Wirsing is a professor in the College of Security Studies. He came to the Asia-Pacific Center for Security Studies from the University of South Carolina where he was Professor of International Studies and a member of the Department of Government and International Studies since 1971. His primary research interests focus on the contemporary politics, international relations, and defense and security issues of South Asia. He holds a Ph.D. in International Studies from the Graduate School of International Studies, University of Denver. Dr. Wirsing has made nearly forty research visits to South Asia since 1965. Dr. Wirsing is the author, editor, or co-editor of eight books, most recently (author) *Kashmir in the Shadow of War* (M.E. Sharpe, 2003) and (co-editor) *Religious Radicalism and Security in South Asia* (APCSS, 2004).

DR. ROUBEN M. AZIZIAN. Dr. Azizian came to the Asia-Pacific Center for Security Studies in January 2002 from the Department of Political Studies at the University of Auckland, New Zealand. Dr. Azizian has edited four books and published numerous book chapters, journal articles and working papers on foreign policy and security of Russia, Central Asia, South Asia, Northeast Asia as well as New Zealand. His major publications include: *Nuclear Developments in South Asia and the Future of Global Arms Control* (CSS, Wellington, 2001); *Russia in Asia: An Unwelcome Intruder or Accommodating Player?* (CSS, Wellington, 2000); *Strategic and Economic Dynamics of Northeast Asia* (CSS, Wellington, 1999); *Ethnic Challenges Beyond Borders: the Chinese and Russian Perspectives on Central Asia* (with Yongjin Zhang, Macmillan, London, 1998). Prior to becoming a full-time academic, Dr. Azizian had an extensive career in the Soviet and later Russian Foreign Service, which included assignments in Nepal (1972-1978) as Attaché and then Third Secretary; Sri Lanka (1980-1985) as Second and then First Secretary; and New Zealand (1991-1994) as Counsellor and Deputy Chief of Mission.

DR. AILEEN SAN PABLO-BAVIERA. Dr. Baviera is an Associate Professor and Dean of the Asian Center, University of the Philippines. She holds a Ph.D. in Political Science, and an M.A. in Asian Studies. Her current major fields of interest include Asia-Pacific regional security, China-Southeast Asian relations, Asian regionalism and community building, and maritime security. Among her publications are *Bilateral Confidence Building With China In Relation to the South China Sea Disputes: A Philippine Perspective* (Ottawa, 2002); "The China Factor in US Alliances in East Asia and the Asia-Pacific" (AJIA, 2003); "Philippine Perceptions of a China Threat," in Herbert Yee and Ian James Storey, eds. *The China Threat: Myths, Perceptions, and Realities* (London and New York, 2002); and as co-editor, *Philippine External Relations: A Centennial Vista* (Pasay City, 1998).

DR. SANJAY CHATURVEDI. Dr. Chaturvedi, a Leverhulme Fellow of the University of Cambridge, England, is the Chairman, Department of Political Science and Coordinator, Centre for the Study of Geopolitics, Panjab University, Chandigarh. His research interest is the theory and practices of geopolitics, with special reference to Polar Regions and the Indian Ocean. He is the author of *Polar Regions: A Political Geography*, John Wiley & Sons, 1996 and co-editor of the forthcoming *Rethinking Boundaries: Geopolitics, Identities and Sustainability*, (Manohar, Delhi). He has contributed articles to several journals including *Third World Quarterly*; *Journal of Social and Economic Geography*; *Ocean Yearbook*, and *Environment and Planning D: Society and Space.* More recently, he has been a Fellow at Columbia University Institute for Scholars, Reid Hall, and Maison des Sciences de l'Homme, Paris, under the International Programme of Advanced Studies (IPAS). Dr. Chaturvedi serves on the international editorial board of *Geopolitics*, a journal published by Frank Cass, London.

DR. GRAEME P. HERD. Dr. Herd is currently the Professor of Civil-Military Relations, and Associate Director, Senior Executive Seminar, College of International Security Studies, George C. Marshall European Center for Security Studies, Garmisch-Partenkirchen, Germany. Prior to assuming his present duties on September 1, 2002, Dr. Herd was a Lecturer in International Relations and Deputy Director, Scottish Center for International Security (SCIS), University of Aberdeen, Scotland. He has published over 50 book chapters or articles on aspects of post-Soviet security politics in, inter alia, *Security Dialogue*, *Mediterranean Politics*, *European Security*, *Journal of Peace Research*, *Journal of Slavic Military Studies*, *The World Today*, *Strategic Comments* and *Co-operation and Conflict*. He is a Research Associate at Conflict Studies Research Centre (CSRC), Defence Academy, UK, and Associate Fellow, New Security Issues Programme, Chatham House. His latest book (co-edited with Anne Aldis) is entitled *Russia and the Regions: Strength through Weakness* (London and New York: Routledge Curzon, 2003).

MR. ASAF HUSSAIN. Mr. Hussain is a Research Fellow and Consultant at the Institute for the Study of Indo-Pakistan Relations at the University of Leicester in Britain. He teaches religions and cultures, and is engaged in research projects relating to security studies and issues both in South Asia and Britain.

MR. BERTIL LINTNER. Mr. Lintner is a correspondent and senior writer for the *Far Eastern Economic Review.* Mr. Lintner was born in Sweden in 1953 and left for Asia in 1975. He spent 1975-79 traveling in the Asia-Pacific region (the Middle East, the Indian subcontinent, Southeast Asia, Hong Kong, Japan, Australia and New Zealand), but he has been living permanently in Thailand since December 1979, working as a journalist. Mr. Lintner was a free-lance journalist until March 1988, at which time he was employed by the *Far Eastern Economic Review* of Hong Kong as its Burma correspondent. However, he began writing for the *Far Eastern Economic Review* on a free-lance basis in 1982. In addition to his job now as a senior writer for the *Far Eastern Economic Review*, as of 1995 he is also the East Asia correspondent for the Swedish daily *Svenska Dagbladet.* He has also contributed to numerous other newspapers and magazines in Asia, Australia, North America and Europe. Mr. Lintner served as President of the Foreign Correspondents Club of Thailand (FCCT) from January 1993 to January 1995. Mr. Lintner has written five books about Burma: *Outrage: Burma's Struggle for Democracy* (about the 1988 uprising for democracy in Burma) *Land* *of Jade: A Journey through Insurgent Burma* (an account of a trek through northern Burma in 1985-87); *The Rise and Fall of the Communist Party of Burma* (a history of Burma's now defunct communist movement); *Burma in Revolt: Opium and Insurgency Since 1948* (a history of the Golden Triangle opium trade); *The Kachin: Lords of Burma's Northern Frontier*; and one about organized crime in the Asia-Pacific, *Bloodbrothers: The Criminal Underworld in Asia*. Mr. Lintner's latest project is a book about North Korea.

DR. VLADIMIR PORTYAKOV. Dr. Portyakov is Senior Research Fellow and Deputy Director, Institute of Far Eastern Studies, Russian Academy of Sciences, Moscow. Also, from January 2004, he has served as Head of Research Centre on Russian-Chinese Relations. His major research areas consist of contemporary China (policy, economy, contemporary Russian-Chinese relations). Dr. Portyakov's previous positions include: 1999-2003 – Counselor, Embassy of Russian Federation in PRC, Beijing; 1992-1999 – Deputy Director (China's Economy), Institute of Far Eastern Studies, Moscow; in addition, from 1996-2000 – Vice-President of the European Association for Chinese Studies. He also worked in Trade Representation (1973-1975) and the Embassy of former Soviet Union in the People's Republic of China (1978-1982), and in various research institutes of the Soviet Academy of Sciences. Dr. Portyakov's major publications include: *Economic Policy of China Under Deng Xiaoping* (1998, Moscow, in Russian language); *Economic Policy of the PRC in the 1990's* (1999, Moscow, in English); *Economic Reform in China* (2002, Moscow, in Russian). His publications on Chinese migrants and Russian Far East include: "Migration in Russian Far East" in: *Migration Process in Russian Far East and Russia's Policy* (Carnegie Endowment for International Peace, Moscow Center, 1996, pp. 37-57, in Russian); "Are Chinese coming?" *International Life* (Moscow, 1996, No 2, pp. 79-86, in Russian); "Russian - Chinese Trade and Chinese Migration to Russia" in: *Economic Policy of the PRC in the 1990's* (Moscow, Institute of Far Eastern Studies, 1999, pp. 174-182, in English); *Russian Far East and North-East Asia (Economic Cooperation Problem)*, (Moscow, Russian Academy of Sciences, 1998 in Russian); co-author; "Integrating Russian Far East into World Economy",

Politekonom, (Moscow, 1997, [1] 3-4, pp. 149-160, in Russian); China's Role in World Economy and Russian-Chinese Trade – paper presented at the Conference "Integrating Russian Far East into World Economy" in Khabarovsk, November 24-25, 2003 (in Russian). Dr. Portyakov's most recent publications include: "SARS Epidemic in the PRC-Far Eastern Affairs" (A Russian journal on China, Japan and the Asia-Pacific region), East View Publications, 2003 (No 4, pp. 49-57 – in English); and "Eastern Oil Triangle," *Vremya Novostey* (News Time), December 17, 2003, Moscow (in Russian). He also has a research project in progress: "From Jiang Zemin to Hu Jintao. The PRC at the Beginning of Twenty First Century."

DR. ARTHUR RUBINOFF. Dr. Rubinoff is currently Professor of Political Science and South Asian Studies at the University of Toronto, where he has taught since 1972. He holds a Ph.D. from the University of Chicago. He is the author of six books, including *The Construction of a Political Community: Identity and Integration in Goa* (Sage: 1998). He has written more than fifty articles for such journals as *Asian Affairs*, *Asian Survey*, and *Pacific Affairs*. Professor Rubinoff has received grants from the Ford Foundation, the Fulbright Foundation, the Shastri Indo-Canadian Institute, the Smithsonian Institution, the Woodrow Wilson Center for International Scholars, and, most recently, the Social Sciences and Humanities Research Council of Canada for a three-year project on "Identity and Difference in India." He is currently writing a monograph on "The Role of Congress in the Formulation of U.S. South Asian Policy."

DR. ELIZABETH WISHNICK. Dr. Wishnick is a Research Associate at the Weatherhead East Asian Institute at Columbia University and an Adjunct Assistant Professor in the Department of Political Science at Columbia University. In 2003-2004, she was a Fulbright Visiting Scholar in the Department of Politics and Sociology at Lingnan University in Hong Kong. She also taught at Barnard College, Yale College, and the Graduate Faculty of Social and Political Science, New School University, and was a research fellow at Taiwan's Academia Sinica, the Hoover Institution, and the Davis Center at Harvard University. She is the author of *Mending Fences: The Evolution of Moscow's*

China Policy from Brezhnev to Yeltsin (Seattle: University of Washington Press, 2001), and of numerous articles on great power relations and regional development in Northeast Asia. She is published in *Asian Survey*, *NBR Analysis*, *SAIS Review*, *Journal of East Asian Affairs*, *Issues and Studies*, and *Perspectives Chinoises*, as well as in several edited volumes. Dr. Wishnick's current research examines how globalized networks generate security and insecurity for states, regions, and communities, and pose new challenges for security governance. Her Asia-related projects address transnational threats from China and their impact on regional threat perceptions; the security consequences of Chinese migration to the Russian Far East; and great power relations and the Korean nuclear crisis. Dr. Wishnick received her B.A. from Barnard College, her M.A. in Russian and East European Studies from Yale University, and a Ph.D. in Political Science from Columbia University.

DR. IGOR ZEVELEV. Dr. Zevelev is a Professor of Russian Studies at the George C. Marshall European Center for Security Studies. Prior to joining the Marshall Center, Dr. Zevelev was Head Research Associate at the Institute of World Economy and International Relations of the Russian Academy of Sciences (IMEMO), where he had also served as Head of Department and Deputy Director of the Center for Developing Countries. From 1992-99, Dr. Zevelev taught at the Jackson School of International Studies of the University of Washington, University of California at Berkeley, San Jose State University, and Macalester College. He was a Fellow at the Woodrow Wilson International Center for Scholars from 1996-97 and a Senior Fellow at the United States Institute of Peace from 1997-98. Dr. Zevelev has written five books and numerous articles on the politics of Russia, Asian countries, human rights, international relations, and security issues. Among his books are *Russia and Its New Diasporas* (2001); *Global Security Beyond the Millennium: American and Russian Perspectives* (co-edited with Sharyl Cross, 1999); *Urbanization and Development in Asia* (1989); and *Southeast Asia: Urbanization and Problems of Social Development* (1985).

DR. CHARLES E. ZIEGLER. Dr. Ziegler is Professor and Chair of the Political Science Department at the University of Louisville. He received his Ph.D. from the University of Illinois, Urbana-Champaign in 1979. A specialist on Russia and Eurasia, Professor Ziegler is co-editor (with Judith Thornton) of *The Russian Far East: A Region at Risk* (University of Washington Press, 2002), and author of *The History of Russia* (Greenwood Press, 1999); *Foreign Policy and East Asia* (Cambridge University Press, 1993); and *Environmental Policy in the USSR* (University of Massachusetts Press, 1987). In addition, he has written over fifty book chapters and articles for such professional journals as *Comparative Politics*, *Political Science Quarterly*, *British Journal of Political Science*, *Problems of Post-Communism*, *Asian Survey*, and *Pacific Review*. Dr. Ziegler has held an International Research and Exchanges Board Advanced International Research Opportunity grant, a Senior Fulbright Fellowship to Korea, an International Affairs Fellowship of the Council on Foreign Relations, and the Hoover Institution National Fellowship. He currently serves as Executive Director of the Louisville Committee on Foreign Relations, and is listed in *Who's Who in America*. Dr. Ziegler's current research focuses on energy in Russia and East Asia. His most recent papers are "Energy and Security in Central Asia: Russian and Chinese Interests" in *Foreign and Security Policy in the 'New Europe' and Eurasia*; and "Russia, China, and Energy in Central and East Asia," in *Energy Wealth, Governance and Welfare in the Caspian Region.*

CONTENTS

Part Four : The Diaspora in Russia's Security Strategy

Part One
Introductory Perspectives

The Great Powers & Contemporary Ethnic Diasporas: Comparative Perspectives

Chapter 1

The Great Powers & Contemporary Ethnic Diasporas: Comparative Perspectives

Rouben Azizian

Diasporas can have a significant impact on the domestic and foreign policies of states.* The American Jewish community, for example, constitutes a powerful voice within the United States in support of Israel, and shapes American policy toward the Middle East. For years, the Armenian community has influenced U.S. policy toward Turkey and the Caucasus, while Florida's Cubans have pressured Washington to maintain a hard line against Castro's regime. Ethnic Chinese living in the United States, Canada, Australia and Southeast Asia have invested heavily in the People's Republic of China (PRC) and contributed substantially to the mainland's phenomenal economic growth. When the Soviet Union collapsed, some twenty-five million ethnic Russians were living in the fourteen non-Russian republics, with several million more scattered around the globe. Finally, the Indian Government has made relations with its overseas diaspora a major priority in its foreign policy, while Indians abroad are paying much more attention to economic development and policies in their motherland. Publications on diasporas grow in numbers and attract keen interest from specialists and the broad public alike. Here is another opportunity to broaden horizons on the theme for those who are interested.

This book brings together a dozen outstanding international specialists to assess the importance of overseas, migrant, or "diaspora" ethnic minorities in the strategic calculations of three Asian great powers – India, China, and Russia. Drawing in part on papers presented at a recent international conference at the Asia-Pacific Center for Security

* The views expressed in this chapter are those of the author and do not necessarily reflect the official policy or position of the Asia-Pacific Center for Security Studies, the U.S. Pacific Command, the U.S. Department of Defense, or the U.S. government.

Studies in Honolulu, Hawaii, this book provides both fresh descriptive data on overseas ethnic minorities as well as penetrating analyses of how these three Asian giants seek to take advantage of the diaspora phenomenon in their regional and global foreign policies.

My colleague and co-editor Robert Wirsing offers in Chapter Two a useful historical background for the comparative study of contemporary diaspora issues. In his essay titled "The Strategic Potential of Ethnic Diasporas: Lessons from Nazi Germany's 'Fifth Column'," he elaborates on the emergence during the World War II era of the terms fifth column and Trojan horse which were frequently and indiscriminately applied to foreign-dwelling German, Italian, and Japanese minorities. New variants of ethnic fifth column activity, along with the suspicion this kind of activity generates, have often surfaced in the years since World War II. There are several circumstances responsible for this. For one thing, powerful new states have emerged, some with expansionist–or at least potentially expansionist–ambitions. For another, endless tides of international migrants continue to generate large and new (and potentially manipulable) diaspora minorities. In addition, provocative new ideologies exist with which to woo these minorities. According to Robert Wirsing, if anything emerges clearly from the historical record of the Nazi German ethnic fifth column, it is that the world's reactions to it, in particular the infliction of collective punishments on the "guilty" ethnic German minorities, were not only unnecessary but also almost certainly did far more harm to humanity than the fifth columns themselves.

Thematically, the volume is divided into four parts. While **Part One** serves as an introduction, the subsequent parts focus on the diaspora of each of the three great powers.

Part Two is devoted to India and its diaspora. The Indian Diaspora spans the globe and stretches across all the oceans and continents. The population of the Indian Diaspora is estimated to be about 20 million. They live in different countries, speak different languages and are engaged in different vocations. According to the *Report of the High Level Committee on Indian Diaspora* Government of India, 29 December 2001, what gives them their common identity are their Indian origin, their consciousness of their cultural heritage and their deep attachment to India.

It was against the backdrop of economic compulsions generated by colonialism that people of Indian origin began to migrate overseas in significant numbers in the 19th century, and initially to the countries of Africa, Southeast Asia, Fiji and the Caribbean. This wave was triggered by the enormous demand for cheap labor that arose in the wake of the abolition of slavery by the British in 1833-34. Forcefully engaged in the plantations of East and South Africa, as well as the West and East Indies, these lower caste and class peasants and laborers largely escaped the attention of the Indian government and elite. Moreover, since in the countries of their residence they usually were far down in socio-political hierarchies, they rarely figured in the mental maps of a rather status conscious Indian elite. Some change in this regard was noticeable only after Gandhi organized the resistance in South Africa in the early years of the 20th century. The second wave of Indian migrations abroad occurred in the second half of the 20th century, with a steady outflow of some of India's best professionals to the developed countries of the West, and of India's skilled and semi-skilled labor in the wake of the oil boom in West Asia and the Gulf in the 1970s.

According to Sanjay Chaturvedi (Chapter Three), it is only recently that Indian Diaspora has started receiving serious and systematic attention from the intellectuals and institutions of statecraft in India. In sharp contrast to China's long-standing policy framework for overseas Chinese, leveraging the expatriate community for "national" ends, the Indian government has just begun mapping out the Indian settlements/communities abroad.

Like the Indian government, many foreign governments have had to reassess their attitude to Indians living in their respective countries and appreciate their potential role in enhancing bilateral relations with India. Arthur Rubinoff in Chapter Four examines the impact that the Indo-American community has had on transforming the historically hostile bilateral relationship between Washington and New Delhi. He finds the role of Indians in the United States to be decisive in altering perceptions of decision-makers in two countries that had limited contact and conflicting interests. In the first years of India's existence as an independent state, when the Indian community in the United States was small and uneducated, its impact on foreign policy was negligible. However, in subsequent years, the diaspora's influence in the United States has grown as its skills, education, income, and size have increased. It is apparent that the prosperous and demographically significant Indo-American community, typified by physicians and Silicon Valley computer technicians, has remarkably changed not only its image, but the perception of its home country in the United States. In a single generation, the image of Indians in the United States and the subcontinent has been transformed from that of a malnourished skeleton in a filthy *dhoti* to a highly educated prosperous professional in a designer business suit who is a threat to American jobs—an impression reinforced by the impressive number of widely-read and acclaimed novels written in English by expatriates.

The diaspora, currently numbering 1.7 million Indian-Americans—up from 387,000 in 1980—serves as a reservoir of support for New Delhi in Washington. It has also played a major role in transforming Indian society by infusing new ideas—whether formally or informally—as well as economic, human, and social capital from the United States. Its entrepreneurial success in the United States has also influenced Indian policy makers as they undertook economic reforms, a reality acknowledged by Prime Minister and former Finance Minister Manmohan Singh on his visit to the United States in 2006.

Asaf Hussain (Chapter Five) sees a similar and perhaps deeper trend with regard to India's 1.5 million strong diaspora in Britain, where the Indian ethnic community has made a major impact upon British society through the creation of cultural spaces within it. The Indian culture has penetrated British society in a number of ways. First, as Hindu temples were built in Britain, they opened their doors to the British public (unlike the mosques). Second, the festivals of Hinduism were open to the broad British public. In many cases civic dignitaries were invited to partake in such festivals. Diwali was also celebrated in the House of Commons with many members of the Indian community present. Third, the most effective means of cultural penetration was through the development of food-consuming markets in Britain. Indian foods particularly appealed to many vegetarians and vegans in British culture. Thousands of Indian restaurants had popularised Indian foods all over Britain. Fourth, the Indian world of fashions penetrated British culture as well. It was not only that some British women wore saris, dupattas, and shalwar khamises, but some from the younger generation had pricked their noses so as to wear nats (nose rings) or tried henna decorations on their hands. Fifth, Indian films had created a version of Bollywood in Britain. Not only were many of their film scenes shot in British locations by film producers, but some British stars wanted to act in Bollywood films. Sixth, classical Indian music has had a lot of influence in Britain. Great musical artists like Ravi Shankar have made their mark on Britain. Seven, most of the above aspects of culture received strong support from radio and TV stations operating from the major cities in Britain. Furthermore, linkages have been made by Indians with national radio and TV stations like the BBC to project Asian music. British Prime Minister Tony Blair recently summed up this intercultural process by commenting that the people of Indian origin in Britain are "at the heart of our relationship" for "their cultural values contribute significantly towards making Britain the vibrant, dynamic society that it is today. They are a vital bond between our two communities."

Part Three examines the role of the Chinese Diaspora. As many as two million people from the People's Republic of China have migrated legally and illegally since 1978. About 30,000 to 40,000 a year go to the United States–the preferred destination. Chinese migration has become globalized and is already beginning to change traditional demographic patterns in places such as the Russian Far East and the Pacific region. According to Bertil Lintner (Chapter Six), most of the new migrants are not hostile to the Chinese government. On the contrary, as worldwide demonstrations by groups of overseas Chinese protesting the embassy bombing in Belgrade in May 1999 showed, many remain patriotic and identify themselves with the "motherland." As a sending country, PRC pursues policies of enhancing ties with overseas Chinese. The resurgent Chinese nationalism overseas is clearly linked to the PRC's great power aspirations. It is obvious that the Chinese authorities, while pledging to cooperate with the West to stem the flow of illegal migrants, are also actively encouraging migration. There are three main reasons for this policy: to ease population pressure, receive remittances from overseas Chinese, and ensure friendly footholds in the host countries of the migrants. The third reason is no doubt the most controversial, and could cause conflicts in some countries with a growing ethnic Chinese population. Ideas of demographic expansion by China as well as revived fifth-column theories are on the rise in various quarters: among politicians in the Russia Far East, journalists in Southeast Asia, and sometimes in the U.S. media, as in the recent spying case involving a Chinese-American physicist.

Aileen S.P. Baviera (Chapter Seven) examines the phenomenon of the Chinese Diaspora in Southeast Asia, with particular emphasis on the Philippines, asking whether or not the diaspora plays a significant role in the "security strategy" of China. According to the author, the answer to this question lies in an understanding of (1) what is meant by "the Chinese Diaspora" and "the ethnic Chinese," (2) the history of migration and the evolution of their presence, (3) their relations with the government of their country of residence, and (4) the nature of their ties with China through the years. The chapter argues that based on these considerations, the ethnic Chinese minorities in the region have not been and are not likely to be useful as *significant* instruments for the *deliberate* advancement of China's security goals and interests in Southeast Asia. This is especially the case if security is understood here in its traditional (realist) sense of a great power China that seeks political supremacy in the region or even military parity with or an advantage over other great powers.

It is more plausible to argue that the contributions of Southeast Asia's ethnic Chinese to China have been in the aspects of economic security rather than military security, and perhaps even human security, through direct contributions to their relatives and hometowns and villages, and on a much lesser scale direct investments in the local economies of said hometowns and home provinces (with the exception of Singapore, whose investment was not mainly tied to hometowns or pre-existing local linkages but was more policy-driven). If one were to define China's "security strategy," as framed by its desire to become an "advanced socialist state" or in terms of "comprehensive security," then certainly it may be said that the ethnic Chinese of Southeast Asia have had a significant role, although the impact was felt more at the local rather than at the national dimension.

At the same time, these propositions do not exclude the possibility that certain individuals, families, business interests, or organizations may have played a direct or indirect role in covertly or overtly, deliberately or inadvertently, influencing decision makers in Southeast Asia towards certain policies that again, directly or indirectly, favor China's security goals. This may be particularly true for those with strong economic ties and political connections to the central government or key ministries in Beijing. It would also not be surprising if China—like any other great power—occasionally relies on its nationals, compatriots or former citizens to provide political and economic assessments on the country in question. In very open societies such as the Philippines, ethnic Chinese who freely move among the elites would certainly be well-placed to serve as listening posts, if indeed they were under the influence of China. Yet the irony of the situation of the ethnic Chinese is that those who are best-placed to serve China, presumably because of their own influence and access to information, are those who have already integrated with the mainstream societies in their adopted countries and are therefore least likely to respond to appeals or instructions from Beijing. Granted that there are such occurrences, by their very nature they are not well-documented other than through anecdotal reports; thus their impact will be difficult to prove.

What do patterns of perception and mistrust towards Chinese populations outside of China illustrate? From the perspective of the ethnic Chinese, the patterns possibly illustrate the continued perception that they are still a "foreign" or "alien" presence in their adopted countries, which makes them vulnerable to criticism and pressure from different groups, particularly in periods of economic crisis. Yet from the perspective of the local indigenous population, and in particular the majority cultural group and economic elites, the mistrust may be partly attributed to a fear of challenges to their own culture, values, and resources that may arise from the ubiquitous and culturally cohesive ethnic Chinese, especially those that may have strong ties to an emerging power such as China.

Elizabeth Wishnick (Chapter Eight) addresses these very issues and challenges by elaborating on the perceptions of the Chinese Diaspora in the Russian Far East. Despite significant improvement in Russo-Chinese relations, adverse demographic and economic trends in the Russian Far East have prompted Russian officials on the national and regional levels, as well as the public in these areas, to describe Chinese migration as a threat to the integrity of the Russian state. Russian concerns about Chinese illegal immigration today are fuelled by a perception of demographic pressure from China. By 2004, the Russian Far East had a population of 6.68 million inhabiting a territory of more than 6.2 million square kilometers, compared to 107 million Chinese living in the three Northeastern provinces (Heilongjiang, Jilin, and Liaoning) with a territory of 1.9 million square kilometers. Due to the high cost of living and underemployment, the Russian Far East lost seven percent of its population by the mid-1990s. Although the northern regions of the Russian Far East experienced the most substantial outflows, the population of Primorskii Krai and Khabarovskii Krai declined by 1.5 percent and 3.3 percent respectively.

The Chinese people who work in the Russian Far East disproportionately come from the Chinese Northeast, primarily from the Heilongjiang province (62.4% of respondents in the July 2004 survey, compared to 18% from Jilin, 17.2% from Liaoning, and 4% from Inner Mongolia, with 2.4% from other parts of China). Chinese policymakers support legal labor cooperation with Russia because they contend that it takes advantage of the natural economic complementarities (*hubuxing*) between the two countries—Russia has land and resources, but suffers from a shortage of workers, while China lacks land and resources but has an oversupply of labor. Nevertheless, Chinese officials consistently deny Russian allegations that China is promoting illegal migration. Inadequate economic security in the Chinese Northeast creates a combination of push and pull factors that provide powerful economic incentives for Chinese residents of the Chinese Northeast to seek temporary employment in the Russian Far East, despite hardships. Residents in the Russian Far East, however, interpret the steps that Chinese traders take to enhance their economic security as a threat, creating a "security dilemma" with potentially adverse implications for Sino-Russian bilateral and regional relations. Although Chinese provincial level authorities and non-state labor export companies are largely responsible for sending Chinese workers to the Russian Far East, officials in Beijing have welcomed labor cooperation as a natural component of economic globalization and regional economic cooperation with the Russian Far East. However, the Chinese government's tendency to discount Russian security concerns has only served to increase distrust between the two countries, a factor that continues to stymie regional economic cooperation between the Chinese Northeast and the Russian Far East.

Vladimir Portyakov (Chapter Nine) examines the Chinese demographic factor in a broader context of Russia's population trends, political culture and general politics. He explains that the Russian society was poorly prepared psychologically for the influx of Chinese migrants. Indeed, apprehensions of a "creeping Chinese expansion" were voiced and, much to the discredit of the Chinese, fueled by the impression of high criminality of the migrants and their irresistible desire to stay, rightly or wrongly, in Russia forever. The Chinese migrants' evident reluctance to integrate into Russian society looked suspicious, too, even if it was largely caused by language problems (few migrants could speak Russian) and low ethnic tolerance among a great majority of common Russians. Rumors of mounting numbers of Chinese in Russia, with some papers citing millions of migrants, prompted the country's authorities to tighten controls over guest workers in general and Chinese migrants in particular.

The Russian authorities' official attitude toward Chinese migrants can be described in the following terms. Guided by its interests in strengthening Russian-Chinese relations, the Kremlin has opted to keep a low profile on Chinese migrants and refrains from fanning tempers that flare up now and then in the Russian media over the issue. During private meetings with their Chinese counterparts, however, Russian officials regularly voice, even if in subdued tones, their concern over the issue and their readiness to seek a mutually acceptable settlement. That is actually the underlying purpose of the proposed working group on migration.

Judging by its policies, Moscow is well aware of the importance of a stable population in its Far Eastern areas and the significance of its economic development for the destiny of the Russian state. In this context, a definite clue can be found in the speech Russian President Putin made during his visit to Blagoveshchensk in summer 2000: "Unless we make real efforts to develop our Far Eastern areas soon, the ethnic Russian population will, within a few decades, have Japanese, Chinese or Korean as their native language." The "new Chinese migration" in Russia is a complex and many-sided phenomenon that could have various repercussions for the recipient country and, for this reason, spawn diverging judgments. From the author's point of view, this phenomenon may be a source for both harmony and conflict in Russian-Chinese bilateral relations and, to some extent, for harmony and conflict in international relations in Northeast Asia as a whole. The constructive cooperation between Russia and China on migration and economic issues, a stronger social platform for their bilateral relations as well as robust economic development of the Russian Far East and Northeast China could minimize "the conflict side" and enforce the harmonizing effect of Chinese migration into Russia. Most real and imaginary fears and suspicions of Russian citizens regarding the "Chinese presence in Russia" can be dissolved by showing genuine concern for the transformation of Siberia and the Far East into a really liveable place.

Graeme Herd's Chapter Ten bridges **Part Three** and **Part Four** (Diaspora in Russia's Security Strategy) by continuing the Russian demographic theme and the Chinese impact on it through an examination of the relationship between demographic decline and associated migration patterns within the Russian Federation and ethno-strategic vulnerabilities. The author identifies the effects of demographic decline on political processes and socioeconomic conditions in Russia and demonstrates their security implications and consequences, with particular reference to minority separatism. Secondly, he considers the more complex and speculative question: what is the current and maybe projected impact of Russia's demographic decline and changing migration patterns and Russia's exposure to ethno-strategic vulnerability and minority separatism? The chapter concludes by proposing policy recommendations to better manage demographic decline by countering the worst effects of the destabilizing security dilemmas that arise within and between the political, economic and societal security sectors.

The current and future presence in Russia of the Chinese is one of the highlights in the chapter. By 2050, the proportion of immigrants in the labor reserves of Russia will rise to at least 20%, while some sociologists have forecasted that 7-10 million Chinese will live in the Russian Federation. Some Russian experts believe that by 2050, the Chinese in Russia may become the second largest ethnic group after ethnic Russians. Chinese will constitute an inalienable component of the Russian work force, capable of reviving the national sector of services, construction, municipal transport, and agriculture. However, notes the author, on the basis of the current Chinese population in the Russian Far East (RFE), these assessments appear exaggerated. The most realistic assessment is that no more than about 300,000 Chinese migrants can be found in the RFE on any given day and around 90 or so percent of them are most likely to be transient, temporary cross-border migrants. The issue of Chinese migration can easily be politicized, and in the context of the de-Europeanization of the Russian Far East as "ethnic Russians" migrate westwards, it is highly likely that the economic role of Chinese migrants will increasingly be framed within political and societal security contexts.

In recent years, Russia has been trying to lure some its huge diaspora overseas, particularly in the former Soviet republics, to move to Russia and ease the demographic decline. These efforts have, however, been problematic as Moscow has been unable to develop a consistent demographic policy. Attitudes to its diaspora remain mixed while policies are controversial. Igor Zevelev (Chapter Eleven) examines these issues in detail at both theoretical and empirical levels. After the break up of the USSR in 1991, Russia had to deal with twenty-million-plus diaspora of ethnic Russians in neighboring states. The term "diaspora" became popular in Russia since the mid-1990s. It has often been used together with or instead of such terms as "Russians and

Russian-speakers" or "compatriots" which appeared in political and theoretical discourse earlier in 1991-1994. Re-conceptualization of large groups of the population in neighboring states as Russian Diaspora reflected the attempt to emphasize the connection of these people to Russia proper, a collective memory and myth about common homeland, a traumatic experience, and a troubled relationship with host societies.

All Russian official documents and policies, as well as political discourse, suggest that Russian Diasporas in neighboring states are viewed first of all as people whom the Russian state has an obligation to protect. It is clear that policies of "protection" may constitute an instrument of influence in the post-Soviet space. Russia's future attempts to help the Russians in the near abroad could range from neo-imperialistic ambitions to efforts to ensure their human rights. Russia may respond to the problems confronted by its diasporas in the former Soviet states in a variety of ways—some of them quite constructive. The tendency today is to automatically assume that any talk about the Russians in the successor states is potentially aggressive, but this is not necessarily the case.

After the collapse of the Soviet Union, Russia had an opportunity to create a functioning active Russian Diaspora in the neighboring states out of those people who were ethnic Russians or non-Russians feeling affinity with the Russian Federation. The Russian state, with the help of its official rhetoric and laws, did take some steps in this direction, but the results have not been impressive thus far because they were not always supported by concrete and consistent policies. The members of the (potential in many cases) Russian Diasporas in the neighboring states are not politically, socially, or civically organized, and they expect the Russian Federation to do good for them, not necessarily vice versa.

Charles Ziegler (Chapter Twelve) reinforces this argument by noting that the ethnic Russian Diaspora overseas is diverse and therefore can not be easily organized. He dwells on the situation in Central Asia in particular. It is important not to view Russians in Central Asia as homogeneous. Just as they differ in terms of how long they have lived in Central Asia, whether or not they were born there, and what the circumstances were that brought them there (voluntary or involuntary), so too their attitudes may vary considerably. For example, it would be misleading to assume that all ethnic Russians in Central Asia identify closely with their Russian homeland. Nor should it be assumed that all Russians in northern Kazakhstan favor reunification with the Russian Federation. Identities, particularly those in the post-Soviet space, tend to be complex and difficult to categorize.

The actual impact of Russians in Central Asia on Russian politics has been more apparent in the domestic sphere than in foreign policy, with the Kremlin adopting largely symbolic policies. Russian nationalism could, however, reinvigorate the role of Russia's Diaspora in foreign policy. The strong showing of nationalist parties in the latest parliamentary elections and the surge of Russian patriotism generally may lead to greater pressures to "defend" Russians abroad. A triggering event would be more likely to occur in Kazakhstan than in any other Central Asian country. However, the leaders of both Kazakhstan and Russia are in firm control of their governments and both, realizing the potential for instability and bloodshed, have rejected using the ethnic card in foreign relations.

The twelve chapters of the book represent, in sum, a fascinating, complex and mosaic picture of ethnic diasporas and diaspora policies of great powers. Unlike the traditional and usually small country diasporas of Ireland, Israel, Greece and others, the diasporas of China, India and Russia reflect a new phenomenon and process that needs further investigation. As the above countries continue to assert themselves economically and geopolitically, how will the diaspora factor evolve in their policies? Is it likely to cede its importance to other traditional elements of national power or is it to grow in importance? As the three giants are trying to cope with their demographic challenges, namely China and India with mounting growth and pressure while Russia with continuing population decline, how is this going to impact their internal and external security priorities? If globalization is unstoppable and leads to the erosion of traditional borders, how realistic is it for Russia but also for South and Southeast Asia, as well as Oceania, to count on regulation of Chinese immigration? Should the term and challenge of the rise of China also include the demographic expansion of the Chinese, along with the expansion of China's economic and diplomatic power? If so, is the region ready? The recent anti-Chinese clashes in the small and remote Solomon Islands demonstrated that the Chinese factor has become an integral part of politics of many countries in the region. China has been quite restrained so far in dealing with violations of Chinese human rights overseas. Will a stronger and more ambitious China review its stance?

The future of Asia-Pacific and its security depend on many variables, with the ethnic diasporas undoubtedly being one of them.

The Strategic Potential of Ethnic Diasporas: Lessons from Nazi Germany's "Fifth Column"

Chapter 2

The Strategic Potential of Ethnic Diasporas: Lessons from Nazi Germany's "Fifth Column"

Robert Wirsing

Introduction†

Throughout most of the 20th century, the notion that certain ethnic minorities were especially susceptible to political disloyalty found a receptive and, inevitably, suspicious audience in many countries of the world. The two world wars gave birth to much of the suspicion, since they happened to involve aggressor states whose ethnic majorities were both virulently nationalist and, as a result of earlier massive migrations, heavily represented among the world's far flung ethnic diasporas. During the World War II era, in particular, the terms fifth column and Trojan horse came into common use and were frequently and indiscriminately applied to foreign-dwelling German, Italian, and Japanese minorities, whether or not they were foreign born. The war witnessed some extremely brutal measures undertaken by governments against these minorities on grounds that they were–or were capable of becoming–dangerously sympathetic with the subversive intentions of the Axis powers. The war's end brought with it, in more than a few cases, harsh forms of retaliation against them as well as against other minority communities identified with Axis-allied states. Many of the allegations that had been hurled against these minorities were eventually challenged, and the countless reports of their alleged sabotage and disloyalty that had vastly excited an earlier generation were in some instances discredited. The fifth column stigma that was attached to them in those traumatic wartime years never entirely disappeared, however, and in fact, it still remains in at least a few cases a sensitive political issue.[1]

†. The views expressed in this chapter are those of the author and do not necessarily reflect the official policy or position of the Asia-Pacific Center for Security Studies, the U.S. Pacific Command, the U.S. Department of Defense, or the U.S. government.

New variants of ethnic fifth column activity, along with the suspicion this kind of activity generates, have often surfaced in the years since World War II. There are several circumstances responsible for this. For one thing, powerful new states have emerged, some with expansionist—or at least potentially expansionist—ambitions. For another, endless tides of international migrants continue to generate large and new (and potentially manipulable) diaspora minorities. In addition, provocative new ideologies exist with which to woo these minorities. Ideologies of ethnic nationalism, for instance, have carried the mesmeric idea of national rebirth far beyond its European birthplace to all parts of the globe and intensified awareness of cultural identities, undermined pre-existent political loyalties, and provoked autonomist and separatist movements. Along with these nationalist ideologies, however, have come new species of mobilizing doctrine that showcases the migrants' religious identity and the danger it faces from foreign adversaries. The potential for external interference, manipulation, and subversion of diaspora minorities, though not necessarily of a sort patterned on the Nazi German model, has inevitably spread along with these ideologies. Just as important among the conditions congenial to new ethnic fifth column activity, however, are the spectacular developments in communications technology, which enable nearly continuous contact and trafficking between homeland and diaspora on a scale without precedent in history.

Fifth column activity has almost invariably spawned counter-fifth column activity of its own. Judging from the hysteria and cruelty that sometimes characterized these counter-fifth column reactions in the past century, the counter-fifth column "remedy" has not infrequently been at least as terrifying and destructive as the fifth column "disease" it was meant to cure. It is this paradox—the awful dangers inherent in both the actions of and reactions to ethnic fifth column phenomena—that is the focus of this chapter. Taking as its starting point that the concept of fifth column, suitably redefined to fit contemporary circumstances, remains as applicable today as ever, this chapter takes a retrospective look at the so-called Nazi German fifth column of the Second World War period, seeking in its uniquely rich record clues both to the political potential of present-day efforts to manipulate and subvert ethnic minorities as well as to the dangers inherent in the misinterpretation and exaggeration of this potential.

The Concept of a Fifth Column

The expression "fifth column" was born in the early months of the Spanish Civil War (1936-39) when General Emilio Mola, in command of General Francisco Franco's rebel Nationalist forces on the Madrid front, made the menacing comment in an interview that the Loyalist-held center of Republican Spain would soon fall not to the four columns of rebel troops then converging on the city for a final assault, but to a fifth—already lying in wait within its gates.[2] Mola's choice of metaphor quickly achieved international notoriety as a synonym for the worst sort of treachery.[3] In the attack on Madrid, of course, *ethnic* loyalties had little or nothing to do with the presence of a fifth column; in that instance, the term was applied to native pro-rebel Spaniards who had or were suspected of having fascist ideological sympathies. The term continued to convey the idea of ideological (fascist or communist) conspiracy, even as it gained acceptance outside of Spain. However, since ethnic minorities, especially those having blood ties with Europe's other fascist states, inevitably seemed least trustworthy to the apprehensive majorities, the fifth column appellation increasingly implied an *ethno*-ideological conspiracy. The beleaguered inhabitants of Madrid expected the *quinta columna facciosa* to perform acts of sabotage, interfere with communications and transport, seize or incapacitate vital targets, and in other ways lend aid to the invading forces while harassing and demoralizing the defenders, thus attaching a distinctly military or para-military connotation to the concept. Reports of such activities were plentiful in Poland after the outbreak of war on September 1, 1939, and in every other European country that fell victim to the Nazi *blitzkrieg*. It was quite apparent, however, that as much or more damage had been or could be inflicted by other than military means, in advance or even in lieu of a military assault. Hence, the meaning of a fifth column was soon stretched to accommodate longer-range political actions (organizational infiltration, labor agitation, public demonstrations and, especially, the spreading of morale-weakening propaganda), which seemed designed to achieve the same objective—the undermining of an adversary state. The term's meaning was further confused by the failure, natural in wartime, to make a sharp distinction between fifth columnists *dwelling* behind the lines and small groups of enemy commandos *dropped* behind the lines. In fact, anything from a band of enemy paratroopers, dressed innocently in priestly cassocks and airlifted to the target country the night before an invasion, to a mass of unassimilated ethnic descendents of long dead migrant ancestors could be, and often was, described as a fifth column in the frantic wartime years.[4]

The topic of fifth columns achieved astonishing popularity among an earlier generation of journalists and political analysts.[5] However, the significance of the subject to the people of the World War II era went well beyond its immediate literary appeal.

Suspicion of disloyalty was widespread in many countries, with enormous implications for large parts of their population. Unfortunately, suspects were often entire ethnic minority groups. The forced mass transfer in wartime of Americans of Japanese descent and Russians of German and Tatar descent and, after the war, of Poles, Czechoslovaks and Hungarians of German descent are well known examples. Victims of the Nazi conquest, rather than admit lack of ability or courage on the part of their soldiers or political leaders, often and understandably attributed their failure to stop Hitler's forces to internal conspirators, and frequently took harsh reprisals. On many occasions, fear inspired paroxysms of public hysteria. Overzealous patriots, determined to ferret out the seemingly ubiquitous "quislings" in their midst, sometimes engaged in senseless brutality and at other times in downright ludicrous behavior. Louis De Jong has catalogued an extensive record of both.[6] How many innocents were beaten, stripped of their possessions, interned or killed will never be accurately known. The figure, from all accounts, is large.

Many major political and military decisions made in that period in Europe, America, and elsewhere were inspired by fear of fifth columns. Alarmed by Nazi successes in Europe, President Franklin D. Roosevelt warned Americans in a fireside chat on May 26, 1940 that "we know of new methods of attack. The Trojan Horse. The Fifth

Column that betrays a nation unprepared for treachery. Spies, saboteurs and traitors are the actors in this new tragedy."[7] Only a few days earlier, Major Matthew B. Ridgway, at the time head of the War Plans Division of the War Department (eventually made General and Army Chief of Staff), had called for active intervention, even preventive occupation, in areas of South America with large settlements of ethnic German and Italian minorities.[8] The still neutral U.S. government soon launched extensive diplomatic and military operations to secure the hemisphere against ethnic fifth column activity. While the necessity or desirability for this particular action was once the subject of debate, the truth remains that even where later investigation revealed no trace at all of a bona fide fifth column, the popular and often official assumption that one existed sometimes had substantial consequences.[9] Obviously, the magnitude of fifth column activity was exaggerated, as was, undoubtedly, its importance in determining the course of events in particular cases. Nevertheless, even when due allowance is made for exaggeration and partisan interpretation, three judgments seem inescapable:

(1) The extent to which institutional capability for the systematic manipulation and subversion of ethnic German minorities was made an integral part of Nazi foreign policy machinery was without parallel anywhere. Nothing in history had even remotely approximated the organizational resources available to Nazi leaders in their attempts to politically exploit expatriate minorities in alien lands.

(2) Captured Nazi records make it abundantly clear that enormous energy and resources were poured into efforts to stimulate mass disaffection and disloyalty among ethnic Germans abroad. Efforts were uncoordinated, inconsistent, and sometimes counter-productive. However, there is no question that the Nazis not only tried, but *tried hard*, to manipulate and subvert ethnic German minorities settled abroad.

(3) In spite of all kinds of obstacles, some generated by themselves and some the result of conditions beyond their

> power to control, the Nazis were able in some instances to subvert the loyalties of substantial portions of ethnic German minority populations and, on occasion, to place their mass disloyalty at the service of Nazi foreign policy.

The Nazis scored many conspicuous failures, but they did not always fail. Fifth column-like formations were assembled in some lands, many of them from ethnic German minorities. These formations did engage in a wide variety of unequivocally subversive activities on behalf of the enemy, and sometimes, most notably in parts of Central and Eastern Europe, with devastating effects. To dismiss the Nazi German fifth columns as complete fabrications of wartime hysteria would be as much a mistake as to inflate the extent of their mobilization or to credit them with too great of a responsibility for the short-lived triumph of Nazi Germany in Europe.

The following is a closer look at the development of the German fifth column and the factual bases for these assertions.

Operation of the German Fifth Column, 1933-1945

Nazi Germany approached World War II with a population of roughly 67 million. To this, the annexation of Austria (*Anschluss*) in March 1938 added another 6.2 million. German-speaking minorities then still resident outside the Reich (*Auslandsdeutschen*) in Europe and overseas numbered about 11 million. Well over half of this number was located in Europe (in more than a dozen countries, most prominently in Czechoslovakia, France, and Poland), but there were substantial settlements in the Soviet Union and North and South America.[10] Properly speaking, some of these were *Reichsdeutschen*, namely persons who, for a variety of reasons, retained German citizenship.[11] The overwhelming majority and the focus of this discussion, however, were so-called *Volksdeutschen* (ethnic Germans), namely German in culture or cultural background but citizens of alien countries.[12] These *Volksdeutschen* groups, whether cultural survivors of historic mass migrations, such as to Czarist Russia, the Americas in the great transatlantic crossings of the 19th and early 20th centuries, or victims of the Versailles peace settlement and the break-up of the Austro-Hungarian Empire in 1919, varied considerably in size, proximity to the German state, and the amount of interest which they held for the wielders of power in the Nazi system. Linked to the fatherland by a theory of organic nationhood that originated in racist and nationalist philosophies of the 19th century, *Deutschtum im Ausland* (Germandom abroad), conveniently supplied excuses for Nazi territorial expansion and was quick to participate prominently in the events precipitating another global war.

Institutional Capability

German concern for ethnic Germans abroad considerably antedated the Third Reich. It first became noticeable in the latter part of the 19th century, but then was mainly confined to Germans of the Hapsburg monarchy, whose cultural dominance was increasingly under challenge from Italian, Magyar, and Slavic nationalisms. Cultural protective societies (*Schutzvereine*) appeared in virtually every German-Austrian community, and by the first decade of the 20th century, numbered in the thousands.[13] The tempo of *Volksdeutschen* activity was far slower in Germany itself, where Germans were under no particular cultural threat and, indeed, were basking in the glories of a growing empire. What interest there was manifested itself mainly in efforts to thwart assimilation by supporting German-medium schools among Germans abroad. Thus, the *Verein fuer das Deutschtum im Ausland* (League of Germandom Abroad, or VDA), by far the most powerful nongovernmental organization engaged in *Volkstumsarbeit* (Germandom work) by the time of the Nazi accession to power in 1933, began its career in Berlin in 1881 as the *Allgemeiner deutscher Schulverein* (Universal German School Society).[14]

German dilettantism was blown away for good with World War I. That conflict, since it dispossessed Germany of a large part of its pre-war territory and made "minorities" of millions of Germans hitherto unaccustomed to a subordinate social status, radically transformed the nature of *Volkstumsarbeit*. Preserving language gave way to more ambitious notions. The important *Deutscher Schutzbund* (German Defense League), for example, formed in 1919 with the help of numerous refugee groups from former German territories, abandoned the simple defense of minority cultural values in favor of an aggressive assertion of German national unity—a unity transcending political boundaries. Thus was born in Germandom work the potentially treasonous idea that citizenship of the *state* ranked beneath membership in the *nation*: "*Schutzarbeit* became *volksdeutsche Arbeit.*"[15]

The war also inspired a stupendous increase in the attention paid by Germans to ethnic German affairs. The *Deutsches Ausland-Institute* (German Foreign Institute, or DAI), founded in Stuttgart in 1917 originally to counter Allied propaganda in neutral countries with large ethnic German minorities, mirrored this heightened interest in its acquisition over the next two decades of a mine of information on Germandom abroad. By 1939, the Institute's library held over 100,000 volumes and subscribed to some 1,700 newspapers and periodicals. The Institute's ample staff sorted thousands of letters, postcards, and photos received daily, sponsored exhibitions and public lectures, operated a large museum, prepared numerous publications of its own, and maintained a file of over 40,000 ethnic German societies abroad.[16] By the early 1930s, the VDA, whose activities glittered even more impressively than those of the DAI, had well over 3,000 local affiliates within Germany and a worldwide membership in excess of two million.[17]

Volkstumsarbeit, stimulated after Versailles as much by reports of cultural, social, and economic repression in some areas where ethnic Germans dwelled as by the evident speed of assimilation in others, did not fully come into its own, however, until 1933, when it was marshalled into the service of National Socialism. With this momentous change in its fortunes, political work among Germans abroad (*Volkstumspolitik*) increasingly took precedence over cultural and other Germandom concerns. The concept of German unity itself took a significant step forward, for the interests of the German *nation*, wherever it dwelled, now became synonymous with the interests of the German *state*. While the Weimar Republic (1919-1933) had itself discreetly supplied encouragement to the political ambitions of *Volksdeutschen*, there would soon be nothing to compare with the exertions of Nazi Germany in this regard.

Among other things, the Nazi revolution meant the almost complete renovation of organized German life, and did not exclude Germandom organizations. A variety of governmental and party agencies, some with vague purposes and overlapping objectives, were added to an already bewildering array of public and private groups inherited from the Weimar period. Though the distinctions were sometimes blurred with the progress of Nazi *Gleichschaltung* (coordination), there were three basic categories into which fell the 82 Third Reich agencies (in 1936) with direct interest in one aspect or another of ethnic German affairs. As listed in a compilation (Main Agencies for the Promotion of Germandom Abroad) prepared by the DAI and dated February 20, 1936, these were:

A. State agencies (a total of six), including the *Kulturabteilung* (Cultural Affairs Department) of the *Auswaertiges Amt* (Foreign Office) and the *Reichsministerium fuer Volksaufklaerung und Propaganda* (Ministry for Public Enlightenment and Propaganda);
B. Party agencies (a total of sixteen), foremost among them the *Auslandsorganisation* (Foreign Organization) of the *Nationalsozialistische und Deutsche Arbeiter Partei* (National Socialist and German Workers Party, NSDAP), formally responsible for carrying on party work among German *citizens* abroad; and
C. Free functional agencies (a total of sixty), classified into four subgroups, namely
   (a) Central organizations (twenty four), including such functionally varied groups as the multipurpose *Volksbund* (until 1933, *Verein*) *fuer das Deutschtum im Ausland*, the *Gesellschaft fuer Siedlung im Ausland* (Society

for Foreign Settlement), the *Deutsch-Akademischer Austauschdienst* (German Academic Exchange Service), and the *Bund auslanddeutscher Studenten* (League of German Students Abroad);

(b) Religious organizations (five), such as the *Reichsverband fue die katholischen Auslanddeutschen* (League of Catholic Germans Abroad);

(c) Institutes (twenty two), the most important of which was the DAI, mentioned above; and

(d) Germandom Leagues (nine), federations such as the *Bund deutscher Osten* (Federation of Eastern Germans), *Sudetendeutscher Heimatbund* (Homeland Federation of Sudeten Germans), and *Bund deutscher Westen* (Federation of Western Germans), representing minority ethnic German interests in several regions of Europe.[18]

To be sure, these agencies were far from equal in their importance to ethnic German affairs and in the amount of influence they could exert on Nazi foreign policy. Many of them, which included the great majority of the so-called "free" agencies, had little or no policy function, and those that did were soon brought securely under party control. Organizational leaders lacking in enthusiasm for National Socialism, or out of sympathy with the aggressive and opportunistic political edge which the Nazis gave to *Volkstumsarbeit*, were gradually eased from positions of authority.[19] Nazi party entrepreneurship in the sphere of Germandom affairs inspired a vast amount of envy and resistance from the "traditional" agencies (most particularly from the conservative career diplomats of the Foreign Office), and the interminable feuding that ensued unquestionably rendered the organization of ethnic German matters under Hitler colossally inefficient. On the other hand, it was the steady encroachment on the work of non-party agencies by the omnivorously aggressive Nazi party organization that guaranteed the subservience of *Volkstumspolitik* to Nazi Germany's foreign policy objectives. By the onset of war in 1939, Germandom's huge organizational machinery *within* the Reich had been fully bound to the purposes—and cross-purposes—of the Nazi state.[20] The obvious corollary step was to obtain the cooperation of ethnic Germans abroad.

Nazi Subversion of Ethnic Germans

In its efforts to foster contacts with *Volksdeutschen* in alien countries, the Third Reich was assisted as much by the persistence of German culture in many areas as by the close bonds with the homeland that often existed. In many countries, local ethnic German communities maintained schools that provided instruction in the mother tongue, often with the material and moral assistance of Germandom organizations in the Reich. German-minority districts in the successor states to the Austro-Hungarian Empire naturally were particularly rich in *Volksschulen*; their number, however, was impressive even in some overseas communities. Brazil, for example, had an estimated 1,260 German-language schools and enrolled over 50,000 students in the year 1932-33.[21] Teacher and student exchanges that brought *Volksdeutschen* to Germany had long been a feature of *Volkstumsarbeit*, and there were vast numbers of literary, religious, veteran, youth, and sporting associations in areas of ethnic German settlement which drew support and included a rich correspondence from Germandom organizations in the homeland in their drive to sustain cultural identity.[22]

A German-language press had flourished, at least temporarily, wherever ethnic Germans had settled.[23] Indigenous publications were often augmented with books and other materials supplied from Germany. A number of Germandom organizations, including the DAI, actively participated in directing new immigration to selected areas, in a further and relatively unusual bid to replenish existing ethnic German communities.[24] German settlements abroad varied greatly, of course, in their capacity or desire to resist assimilation. However, in general, "the close association of Germans abroad with the homeland," as Smith comments, "has been extraordinary when compared with other lands and migrations."[25]

With Hitler's rise to power in 1933, Nazi leaders wasted no time extending their own reach into German settlements abroad. They did so haphazardly, with little or no guidance from Hitler. His absorption with economic recovery and military rearmament, coupled with an understandable reluctance to antagonize foreign governments unnecessarily, precluded much concern by him with ethnic German affairs in the early formative phase of the Third Reich. The confusion and jurisdictional squabbling which resulted probably justified Smelser's objection to use of the word "conspiracy" to describe the nazification of *Volkstumspolitik*.[26] The Nazis spent as much or more of their time warding off one another's assaults in the uniquely unrestrained intramural power struggle Hitler tolerated among his lieutenants as they did systematically planning the conquest of power abroad. Nevertheless, there was very soon a visible and bustling Nazi presence in Germandom activities in areas of ethnic German settlement.

Nazi Germany naturally exploited existing organizational linkages and injected large quantities of National Socialist propaganda into the cultural and educational work of the VDA, DAI, and other ostensibly autonomous functional agencies. Books, pamphlets, and films laden with glowing descriptions of the rebirth of Germany were shipped abroad and disseminated through the long established and generally reputable associational networks of these groups. Much of the work of the "private" agencies continued to be quite innocent, but even seemingly innocent endeavors were sometimes turned to political advantage. At one point, the DAI, acting through German consular officials, sought to launch a "pen pals" program for German-Americans in which a distinctly German world outlook was to be instilled in the Americans by reliable National Socialists in other foreign outposts.[27] Under the especially spirited leadership of Rudolf Hess' protégé Ernst Wilhelm Bohle, the party's *Auslandsorganisation* (AO) moved quickly to bring the approximately half-million German citizens resident abroad (*Reichsdeutschen*) into line with the ethos of the homeland. In spite of frequent demands by his German rivals as well as by foreign governments that he confine his labors to persons of German citizenship, Bohle uninhibitedly asserted responsibility for some of the *Umschulung* (retraining) of *Volksdeutschen* as well. Bohle made no secret of his intent to transform the *Reichsdeutschen*, at least, into potent fifth columns. Designating them "pioneers of the New Germany," Bohle repeatedly demanded that they become a *gefuegiges Werkzeug* (pliant tool) in the service of Nazi foreign policy.[28] To them fell much of the task of distributing the vast amounts of National Socialist propaganda sent abroad by the AO "in packages, on ships, by mail, rail and air, and by personal emissaries ..."[29] The AO brought thousands of *Parteigenossen* (party comrades) from the ranks of *Reichsdeutschen* to Germany each year to celebrate the organization's anniversary, and it seized upon the opportunity to reinforce their dedication to Nazi ideals.[30] On occasion, resort was made to more unsavory devices. In Jacobsen's reasoned opinion, the AO, perhaps acting in league with the dreaded secret police, the *Gestapo*, probably relied quite often on intimidation of both *Reichsdeutschen* and *Volksdeutschen* to hasten conversion amongst the obstinate.[31]

While they are, of course, virtually impossible to prove, there were numerous allegations in the 1930s of beatings, arson, and boycotts arranged against "uncooperative" ethnic German businessmen or newspaper editors.[32]

Political movements among ethnic Germans sympathetic with National Socialism were often recipients of generous Nazi financial subsidies. Konrad Henlein's *Sudetendeutsche Partei*, for example, in addition to a large and regular monthly stipend, was apparently furnished a particularly large sum on one occasion to aid in contesting the 1935 parliamentary elections in Czechoslovakia.[33]

In countries on the German border, particularly Czechoslovakia, Nazi interference in minority politics became epidemic and began around 1935. "There are countless references," writes Smelser, "to uncountenanced activities of local party as well as SA [Sturm Abteiluing] and SS [Schutzstaffel] units; to inflammatory and compromising materials being sent across the border; to the establishment of wildcat guerrilla camps; and to interference in the municipal politics of border towns."[34] With the centralization of Germany's involvement in *Volkstumspolitik* under Nazi state security services—Heinrich Himmler's SS and Reinhard Heydrich's *Sicherheitsdienst* (SD)—achieved in 1937 with the creation of the powerful *Volksdeutsche Mittelstelle* (Central Office for Ethnic German Affairs, or VoMi), interference grew more thorough and more sinister.[35]

Thanks in no small measure to Josef Goebbels' extraordinary faith in the power of the spoken and printed word, Nazi Germany was the first state in history to bring modern communications technology fully into the service of political propaganda. Much use of it was made in the Germandom cause. The press and radio spewed forth the Nazi line in enormous quantities to ethnic Germans in Europe and overseas. When they could, the Nazis simply commandeered newspapers that served ethnic German communities. When they could not, they compensated with generous offers of subsidized news to the German-language press through the *Deutsches Nachrichten Dienst* (German News Service) and its various subsidiaries, which included Trans Ocean that served overseas areas.[36] In many ways the centerpiece of the Reich's propaganda enterprise, however, was radio. Long- and medium-wave broadcasts to *Volksdeutschen* in Europe from transmitters in Berlin (*Deutschlandsender*) and several other cities rose from 236 in 1933 to 1,500 in 1938.[37] While *Volksdeutschen* in Europe were often accessible by other means, "broadcasting," according to one student of Nazi propaganda, "became the most important means of keeping in touch with the Germans overseas."[38] By 1936, the Nazi External Service had surpassed the BBC's overseas short-wave services, and by 1939 was producing unprecedented daily programming in excess of 70 hours in German and many other languages.[39] The Nazis went to great lengths to assure themselves of a listening audience. They supplied short-wave receivers, created "wireless clubs" to encourage group listening, and developed a "zone service", according to Zeman,

> which was designed to inform the listeners of forthcoming programmes and to remind them of past ones. Every month 75,000 copies of bilingual programme sheets were distributed to various clubs,

> listeners' groups and to individuals; some 3,000 matrices were also sent out to interested newspapers abroad. All these services were provided on request, free of charge. Until America's declaration of war on Germany [in 1941], the programmes of the German short-wave transmitter were published in all specialized radio magazines in the United States as well as in some of the daily newspapers; the 150 German-language papers often published detailed reports on the content of the broadcasts.[40]

Nazi propaganda efforts were often uncoordinated and crude. It was once reported, for example, that sixteen truckloads of SA "brownshirts," thirty men to a truck, had been seen moving near the Czechoslovakian border, shouting a favorite Nazi slogan—*Ein Volk, ein Reich, ein Fuehrer!*—to their ethnic kinsmen on the other side.[41] At other times, their overtures were cloyingly sentimental, like the DAI-initiated birthday congratulations sent from ancestral towns in Germany to ethnic Germans in the United States, or the blue lights with which German families with members living abroad were encouraged to decorate their yuletide trees.[42] In the field of *Volkstumspolitik*, much was not done well by the Nazis, but virtually nothing was left undone. As was pointed out earlier, one incontrovertible fact stands out about all these Nazi attempts to woo, manipulate, and subvert ethnic German minorities abroad: they tried hard.

The Results of Volkstumspolitik

By the 1930s, centuries of immigration had resulted in a Germanic Diaspora with branches in practically every country in the world. No matter how small or inconsequential some of these outposts of Germandom may have been, one suspects that the conscientious representatives of Nazi Germany showed up in virtually all of them. Wherever ethnic Germans were numerous, and regardless of how distant from the homeland, attempts to manipulate, alter, or subvert loyalties were inevitably undertaken unless entirely prohibited, as in the Soviet Union, by lack of Nazi access. In only one of the four regions of the globe (Europe, the Soviet Union, North and South America) where ethnic Germans were to be found in substantial number in the 1930s did anything closely fitting the description of fifth columns materialize as major actors in the drama of wartime events. That, of course, was in Europe. Virtually everywhere else, it was assumed at the time that the seemingly omnipotent Nazis could produce one if they wished. Fear of such an eventuality, as was pointed out earlier, clearly and heavily influenced the course of events. Admittedly, failure of recognizable fifth columns to materialize in 1939 or 1940 outside of Europe does not preclude the possibility that they *might* have arisen elsewhere had the war taken a different course in Europe, or had threatened governments neglected to take stern precautionary measures against them. The fact remains, nonetheless, that the German fifth column, most certainly as a *military* weapon and to a large extent also as a *political* weapon, was essentially a European phenomenon.

Within Europe, moreover, the Nazis achieved very mixed results. In his major study of the German fifth column, the Dutch scholar Louis De Jong found little evidence of fifth column activity in those areas of Western Europe (Scandinavia, the Low Countries, France and Britain) that were targets of Nazi aggression. The evidence he sifted mainly had to do with the mobilization of *military* fifth columns at the time of German invasion. Notwithstanding the possibility that significant *political* fifth column activity had occurred earlier, there is still no particular reason to dispute his findings.
Observe that ethnic Germans were especially numerous only in France, however, so De Jong, in this part of Europe, was necessarily hunting mainly for *ideological* rather than *ethno*-ideological fifth columns.

With regards to East Central Europe, De Jong reached far different conclusions. He judged that the Nazis constructed formidable *political* fifth columns from the ethnic German minorities in five countries–Czechoslovakia, Poland, Yugoslavia, Hungary, and Rumania. Two of them (in Poland and Yugoslavia) ultimately also served Hitler as *military* fifth columns.[43] In the other three cases, according to De Jong, either feckless European diplomacy (Czechoslovakia) or an alliance with Germany (Hungary and Rumania) supplied Hitler his wants and rendered unnecessary military activation of the ethnic German minorities.[44] Of course, not everyone agrees with this assessment. The actual role, or even existence, of an ethnic German fifth column in Poland has been questioned by historians many times.[45] Sharp controversy arose, also, over the role of the Sudeten Germans and their leader, Konrad Henlein, in the destruction of the Czechoslovakian state in the late 1930s.[46] Nevertheless, even those analysts who have emphasized the element of exaggeration in descriptions of fifth column activities generally conceded some significance, at least, to those activities. Smelser, for example, whose study of the Czechoslovakian crisis makes the controversial point that Henlein was not a willing and obedient tool of Hitler (a "crypto-Nazi") at the outset, still freely concedes the existence of a powerful *Volksdeutschen* fifth column in the Sudetenland by 1937.[47] Even the tribute to Nazi ingenuity implicit in De Jong's reckoning comes in a study which pays most attention to the *imaginary* character of much German fifth column activity.

Judged by its European record, the German fifth column was at least modestly successful. Judged on a global scale, it was much less so. Its success, while limited, is far more enigmatic, however, than would have been its complete failure. The Nazis made heroic efforts to politically exploit and subvert ethnic Germans abroad; but they simply faced spectacular obstacles.

Obstacles to the German Fifth Column

Obstacles to the German fifth column were basically of two kinds. First were *extrinsic* obstacles—those common factors which, in varying combination, would obstruct virtually any fifth column-like movement and were essentially imposed upon the Nazis by the environment in which their foreign policy had to operate. Second were *intrinsic*—those rather less common factors which the Nazis essentially imposed upon themselves. The extrinsic sort stemmed from: (1) the requirements of international diplomacy and the competing objectives of Nazi foreign policy; (2) the adversary states' varying abilities to prevent or contain Nazi German penetration and manipulation of the

Volksdeutschen communities; and (3) the origin, character, and status of the minority communities themselves. These kinds of obstacles are the more obvious and can be dealt with fairly swiftly.[48]

Extrinsic Factors

In large part due to the circumstances surrounding World War I, ethnic Germans were often distrusted and detested, and more so the closer to German borders they dwelled. Virtually anything that any German government did overtly in the 1920s and 1930s to render aid and comfort to them would likely have provoked antagonism and sometimes retaliation. Since the latter could affect German security as well as international trade and investment behavior, even Nazi diplomacy, and as obtuse and obdurate as it often was, was bound to respond with a certain amount of circumspection and hesitancy in its dealings with German co-ethnics abroad. Admittedly, Hitler may have been inclined on most occasions, when his party's aggressive brand of *Volkstumspolitik* ran afoul of more conventional foreign policy objectives, to simply ignore the resulting contradictions. There were times, however, when patently subversive activities among ethnic German minorities were so embarrassingly obnoxious and politically counterproductive that they could not be ignored. Nazi Germany was desirous, for example, that the United States be neutral in any European conflict that might develop. Increasingly persuaded that the boisterous activities of the *Amerikadeutscher Volksbund* (German-American League) were alienating most Americans, including many of German descent, and seriously hampering Germany's efforts to improve relations with the United States, Berlin severed its formal ties with the *Bund* early in 1938 and desisted from any further serious attempt to organize the vast but apparently unsympathetic American *Volksdeutschen* population.[49]

When *Volkstumspolitik* touched upon the interests of Germany's allies, or would-be allies, diplomacy again sometimes intervened to cool the ardor of fifth column proponents. Solicitous of Mussolini's favor, for example, Hitler effectively stifled the powerful irredentist movement among the more than 250,000 ethnic Germans of the Alto

Adige (South Tyrol). So concerned was the Nazi leadership with the Italian alliance in the pre-war period that Germany even consented (in 1939) to the mass transfer to the fatherland of the German-Italian population.[50] At least in one sense, ethnic Germans in Poland were also the victims, temporarily, of political pragmatism. After the German-Polish treaty of friendship was concluded in January 1934, Berlin and Warsaw came to a further understanding in regards to restrictions on mutually hostile propaganda. The Nazi broadcasters agreed "to omit all references to the oppression of the German minority by the Polish government. The order affected the German press as well, and it remained valid–and it was in fact enforced–until 1939."[51]

The progress of Nazi manipulation of ethnic Germans abroad was even more strongly affected by the capability of the host states to control political activity among, and Nazi access to, ethnic Germans. Obviously, this had a lot to do with the size of the ethnic minority. As compared with the 40,000 ethnic Germans in Denmark, the 3,500,000 or so settled in Czechoslovakia (over 22 percent of the country's population) were a formidable group whose control by Prague would have been problematic under the best circumstances. Naturally, host state capability also had a lot to do with geographic position. Several million ethnic Germans, the so-called *Grenzdeutschen* (borderland Germans), lived on frontiers adjacent to Germany and, indeed, in some cases had been part of it until Germany's defeat in World War I. They were an integral part of the Central European German culture area, and they were in most instances readily accessible to Nazi penetration. This helps to account no doubt for the powerful display of Nazi influence in Poland, Czechoslovakia, Hungary, and Yugoslavia; as well as the much less impressive showing Nazism achieved in the Americas and the Soviet Union, where distance alone was such a huge barrier.

Size and geographic placement were hardly the sole determinants, however, of a state's ability to control the outward political display of a minority's discontent. Among the various European states with ethnic German settlements, including those sharing a frontier with Germany or Austria, there were substantial differences in the degree of tolerance exhibited towards ethnic minorities, as well as in the willingness of governments to throw the weight of state enforcement machinery against foreign-directed subversive activities among them. Poland—well-armed, authoritarian, and traditionally anti-German—supplied the German minority with very few legitimate means for the effective expression of their resentments. Repression of Nazi activities among ethnic Germans was probably more heavy-handed in Poland than in any other European country. Ironically, Czechoslovakia, uniquely and profoundly committed to Western liberal democracy and the accommodation of ethnic minority grievances, provided the Nazis with their most congenial environment in Europe. It was the last state in Europe to ban the Nazi party, and the only state in the pre-war decade both to permit an explicitly *Volksdeutschen* political party (the *Sudetendeutsche Partei*) to contest a free nationwide parliamentary election (in 1935) and, upon the astonishing triumph of that party at the polls, to invite its leaders to join the government.[52]

Apart from the restraints imposed by international diplomacy and the capability of host states to control foreign-influenced "anti-national" activities stood those sometimes insurmountable obstacles to Nazi penetration and political persuasion that related to the composition and character of the minority communities themselves. Those ethnic German groups whose minority status originated in the Versailles accord, such as elements of the German-Polish population, naturally sheltered exploitable resentments that would have been hard to duplicate among those *Volksdeutschen* in North and South America, for example, whose beginnings were in voluntary migration. Moreover, even where minority grievances were ancient in duration and inflamed by economic hardship and flagrant propaganda, as in Czechoslovakia, there were still very large numbers of the German minority who, whether on grounds of religious or political conviction, steadfastly resisted the appeals of National Socialism.[53]

The most powerful extrinsic obstacle of all, in some areas, was unquestionably the toll extracted from Germandom by the largely imperceptible but inexorable process of cultural assimilation. In the United States, for example, where in 1910 first- and second-generation Germans numbered over eight million and were the largest immigrant group in the country (almost 9 percent of the country's population of 92 million), maintenance of German cultural identity–and loyalty to Germany–had not always seemed impossible.[54] Nevertheless, the intensity of popular suspicion and resentment reached about Germans after American entry into the war in April 1917 and the resulting severe repression of German ethnic expression no doubt hastened the progress of assimilation. German books were burned, German place names expunged, German employees fired, German churches desecrated, German newspapers harassed with restrictions, and ethnic Germans themselves spat upon, beaten, and lynched (though only once fatally). Caught up in the feverish enthusiasm of super-patriotism, American public officials had then waged their own sort of *Kulturkampf* against Teutonic outposts in America. "By summer of 1918," according to one account, "approximately half of all the states had curtailed or abolished instruction in the German language, and several, along with dozens of counties, cities, and villages, had restricted the freedom of citizens to speak German in public,"[55] Such treatment must have enhanced the attractions of assimilation, which was in any case so painless and lucrative. Thus, it is apparent why even most of America's more recently arrived *Volksdeutschen* chose the favored assimilationist path of earlier German immigrants. It is not altogether surprising, either, that the remaining German-speaking Americans (Reichsdeutschen, still citizens of Germany), who may have numbered as many as 1.6 million in the 1930s, proved to be such a disappointing source of support for the Nazi cause.[56]

The ethnic Germans of South America stood in striking contrast to North Americans of German descent in respect to the assimilation factor. Estimated by the *Auslandsorganisation* of the NSDAP in 1936 at over one million, both *Volksdeutschen* and *Reichsdeutschen* were found in fairly large numbers in Brazil (800,000), Argentina (150,000), and Chile (30,000).[57] By 1938, Nazi influence among these groups had become very strong. According to Frye, most of the German-medium schools in Brazil, for instance, which numbered around 1,300 in 1936, eventually fell under Nazi domination.[58]

There were various reasons for the exceptional appeal of Nazism in this part of the hemisphere, which included the persistence of strong rural German communities (the so-called *bodenstaendige Deutsche*), a sense of cultural superiority over the "natives" that was impossible to sustain in North America, and the absence, until the late 1930s, of any determined official efforts to resist it. Of great importance, however, is the fact that in South America, where interethnic relations were governed by no such paradigm as the "melting pot," there was relatively little public pressure to assimilate. Even in Chile, where the German element, according to a count made at the end of World War I, represented no more than 0.6 percent of the total population, the persistence of German cultural traits and the popularity of Nazism were remarkable.[59]

The foregoing discussion should have made plain that, regional variations notwithstanding, there were limitations on Nazi interventionist activities about which they could do little or nothing. These limitations, here labeled extrinsic, were plentiful everywhere, but were most formidable of course in areas distant from the Third Reich. While they certainly did not prevent the spread of Nazism in every case, they unquestionably hindered its progress.

There remains, however, a set of "intrinsic" obstacles, essentially self-imposed, which handicapped the Nazis, if possible, even more. These obstacles the Nazis *would* not alter, in spite of the fact that they severely hobbled Germany's gigantic Germandom enterprise *wherever* there were German minorities. These obstacles related directly to the National Socialist concept of ethnic identification. German ethnicity, as defined by the Nazis, (1) bound *all* Germans in allegiance to the Nazi state, since it was *pan-Germanic* in application; (2) confined allegiance to the Nazi state to Germans *only*, since nationality was based in *organic* relationships; and (3) certified German superiority *above* all others, since it was determinedly *racist*. How Nazi ethnic theory handicapped the German fifth column supplies especially suggestive clues, by the way, to the *contemporary* potential worldwide for ethnic diaspora fifth column activity.

Intrinsic Factors

Pan-Germanism - The Nazis went to extraordinary lengths in their efforts to concentrate power in an elite party oligarchy and, as much as possible, in the hands of one man. Unlike the Italian fascists, they justified their endeavors by reference not to a theory exalting the state, but to an extravagant idea of nationhood.[60] According to the Nazis, the transcendent German nation (called *Deutschtum* or *Volkstum*), reaching out over political boundaries and across centuries of separation and cultural change, remained bound by blood to a lofty cultural mission. Tangible power, however thoroughly centralized, was intended only to ensure the unity of this unique *Volksgemeinschaft* (national community), whose survival would depend otherwise solely on the tenuous, endangered, and essentially intangible bonds of German culture. This idea—that the power of the state was the armor of cultural integrity—was not invented by the Nazis, but they made political allegiance more contingent on cultural identity than it had ever been before.

The mating of the promiscuous Nazi state with the carelessly defined German *Volk* had some curious results. German-Russians and German-Americans, many of whom had long ago severed their ties with the homeland and even ceased to speak its language, discovered themselves declared *Volksgenossen* (comrades of the German nation) and described thereafter, in a deft and deliberate transposition, as "Russian-Germans" and "American-Germans." That small gesture of verbal imperialism symbolized the entire process of *Gleichschaltung*, by which all elements of the German nation were to be brought into coordination with the collective tasks of the German state. *Gleichschaltung* proceeded at different levels of German society, but with the same fundamental objective. On the individual plane, it sought complete psychological identification with the social group: self-realization through self-annihilation, as one author described it.[61] At the group level, *Gleichschaltung* required unquestioning acceptance of the Nazi blueprint by organizations inside and outside of the Reich. It was noted earlier that leadership of Germandom organizations, after a few years of struggle, was substantially cleansed of non-Nazi elements. The defeated "traditionalists," according to Smelser, were men who were often as convinced as Hitler that Germans everywhere were indissolubly bound to the Germanic cultural community. In contrast to Hitler, however, they were also men "who tended to treat ethnic

Germans not so much as tools of Reich foreign or domestic policy but as unique population groups with viable interests and goals of their own."[62] *Gleichschaltung* meant self-sacrifice equally for individual Germans, for the Germandom organizations, and for the *Volksgruppen* themselves of Czechoslovakia, Rumania, Belgium, Memel, Danzig, and other lands where Germans dwelled.

There is no way of knowing precisely how many *Volksdeutschen* swallowed the dogmas of Nazi pan-Germanism. Their number must have been larger among the embittered *Grenzdeutschen* of East-Central Europe than among the volunteer migrants to the Americas, but the idea, if seriously examined, really should not have had much appeal anywhere. It clubbed all Germans into a mystical monolithic community stripped of the rich social, economic, historical, and intellectual diversity which had been their actual fortune. It rested on the preposterous assumption that human concerns were uniform from one end of Germandom to the other, and that they all could be successfully represented by the Central European Nazi state. It made being culturally German troublesome, sometimes downright dangerous, regardless of one's political orientation. It was totally impenetrable by the fact that there might be *Volksdeutschen* who yearned for a homeland other than Germany, if they yearned for one at all.

Regardless of the actual number who did believe in Nazi pan-Germanic ideals, what seems incontrovertible is that they could but rarely *act* upon them. To be suspected of harboring such convictions was unpopular and likely to generate suspicion, and to make them public risked being charged with treason. Even in Czechoslovakia, where ethnic German politics always carried the thinnest veneer of loyalty to the state, Konrad Henlein might have privately offered himself and his party to Hitler as a "factor in National Socialist Reich policy"; but his public pronouncements emphasized repeatedly his independence of the Nazi movement and loyalty to the Czechoslovakian state.[63] Pan-Germanism inevitably stained the *Volksdeutschen* affirmation of German culture, like speaking the German language in public, with a hint of betrayal. It invited retaliation. While pan-Germanism may have been comforting to those with wounded cultural pride, it was for many ethnic Germans on this planet, as for those who wished to mobilize them, a gigantic albatross.

Cultural Organicism - Hitler's *Mein Kampf* began with the declaration: "Common blood belongs in a common Reich."[64] These words reveal a conception of the nation quite at odds with the conception held by most liberal Europeans of the day. Whereas for them the nation was a society of freely-associating individuals mechanically joined by common culture, for Hitler and his true-believer confederates the nation was a "living" organism joined by blood. "In the Nazi conception of the nation," wrote Bischoff,

> individuals are united, primarily because of common inheritance in blood, into an organic group, a *Gemeinschaft*, in which the particular individual is subordinated to the whole and his value becomes dissolved in that of the nation. There is thus a contrast between a mechanical adding together of like individuals and a chemical synthesis of individuals with a common origin.[65]

What was *organically* exclusive clearly ought to be *politically* exclusive as well: state should coincide with nation. In the organic nation-state, meant alone for the *Staatsvolk*, there was no allowance for ethnic minorities. Here, the Nazis were as disinterested in absorbing non-Germans through cultural assimilation (in de-nationalization, in other words) as they were contemptuous of living with them as equals in a framework of cultural pluralism.

Extreme Nazi cultural organicism was tantamount to the denial of minority rights, at least as they had been defined in the Covenant of the League of Nations. Admittedly, Nazis had spoken at times of the right of "national self-determination," but they quite apparently did not mean nationality to be a matter of subjective individual decision or popular plebiscite: a Jewish-German, no matter how culturally German, could not simply self-select German nationality; a Silesian-German, however content under Polish rule, likewise could not simply self-select Polish nationality. These were matters for the nation, the blood community, to decide.[66]

Committed by their political ideology to a concept of the nation that was incompatible with the notion that a minority *qua* minority had certain inalienable rights, the Nazis, as might have been expected, failed almost entirely to exploit the fifth column potential of *non-German* ethnic minorities. In their life-or-death struggle against the Soviet Union, they made notoriously poor use of the numerous, and often resentful, Soviet minorities, in perhaps fatal disregard of Alfred Rosenberg's plan to turn the non-Russians against the Bolshevik enemy with the offer of dismemberment.[67] By the end of the war, the Nazi External Service was broadcasting in 55 languages. However, these broadcasts, authorities agreed, stressed National Socialist themes heavy with racial and ethnic stereotypes, and they concentrated propaganda "on the foreign audience that they knew best—Germans living abroad."[68] The Nazis did diversify their mass subversive activities from time to time to include non-German minorities.[69] In general, however, the Nazis were more the victims than the beneficiaries of their own ideology. After war had broken out in Europe, "the emphasis in enemy countries had to switch to undermining the morale of the citizens as a whole. But even then," Hale pointed out instructively,

> the logic of an internal propaganda designed to rally a committed audience around the catchphrases of total fascist power spread into the sphere of foreign propaganda. There was no consistent attempt to understand the psychology of the anti-fascist foreign audience, little attempt to modify the hate-language and emotional racist appeals that characterized the RRG's output. When the tone sometimes lapsed into friendly chattiness, or into highbrow monologues on German culture, the intention was only to make more relevant and more respectable the uncompromising political message.

> Although the treatment varied from country to country and from moment to moment, the themes of Nazi foreign propaganda were little more than an echo of the internal line: anti-Semitism, anti-communism, the superiority of the Aryan race and German nation, the wisdom and power of the Fuehrer. There could be no positive message based on the ideology of national socialism or fascism.[70]

"The post-war [World War I] German society," wrote Barbu "was so intensely obsessed with its survival as a separate group that it completely failed to formulate any of its experiences in a system of universal modes of life. As such", and in contrast to communist societies, "it had no open door to humanitarianism."[71] Supremely obsessed with itself, the Nazi state could spare little anguish for the non-German oppressed. It did not succeed in subverting them. It hardly even tried.

Racism - It has already been argued here that Nazi Germany sought, indiscriminately and unwisely, to mobilize *all* Germans, and that it confined its efforts, also unwisely, to Germans *only*. Without question, it compounded its problems by appealing to them with the perverse and self-limiting idea of racism. Pan-Germanism glossed over cultural, political, and economic contradictions and branded ethnic Germans everywhere with the mark of potential treason. Cultural organicism, in its turn, excluded all but German minorities from the attention of the Nazi state. Racism went a step further and insulted virtually everyone who was not of German descent.

In the Nazi scheme of things, a nation's virtue lay in the purity of its blood. Racially purer nations were superior to those which suffered from severe racial mixture. The purest were Aryans, a vague grouping of peoples amongst whom—somewhere to the fore—stood the Germans, or at least those blonde, blue-eyed Nordics amongst them. All others were relatively impure and, therefore, relatively inferior. Against contamination by them, the racially superior nations had to be constantly vigilant, a mission which the Nazi state adopted with relish.

The Nazis never succeeded in adequately defining what they meant by race, and, apart from Jews, Gypsies, and Negroes, were characteristically vague about a group's ranking at any particular moment. When it suited them, Slavic people were all barbarians and *Untermenschen*, inferior humans. When it did not, exceptions were made. In late 1938, for example, the Slovaks, then a target of Nazi propaganda against the Czechs, found Nazi descriptions of their racial origins moving perceptibly closer to those of the German people.[72] When Hitler's early confidence in German-Americans was rewarded with their enthusiastic participation in the war against him, his estimate of their race-worthiness experienced a remarkable decline.[73] Consistency in racial doctrine was not among the more conspicuous achievements of the Third Reich.

To be certain, Nazi Germany was not the only racist society of the day; and the Nazi government was by no means the first, or last, to officially endorse racial inequality. It was the first and only state in modern times, however, to make racism a major political export. No other state had ever before predicated foreign policy so extensively on racist dogma. No state had ever pinned its hopes so completely on its own racial indomitability or the presumed racial weakness of its adversaries.[74]

No state had ever so casually disregarded the realities of racial and ethnic relations in the countries which were the friendly or unfriendly targets of its diplomacy. Nazi racist dogma alienated Germany's potential allies, united its opponents, rendered any sort of collaboration with it sinister, and eliminated all doubts about its virtue and any ideological objections to resisting it. The Nazis blithely disregarded it, but racism, as an approved subject of discourse among civilized nations, was an idea whose time had departed.

The political mobilization, manipulation, and subversion of ethnic minorities, difficult under the best of circumstances, were made needlessly more arduous by an idea with little acceptability. Most non-German (or, at least, "non-Aryan") minorities would certainly be distrustful of a state that had classified them as biologically inferior. Most non-German majorities, in those countries that hosted ethnic German minorities, would clearly have added incentive to be suspicious of German elements–and they would also have ample moral sanction to justify repression of real or imagined fifth column activity by them. Many ethnic Germans, for that matter, found the idea repugnant and a solvent for lingering loyalties to the homeland. When it comes to subverting minorities in this exceedingly multicultural world, one should be advised against an idea so lacking in versatility as racial supremacy.

It bears repeating at this point that these and all the other obstacles to the political mobilization and manipulation of ethnic minorities considered so far in this chapter did not prevent the Nazis from achieving some success in this regard just the same. This is not only surprising but, for reasons now to be considered, acutely pertinent to one's understanding of the contemporary potential for mobilizing and manipulating ethnic diasporas for foreign policy purposes.

Ethnic Diasporas: The Current Strategic Potential

Judging the strategic potential of ethnic diaspora minorities, as the foregoing discussion should have made clear, is difficult even with the advantage of hindsight and when documentation is fairly abundant. However, judging their *current* potential presents even greater difficulties. One reason for this is that today the term "fifth column" is itself in huge disarray. Practically any political project that a writer considers unsavory can be–and often is–designated as a fifth column. In a recent random sampling of commentary drawn from online sources, the following were explicitly identified as fifth columns: the Hawaiian sovereignty movement,[75] the psychiatric profession (numbering about 150,000 around the world),[76] postmodernists,[77] globalization,[78] the Russian mass media,[79] American radicals (including *The New York Times*!),[80] Muslim chaplains in the U.S. military,[81] Chinese politicians and businessmen favoring opening up more direct links with the mainland,[82] Chinese tourists "missing" in Taiwan,[83] resentful Europeans in the United States,[84] and, less surprisingly, Saudi-backed Wahhabists.[85] The subject of fifth column, let there be no doubt, is a semantic minefield.

Indeed, nowadays professional analysts of ethnic conflict make little use of the concept of a fifth column. This is so in part, one supposes, because the metaphor, obviously sprung from full-scale conventional war, seems an inexact or inappropriate description for peacetime efforts to make belligerent use of a state's network of ethnic diaspora communities. Moreover, the term's association in the immediate post-World War II years with a great many witless and merciless pursuits after imaginary enemies loaded it with connotations incompatible with impartial analytical applications. The term's relative absence from scholarly discussions may also be related, however, to the current and longstanding conventional emphasis on *domestic* determinants of ethnic conflict. Very likely, this unfortunate tendency is strengthened by the clandestine nature of much foreign strategic intervention and its consequent inaccessibility to scholarly inquiry. Yet the term's scarcity in the literature of ethnic conflict may also be due to limitations in prevailing concepts of ethnic conflict, which too often view external manipulations as events on the periphery of the domestic arena rather than as events central to the explanation of the conflict's roots, intensification, and outcome. There have been scholarly attempts to remedy the neglect, but, so far, without much effect.[86]

The intimidatory and ill-boding practice of applying the collective label of fifth column to disliked ethnic minorities has, of course, outlived the demise of the Nazi state. The Chinese in Malaya and Indonesia, Christians in Uganda, Arabs in Israel, and Muslims in India (and not only the Kashmiri Muslims), among others, have all been accused at one time or another of mass treachery—or at least of the potential for it—on behalf of a foreign power or powers. In some instances, as in the case of the Chinese minority in Indonesia in the 1960s, the accusations have led to deadly violence. The overseas Chinese in Southeast Asia have probably occasioned the single most extensive debate on the subject of divided loyalties in the post-World War II era. Most scholarly literature in the last several decades, however, has acquitted Beijing of major *politically hostile* activity involving overseas Chinese and, incidentally, probably further tarred the fifth column concept in the process.[87]

The fact of the matter is that the concept of an ethnic fifth column stands today, and for good reason, discredited in the eyes of many. However, the *practices* it was intended to describe—the infiltration, mobilization, indoctrination, and subversive manipulation by hostile external entities of migrant or diasporic minorities—are definitely not out of fashion. The conditions under which any would-be manipulation- or subversion-minded strategist would have to operate today have changed substantially, of course, since the racist appeals and territorial claims of the Axis powers, especially Germany, combined to arouse fear of fifth column activity. Nevertheless, no one should doubt that the political-strategic mobilization and manipulation of ethnic diaspora groups continues in the present era, whether or not it goes by the name of a fifth column. The motivation for such activity is at least as strong now as ever.

To begin with the obvious, there are plenty of aggrieved diaspora minorities nowadays to supply the raw material for fifth column-like movements. Parts of the world overflow with victims of real or imagined minority discrimination, with refugees fleeing from ethnic conflict, historic ethnic communities divided by arbitrary boundaries inherited from the colonial era, and new migrant communities harboring resentments rising from the modern clash of cultures, especially religious cultures. Satisfaction with and unswerving loyalty to the domiciliary state by ethnic diasporas is by no means universal; indeed, there are numerous diaspora-connected separatist- or at least autonomist-leaning movements in progress today around the world—in northern Sri Lanka, southern Philippines, southern Thailand, China's Tibet and Xinjiang provinces, as well as the Kurdish and Shiite zones of Iraq.

There can be little doubt, either, that there are plenty of aggressive outsiders prepared to intervene on behalf of such minorities. The tremendous explosion both in the number and variety of political entities active in international politics has been repeatedly pointed out.[88] Since Hitler first walked onto the world stage, the number of independent countries alone has approximately quadrupled. The strategic utilization of diaspora minorities is not, however, restricted to states. Indeed, some contemporary "non-state actors" with apparent stakes in expatriate ethnic diasporas—notably terrorist, ethnic and religious militant groups—throw far more political and strategic weight internationally than many of the states that have surfaced in the past half century. With regards to the potential outside perpetrators of fifth column activity, there are not only *more* of them now but also more *kinds* of them.

Not least among developments facilitating strategic mobilization and manipulation of diaspora minorities is the stunning revolution going on in communications technology. One of the most impressive achievements of this revolution was to have empowered hordes of non-state actors with communication capabilities far superior to anything presided over even by powerful states no more than a few decades ago. In the mid-1970s, for instance, roughly 100 countries were transmitting internationally via shortwave radio, with over a quarter of them broadcasting more than 100 program hours per week. The largest of them, the Soviet Union, the United States, and China, in the number and power of their transmitters, commanded an astonishing part of the airwaves. The United States alone, if the radio capabilities of the Voice of America (VOA), the quasi-public Radio Free Europe (RFE) and Radio Liberty (RL) are lumped together, was broadcasting (1977) approximately 1,765 regularly scheduled program hours weekly, and employed 155 domestic and overseas transmitters with total power that approached 27 million watts.[89] In its day, the Soviet Union led the way in linguistic diversity of its broadcasts and in the late 1970s transmitted from a dozen major stations in approximately 75 different languages.[90]

Impressive as were the shortwave radio capabilities of major states in those earlier days, they pale in comparison with the communications capabilities now at the disposal of millions—in the form of television, cellular technology, videocassettes, laptop (and hand-held) computers, email, and the Internet. Terrorist web sites alone, monitored by a researcher at the United States Institute of Peace in Washington, DC, for the last 7 years, have grown in number in that short period from 12 to more than 4,000.[91]

According to this source, all known terrorist groups maintain more than one website, and the sites boast different languages. The sites take donations and offer training. The online magazines of some of them offer guidance on kidnapping, poisoning, and murdering hostages. Potential terrorist targets are openly discussed.

The revolution in communications technology that accelerated spectacularly in the 1990s, says Marc Sageman, a leading interpreter of contemporary terror networks, has dramatically transformed the process of mobilizing recruits to what he calls the "global Salafi jihad." Whereas religion-based terrorism had at one time sought recruits primarily through face-to-face interactions, the Internet has made

> possible a new type of relationship ... a seemingly concrete bond between the individual and a virtual Muslim community. This virtual community plays the same role that 'imagined communities' played in the development of the feeling of nationalism, which made people love and die for their nations as well as hate and kill for them. Because of its virtual nature, the Internet community has no earthly counterpart and becomes idealized in the mind of surfers. This community is just, egalitarian, full of opportunity, unified in an Islam purged of national peculiarities, and devoid of corruption, exploitation, and persecution. The appeal of this approximation of paradise can become irresistible, especially to alienated young Muslims and potential converts suffering from isolation or from ordinary discrimination.... Without the restraints from real interactions with the social world, this virtual world allows extreme violence against the presumed conspirators against the virtual umma.[92]

The revolution in communications technology has, in other words, helped enable transformation of the scattered diaspora of (Arab and non-Arab) expatriate Muslims into attractive targets of opportunity for a new breed of non-state strategic entities—jihad-minded radicals. Lawrence Wright is one who endows this transformation with large importance indeed. In an article sub-titled "Were the Madrid bombings [of 11 March 2004] part of a new, far-reaching jihad being plotted on the Internet?" he observes that Muslim immigration has had a profound impact on Europe. "Nearly twenty million people in the European Union," he says,

> identify themselves as Muslim. This population is disproportionately young, male, and unemployed. The societies these men have left are typically poor, religious, conservative, and dictatorial; the ones they enter are rich, secular, liberal, and free. For many, the exchange is invigorating, but for others Europe becomes a prison of alienation.... The Internet provides confused young Muslims in Europe with a virtual community. Those who cannot adapt to their new homes discover on the Internet a responsive and compassionate forum.[93]

Just as analysts disagreed in an earlier day over the power of Nazism's appeal to the scattered Germanic Diaspora, they are far from having reached a consensus position today either on the power of Internet appeals to the equally scattered Muslim Diaspora or, for that matter, on the overall capacity of state or non-state actors to mobilize expatriate Muslim communities for strategic objectives. A degree of skepticism in regards to these matters is essential. However, it should not be pushed so far that it entirely rules out the patterns of behavior that once fell under the rubric of a fifth column. There are in this world simply too many opportunities for exploiting grievances and feeble loyalties to expect ordinary mortals to pass them up. There is today, just as there was decades ago when Walker Connor commented on the incredibly complex circumstances inviting "informal penetration" in the African Horn, an almost irresistible temptation "to ride Trojan horses that graze within another's gates."[94]

Persistent Obstacles

Any contemporary fifth column-like program would have to make allowance, of course, for many of the same obstacles that blocked

Nazi inroads into ethnic diaspora groups. FitzGerald's careful critique of the fifth column hypothesis as applied to the overseas Chinese of Southeast Asia illustrates the point. He argued persuasively that Beijing's overtures to the overseas Chinese since 1949 had been increasingly restrained both by the influence of competing Chinese Communist diplomatic objectives and by the political environment of the overseas Chinese communities themselves. The external costs of maintaining the relationship were prohibitively high, FitzGerald maintained, because

> it involved shoring up those props to the relationship that were most colonial in appearance, which reinforced the characteristics of Overseas Chinese that set them apart from the local people, and which inevitably involved problems in foreign relations. It also meant the assumption of impossible responsibilities for protection. And it meant attempting to dictate the behavior and responses of a population over which the CCP [Chinese Communist Party] could exercise almost no control.

Also, the benefits to China were correspondingly low, he continued, for

> it was precisely because of their special relationship with China and their position in the countries of residence that the Overseas Chinese were both a liability in establishing or developing friendly relations with Southeast Asia, and an unsuitable instrument for the pursuit of more covert objectives. Cultural separateness, economic domination, racial arrogance, and political attachment to China made the Overseas Chinese a suspect minority in Southeast Asia and unlikely channel for effective influence for the CCP.[95]

Cultural assimilation, which so baffled the Nazis in North America, remains there and elsewhere a powerful obstacle to external attempts at diaspora mobilization. With the passage of nearly a century since the last great wave of European migration to the Americas, there is clearly no scope at all there for the mass enlistment of "overseas Europeans" in the political or strategic designs of foreign powers. However, for more recent immigrants–from the Middle East, Asia, or Africa–the potential for mobilization is less easy to gauge. Let it be acknowledged, then, that there are some countries today which are, or seem to be, virtually impregnable targets. Let it also be acknowledged, moreover, that there are ethnic diaspora communities whose mobilization and strategic employment might be so politically costly that no sane government or other political entity would run the risk. The possibility still exists, however, that the raw potential for such employment may have risen, in fact, since the days of the notorious German fifth column.

The Domestication of Ethnic Subversion

Earlier pages have pointed out that the Third Reich's Germandom organizations were freighted with one of the most repugnant ideologies of modern times. This ideology burdened Germany with a concept of ethnicity with limited appeal to many ethnic Germans and with practically none at all for non-German minorities. Nazi Germany's unambiguously imperial, parochial, and racial dogmas stimulated distrust of Germany and Germans, and they imparted an unusually sinister face to Germany's efforts to maintain contact with and to mobilize ethnic Germans abroad. National Socialism was a uniquely powerful mobilizing force within Germany. Outside that country, among non-Germans, it was largely impotent.

An entirely different situation prevails today. Almost all states pay at least formal lip service to an ideology that contrasts at every point with National Socialism and is revered by virtually every ethnic minority. It is liberationist whereas Nazism was imperialistic, universal whereas Nazism was parochial, and egalitarian whereas Nazism was racially supremacist. This new ideology sanctions international (humanitarian) intervention on behalf of ethnic minorities (even though the intervention may put in jeopardy a minority group's loyalty to the host state) whereas Nazism had the blessings of Germany only. It is seductive rather than sinister, and in a way it seems to have "domesticated" what once might have passed as subversion. The bywords of this ideology are three: national liberation, self-determination, and democratization.

National Liberation - In place of Nazi Germany's overtly imperial, expansionist pan-Germanism, which lay claim to all Germans everywhere and, to boot, a substantial amount of territory on which to settle them, today's world boasts a species of ethno-nationalism that is aggressively minority- rather than state-centric, and separatist rather than in-gathering. National liberation means the creation of new identities and new states—the forging of new allegiances from the wreckage of old ones. It affirms the historical, geographic, and socio-economic discontinuities that undermine the cohesion of ancient cultures as stoutly as pan-Germanism denied them.

All of the major pandemic movements that flourished at the beginning of the last century (pan-Turkism, pan-Slavism, and pan-Germanism) are today either dead or dying. In contrast, pan-Arabism and the related but more comprehensive pan-Islamism have obviously achieved impressive organizational expression and considerable vitality today, but whether either of these will ultimately be able to substitute a viable pandemic for the quite virile nationalisms and sub-nationalisms within them remains a matter fiercely debated.[96] Nothing is more revealing of the inherently segmented appeal of national liberation than the dilemma endlessly faced by the Palestine Liberation Organization in attempting to spell out its own political mission. Dependent for their independence movement's survival on fellow Arabs and Muslims, Palestinian Arabs by necessity have had to be dutifully respectful in their National Covenant of Arab unity—in other words, of the conglomerate "Arab Nation" and pan-Arabic (along with pan-Islamic) ideals. They have repeatedly emphasized in the same document, however, the autonomy of their movement and the

Palestinian rather than simply Arab (or Muslim) character of its objectives.[97]

National liberation is as fundamentally secessionist in spirit as National Socialism was irredentist. Irredentism flowed naturally from redemptive pan-Germanism, as naturally as secession flows from divisive national liberation. Militant nationalism among the German-speaking minority of the South Tyrol, for example, spread rapidly after that region's transfer to Italy by the Treaty of Saint Germaine in 1919. Throughout the lengthy history of that nationalist movement (it endured into the 1960s), it was always preeminently irredentist and sought *Anschlus* (union) with German Austria. The movement is moribund today, one of the only severe ethnic conflicts to have been folded up so peacefully in the post-World War II era. The explanation for this is almost certainly to be found in the generally diminished appeal of pandemic (in particular, *non-religious* or *non-sectarian*) movements and of pan-German irredentism in particular.[98]

Irredentism survives, no doubt, but it must masquerade nowadays as secession. Irredentist yearnings are clearly out of fashion.

Self-determination - Nazism unequivocally denied minorities rights of their own and it confined its appeals abroad to ethnic Germans only. The doctrine of self-determination, which virtually all contemporary statesmen at least formally applaud, restores these rights, bases them in positive law, and universalizes their application across cultures. Essentially, and in spite of its ambiguities, self-determination makes allegiance a matter of political rather than biological selection. It replaces the idea of cultural organicism (or *primordial* ethnic identity) with a highly voluntaristic and open-ended kind of cultural self-selection (or *plebiscitary* ethnicity).

The first article of the International Covenant on Civil and Political Rights, a major human rights document adopted by the United Nations in 1966 and in force for ratifying states by late 1977, sets forth that "all peoples have the right of self-determination. By virtue of that right they freely determine their political status and freely pursue their economic, social and cultural development."[99] This is only one of many signals that the legal doctrine of self-determination today enjoys huge international acceptance, and even those statesmen wary of its implications or uncertain of its meaning hesitate to reject it.[100] Under its protective mantle, every ethnic minority, no matter how inconvenient (or spurious) its claims or inconsequential its role, enjoys the theoretical right to define its own political identity. Self-determination renders unnecessary the intervention of a protective cultural fatherland, since every state, no matter if an ethnic bond exists between it and an aggrieved ethnic minority, is now under some moral compulsion to come to the minority group's defense.

As was the doctrine of cultural organicism, self-determination is neutral as to who uses or abuses it. It too shelters terrorists, rogues, and racists; excuses tyrannical regimes and the repression of political oppositions; and inspires fanaticism and sires bloody strife.

Unlike anything that came before it, however, self-determination is a new and powerful moral weapon in the armory of every ethnic minority, diaspora minorities included. It is also a masterful disguise, of course, for old-fashioned political interference and strategic subversion.

Democratization - Nazi Germany espoused racist dogmas that were blatantly partial to Germans. They were also unblushingly elitist. The Master Race was meant to do precisely what the word "master" implied: to rule over all the other more-or-less inferior races. Social Darwinist to the core, Nazi racial theory presumed that manifested *political* weakness grew out of inherent *racial* decadence for which there was no remedy. Even if the non-Germans of Hitler's day had been able to swallow everything else in National Socialism, this doctrine of permanent and racially predetermined political inferiority was surely indigestible.

The political aspirations of diaspora minorities today are whetted from one end of the globe to the other with the promise of democracy. No greater contrast with Nazi race theory could be found. Democracy makes axiomatic that all shall stand as equals in the political kingdom: that for every man there shall be one vote. This is hardly a guarantee that power will be shared equally, only that all—disencumbered of any sense of racial inferiority or superiority—will have equal formal access to it. Nor is there any reason to believe that government will be wise and just, or even very democratic, just because the popularly elected have taken the seats of the racially selected. Skeptics are right: democratization does not abolish inferiority. However, it does destroy the relevance to politics of the theory of biologically-determined racial inferiority.

National liberation is the doctrine that challenges ethnic minorities to create a nation; self-determination justifies their claims and supplies the moral encouragement and legal sanction of the entire world community; democratization, in turn, provides those who will inherit the new state with promise of an equal political stake in its future. These are stellar attractions. They appeal to people in ethnic diasporas. They also appeal to those who seek political advantage in crumbling loyalties. They have the potential to make the political mobilization and strategic manipulation of ethnic diasporas easier than ever.

Conclusion

Appreciation for the role the German fifth column actually played in the World War II era was inevitably colored by the experience particular countries had of it. Americans, for instance, had a fairly limited and, in most ways, exceptional encounter with it. What they were introduced to as a "fifth column" bore little resemblance to the sometimes deadly species that became prevalent in Europe. The American *Bundesfuehrer* Fritz Kuhn may have intended far more sinister activities for the *Amerikadeutscher Volksbund* than those in which it commonly engaged before its dissolution, but all the Nazi salutes and swastika-brandishing flags in the world could not have turned his ragtag band of self-styled "storm troopers" into anything justifying General Mola's threatening metaphor. The *Bund* never attracted more than a few thousand of the millions of Germans who had settled in America, and it was regarded as little better than a pest by its adored Nazi leadership in Europe. The excitement generated by overtly pro-Nazi elements in the United States in the 1930s was, with little exaggeration, in near perfect inverse correlation with their political importance.[101] By the same token, security measures taken by the U.S. government not only against U.S.-based Germans but also against ethnic Germans in parts of Latin America, according to recent scholarship, may also have significantly exaggerated the threat.[102]

Others, less fortunate than the Americans, were fated to more than a harmless caricature. Many Eastern Europeans, Czechoslovakians above all, would tie the ultimate destruction of their countries by the Nazis in important measure to the "enemy within." Even when, with hindsight the German fifth column is granted a much less exalted role even in Europe than was claimed for it at the time, one must pay due regard to the enormous and often tragic consequences which the mere suspicion of disloyalty inspired.[103]

The practice of mobilizing and manipulating co-ethnic expatriate minorities, to which the Nazis were often drawn, did not perish in April 1945. After all, the absence of statesmen with declared *Volkstum* concerns like those of the Nazis does not mean that there are none prepared to orchestrate in their own way the ubiquitous discontents of the contemporary era's ethnic minorities. There ought to be then some lessons for the present to be drawn from this reappraisal of the vanquished German fifth column. Four seem worthy of further reflection.

1. *Any contemporary ethnic fifth column-like formations are highly unlikely to be as easy to detect and identify as was the German fifth column.* The Nazis inherited a vast complex of Germandom organizations at home and abroad, which, augmented with many more of their own, they proceeded to bring into conformity with Nazi policy. These organizations, even when their activities were relatively innocent, were widely suspected of providing cover for ill-intentioned Nazi penetration, and they were often brought under close state surveillance. Nazi efforts to conceal their connections with these organizations were absurdly ineffective and, indeed, half-hearted. It did not help either that many Germandom groups, even when cautioned against it, openly displayed the regalia and integrated the rituals of Nazism into their own local programs.[104] Nazi recruitment abroad generally avoided non-Germans, a fact that made German fifth columnists conspicuous by culture if not by ideology. Indeed, the German fifth column was noteworthy in the open professions of loyalty to Hitler which commonly came from ethnic Germans abroad,

and in the many unequivocal public statements of Nazi expectations of ethnic Germans made by Nazi officials at home.

No contemporary state or non-state entity has at its disposal an institutional infrastructure, public or private, at home or abroad, on the scale of the Germandom organizations of the Third Reich, with the exception, perhaps, of Israel (enormously reliant on diaspora Jewry) and the two Chinas (arch competitors for the economic investments and political sympathies of the Overseas Chinese). Their unusually "busy" trans-world ethnic connectivity no doubt helps to account for the occasional fifth column allegations made against Beijing, as well as allegations of heavy-handed ethnic lobbying hurled frequently against both Taipeh and Tel Aviv. The rest of the world's political entities, whether or not they are interested in mobilizing ethnic diasporas, essentially do without assets of this magnitude.

That may not be a terrible handicap. With regards to organizing the mobilization and manipulation of diaspora minorities, contemporary political entrepreneurs do have to be imaginative and versatile, probably more so than the Nazis with their rich Germandom inheritance. However, the severe limitations of that inheritance have already been reviewed. There clearly are advantages to the cultural "neutralism" that currently prevails in the choice of minority clients, not least the absence of any requirement that there be an organic connection between the cultivator and the perpetrator of fifth column-like activities. This way, it is easier to wash one's hands of efforts that fail or even to deny complicity when they succeed. In the post-German variation, the fifth column relationship may be entirely pragmatic, require few if any emotional bonds, and, should circumstances change, be dispensed with without hint of racial treason. The great advantage in this sort of "random" fifth column conspiracy is that the target state can not be certain where the *other* four columns are coming from!

2. Contemporary ethnic fifth column-like formations are almost certainly not going to be as easy to dislike as was the German fifth column. On the contrary, they may well find it relatively easy to win support for their activities around the world. The activities of ethnic fifth column-like formations are, virtually by definition, going to antagonize some groups—if none other, certainly those which control the state under assault from within. However, there are degrees of antagonism and variations in the size of the groups antagonized, and these are important predictors both of the strength of conspiracy and the target state's capacity to resist it. The Nazis pushed both to their limit and aroused intense enmity from many of their opponents and at least irritated practically all non-Germans. Nazi ideology was not uniformly repulsive in all parts of the globe: anti-Semitism, as was noted earlier in this chapter, found readier acceptance in Eastern Europe than in either Western Europe or the Americas. Yet the proclamation of German racial superiority was obviously a self-limiting feature in mobilizing recruits: there were, after all, only about 11 million *Volksdeutschen* abroad who might be expected to find the doctrine appealing as compared to a far larger number of non-Aryans who most certainly would not.

The currently fashionable ethno-nationalist ideology of national liberation, self-determination, and democratization that was described earlier has stamped with legality at least some forms of contemporary external interference in ethnic minority affairs, while often making those who resist it appear more sinister than the interventionist agents themselves. Many national leaders today do have reservations about the highly "permissive" precedents, such as "humanitarian intervention" and "preemptive war,", currently being set for outside interference in what were once considered "domestic" affairs of "sovereign" states. In spite of these reservations, however, it remains far easier to express moral approval of foreign intervention on behalf of movements seeking national liberation, self-determination, and democracy than it was in the 1930s to betray sympathy for racial supremacy. In fact, *failure* to intervene in the defense of the rights of ethnic minorities, as the world's inaction in the face of the 1994 genocidal slaughter of Tutsis in Rwanda illustrates, is taken in some quarters today as a sign of moral cowardice. In such an atmosphere, one hardly needs a ministry of propaganda to disseminate what is already supplied, free of charge or appearance of self-interest, by an eager international community. Political manipulation and strategic subversion go by other names today, and it is sometimes difficult to distinguish malevolent from benevolent intentions. Having gone respectable, however, manipulation and subversion have not gone away.

Nothing better illustrates the sharp difference between the Nazi era and today's era when it comes to public tolerance of ethnic fifth column-like activities than the difficulties some separatist-troubled countries have had in convincing world opinion that the self-styled "freedom fighters" at work within their borders are better described as "terrorists." In the cases of both Tibetan and Uighur separatism, China, for example, has found its strategic plans for pacifying the minority provinces in its western borderlands up against world views far more sympathetic with the rebellious minorities, especially the Tibetans, than with their Chinese hosts.[105] The bulk of opinion in the West appears convinced of the unmitigated evil visited upon the world by so-called Islamic extremists and their allies among Muslim migrant Diasporas, but the issue of terrorism's evil is far from decided among the world's billion-plus Muslims.

3. *Though they will be up against many of the same obstacles that thwarted the Nazi German fifth columns of World War II, which included those that were self-inflicted, one can be reasonably certain that there will be a fairly steady crop of ethnic fifth column-like entities surfacing in coming years to challenge the contemporary status quo.* This is so not merely because there are so many discontented ethnic minorities reaching out for foreign assistance, although that surely is a factor. Nor is it due solely to the widespread perception of the advantages in modern international conflict of indirect aggression and proxy combatants, although that too is important. It is due also, and significantly so, to the profound changes being witnessed not only in the number and character of international actors but also in their capacity, technologically and otherwise, to affect events. It is in an increasingly transnational world, in which old boundaries and the conventional behaviors that went along with them count for less. New boundaries, including those marking off ethnic and religious identities, may well count for more.

4. *It is of extreme importance, therefore, that world leaders react to alleged ethnic fifth column phenomena with the utmost sobriety and with impartial case-by-case analysis. If anything emerges clearly from the historical record of the Nazi German ethnic fifth column, it is that the world's reactions to it, in particular the infliction of collective punishments on the "guilty" ethnic German minorities, were not only unnecessary but also almost certainly did far more*

harm to humanity than the fifth columns themselves. It is true, of course, that Nazi Germany's fifth column exertions achieved some successes. More notable, however, were its failures. The successes occurred mainly in East-Central Europe under an extraordinary set of circumstances that included a humiliating defeat in war, the collapse of empire, worldwide economic depression, feverish nationalism, and a demonic human will at the head of state. It is wholly logical to question whether without the reinforcement of all of them, the German fifth column would have scored any victories; indeed, whether it would have developed at all.

Circumstances at the start of the 21st century preclude drawing firm conclusions about the precise evolution of ethnic fifth column-like phenomena. One thing, of which we can be certain, however, is that they will supply some of the furnishings of international relations well into the future.

Part Two
The Diaspora in India's Securtiy Strategy

Diaspora in India's Geopolitical Visions: Linkages, Categories and Contestations

Chapter 3

Diaspora in India's Geopolitical Visions: Linkages, Categories and Contestations

Sanjay Chaturvedi

> Between the de-territorialisation of the world's spaces and the myth of origin, between the nation-state and the plural affiliations of multi-national corporations -this is the milieu of today's diasporas. Not so much as a border -in the sense of that which is crossed or that which anticipates new proprietorship—diasporas and their practices produce and inhabit a postcolonial frontier. This is a contradictory landscape. On the one hand, it is global, so that diasporas are emblems of transnational movement. On the other hand, a particular "diaspora community" more often than not forms itself according to the territorial boundaries of nation-states: for example, that of the "host" nation and that of the "homeland."

> The Indian Diaspora spans the globe and stretches across all the oceans and continents. It is so widespread that the sun never sets on the Indian Diaspora. The population of the Indian Diaspora is estimated to be about 20 million. They live in different countries, speak different languages and are engaged in different vocations. What gives them their common identity are their Indian origin, their consciousness of their cultural heritage and their deep attachment to India.[2]

> Whether the state withdraws or is re-imagined, the reinforcement of identities is often at stake. The new trans-national economic reality seems not to diminish the need for a local or national political discourse. The essential question is whether the resulting geopolitical visions and discourses will interface with the new trans-national economic 'reality' or remain just a rhetoric accompaniment that serves essentially to boost pride and diminish pain...It requires much optimism to believe that international relations in the future will remain free from the ideological perspectives of particular groups. The end of history has not yet arrived.[3]

Introduction

Apparently, the globalization of migration has facilitated diasporas of various kinds. At the beginning of the 21st century, migration emerged as one of the most central, complex, and at the same time, ambiguous issue-areas in social sciences. However, international migration involves far more than simple economic strategies and issues of material well-being.[4] In most cases, migration entails a project of transformation, either by individuals or groups, even states, in which new identities are forged and existing orders as well as borders challenged or in some ways changed.

The dynamic landscapes of diaspora, as the first epigraph shows, are rather contradictory, located somewhere on the continuum between local, national and global. The starting point in this paper, therefore, is that diaspora's between-ness is an open-ended, ambivalent space, where the conventional territorialized understanding of both place and scale becomes problematic. Diverse understandings of *who* moves, *where*, *when* and *why* suggest that a rather complex, multifaceted phenomenon called diaspora could work both as "bridges" and "barriers" *between* as well as *within* polities, localities and communities. Correspondingly, diasporas could generate a sense of "security" as well as "insecurity" among various actors—both state and non-state—dependent upon a geopolitical vision as well as the given or perceived social-cultural context in which it operates.

A geopolitical vision could be defined as, "any idea concerning the relation between one's own and other places, involving feelings of (in)security or (dis)advantages (and/or) invoking ideas about a collective mission or foreign policy strategy".[5] It has also been pointed out that it is not necessary to introduce the concept of the state (although "foreign" policy more or less implies it) or assume that the vision be shared by the majority of a national population. The state can at times be an "external" source of insecure feelings for those who live within its territorial borders, and there may be alternative geopolitical visions within a nation state. A geopolitical vision requires at least a them-and-us distinction and emotional attachment to a place. Whether an analysis of geopolitical visions can be separated from a thorough treatment of national identity–with several defining features such as a historic territory, common myths and historic memories, a mass culture, a common economy and common legal rights and duties for all members–is a more difficult question. It is difficult to imagine a national identity without the feelings of trauma and pride that arise from external relations. In this respect, feelings of national identity and geopolitical visions are difficult to separate. Nevertheless, geopolitical visions are more the concrete translations of such feelings into models of the world, including diaspora.

One of the key intentions in this paper is to argue and illustrate that critical geopolitics of diaspora is much more than human flows defying man-made borders. It could also be about the trans-border dissemination of discourses that define and defend bounded identities in terms of inside/outside, citizen/alien and self/other. Such critical perspectives invite one's attention to multiple sites where geographical knowledge(s) of place, identity, belonging and home are being produced and reproduced. As suggested by Mekonnen Tesfahuney,[6] critical perspectives could also be usefully deployed in the analysis of international migrations to address issues of the construction of certain categories of migrants as "threats." Accordingly, "international migrations interface not only with the issue of mobility rights and 'other' rights and freedoms, but their impacts extend into notions of national and cultural identity".[7]

Rather than thinking about migrations as a movement between one bounded place and another, a critical scholarship of diaspora should be critically investigating the geographies of cultural interplay, bordering confluence, and cutting across existing national boundaries or borders–both physical as well as mental.[8] It also needs to be noted that geographies of diaspora are being written and understood rather differently from diverse "locations" and "dislocations." Thus, there is always a possibility that notions of "homeland" or "motherland" might be manipulated, misrepresented, or appropriated by various intellectuals and institutions of statecraft. On the other hand, taking a clue from Foucault,[9] Harvey,[10] Soja[11] and others, one could illustrate how diasporas are actively engaged in transforming the geographies and architecture of "homelands" while they attempt to create and inhabit new spaces of their own.[12] The inside-out experiences *of* a particular diaspora or diasporas may not necessarily match the outside-in perceptions and expectations *from* the communities concerned.

Critical Geopolitical Perspectives on Mobility and Territoriality

When, *how* and *why* does a human mobility or flow get historicized/ politicised as a diaspora and become implicated in the notions of nationalism, trans-nationalism or trans-migration? Border crossing is often talked about as if the border came first and mobility afterwards. Whereas, there is plenty of historical evidence to prove that it is exactly the opposite. While writing the history of "India" and "South Asia" from the point of view of interplay between mobility and territoriality, for example, David Ludden[13] has argued that,

> in order to understand history inside South Asia, we must escape the confines of modern boundaries that enclose and separate civilizations to explore a wider world within which these boundaries have been invented, contested, defended, and redrawn historically...the political boundaries of South Asia have changed dramatically, at various points in time. It is therefore most appropriate to study South Asia as a huge open geographical space in southern Eurasia, rather than imagining it to be a fixed historical region with a single territorial definition.

Examples of endless cultural mobility and dispersion—a spill-over of cultural elements of all sorts in all directions, and across what are today national borders separating and enclosing state territories—abound throughout the globe.

Mapping Diaspora in a Globalizing Geopolitical Economy

Etymologically, the term *diaspora* is derived from the Greek words *dia* (through) and *speiro* (to scatter). Literally, the meaning of *diaspora* is *scattering* or *dispersion.* It was originally mentioned in the context of Jews or Jewish communities scattered in exile outside Palestine. During the later half of the 20th century it was being applied to the dispersal of any ethnic group or community outside the country of their origin. Diaspora is the term often used today to describe practically any population that is considered "deterritorialized" or "transnational"—that is, which has originated in a land other than in which it currently resides, and whose social, economic and political networks cross the borders of nation-states or, indeed, span the globe.[14] The diaspora populations are growing in terms of their numbers and are expected to play a significant role in the life of the countries of their *adoption* as well as the countries of their *origin.* The complexity and intricacies of diaspora will be returned to after a brief comment on the factors and forces behind international migratory flows and related demographic considerations.

According to facts and figures furnished by the International Organization for Migration, at the beginning of the 21st century one out of every 35 persons worldwide was an international migrant (refer to Figure 3.1).[15] The total number of international migrants is estimated at some 175 million (some 2.9% of the world population). Some 48% of all international migrants are women. However, the actual importance of this phenomenon needs to be assessed in light of the fact that due to border controls, however porous, such movements are restricted and "the desire to move must exceed significantly the ability to do so; and the effects of small phenomena can be quite large"[16].

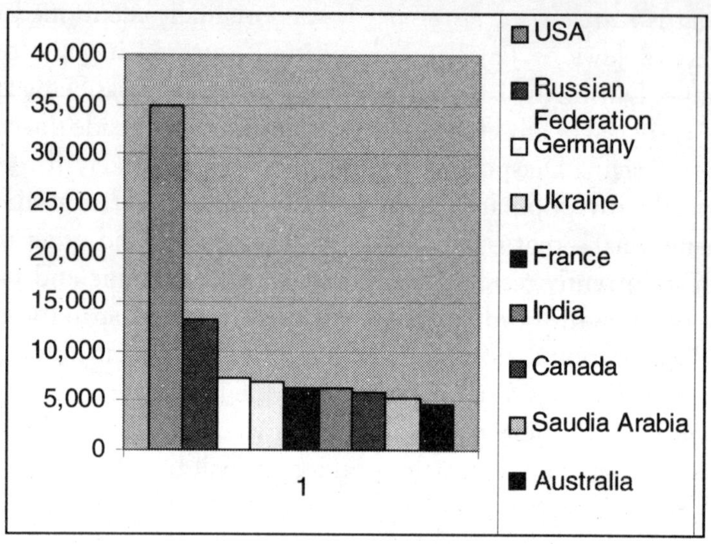

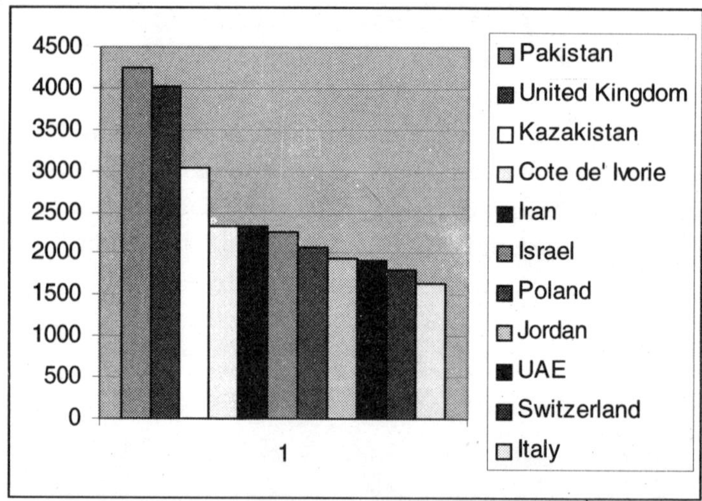

Figure 3.1: Countries with the Largest International Migrant Stock, 2000 (Number of Migrants in the Thousands)

The geopolitical economy of international migration is extremely significant. Over the past 35 years, the number of international migrations has more than doubled. For developing countries, migrant remittances continue to be a major source of income. Worldwide, India (U.S. $11.5 billion), Mexico (U.S. $6.5 billion), and Egypt (U.S. $3.7 billion) received the largest amount of money from their diaspora. However, due to its often informal character, the total volume of remittance is difficult to establish.

Jagdish Bhagwati has forcefully argued in his widely acclaimed book, *In Defense of Globalization*, that rather than trying to restrict immigrations, the governments should find out ways and means to cope with this phenomenon. In his view,

> If it is not possible to effectively restrict illegal immigration, then governments in the developed countries must turn to policies that will integrate migrants into their new homes in ways that will minimize the social costs and maximize the economic benefits...Some nations will grasp this reality and creatively work with migrants and migration. Others will lag behind, still seeking restrictive measures to control and cut the level of migration. The future certainly belongs to the former. But to accelerate the progress of the laggards, new institutional architecture is needed at the international level. Because immigration restrictions are the flip side of sovereignty, there is no international organization today to oversee and monitor each nation's policies towards migrants, whether inward -or outward–bound. The world badly needs enlightened immigration policies and best practices to be spread and codified.[17]

These are no doubt insightful observations. Equally worthy of serious attention is Bhagwati's call for setting up a World Migration Organization which would begin to put together "enlightened" immigration policies and codify best possible practices in this regard, "by juxtaposing each nation's entry, exit and residence policies towards migrants, whether legal or illegal, economic or political, skilled or unskilled."[18] One of the prerequisites of enlightened immigration policies is to ensure that the "bad" effects of diaspora are minimized to the extent possible. Commenting on the "good" effects of diaspora, Bhagwati argues that,

> Enhancing these good effects requires that countries such as India and Taiwan adopt the Diaspora model, extending a warmer embrace to their national abroad, so that the spill over effects can be increased. A *diaspora policy would integrate present and past citizens into a web of rights and obligations in the extended community, defined with the home country as the center*. The diaspora approach is also superior from a human rights perspective because it builds on the right to emigrate, rather than trying to restrict it. Besides, dual loyalty, where migrants retain their loyalty to their home country alongside their loyalty to the country they have come to, is increasingly judged to be acceptable. Nearly thirty countries now offer dual citizenship. Others are inching their way to similar options. Many less developed countries, such as Mexico and India, are in the process of granting citizens living abroad hitherto denied benefits such as the right to hold property and to vote via absentee ballot (emphasis supplied).[19]

However, the "good" and the "bad" effects of diasporas may not necessarily work out in a rather straight-forward manner. They are mediated by a variety of factors, including specific meanings that are being attributed to the very term "diaspora." It is equally important to critically examine how a particular understanding of human mobility—

in the sense of de-territorialization or re-territorialization—acquires a virtual monopoly of the term "diaspora."

For Arjun Appadurai,[20] diaspora implies a de-territorialized fertile ground that is characterized by a global circulation of capital, commodities as well as human beings. The de-territorialised populations in the abiding sense of placelessness and timelessness carry ideas and images from their homeland/motherland/fatherland to the new "host setting." What has received less attention perhaps is the use of diaspora as a spatial strategy by globalizing Westphalian "nation-states," especially major powers of civilizational proportions and predispositions, to re-territorialize its imagi(nation), in the wake of mounting challenges its legitimacy, authority and effectiveness.

The Origins and Evolution of the 'Indian' Diaspora: Geo-economic Perspectives

A long history of human mobility and migration notwithstanding, it is only recently that the Indian Diaspora has started receiving serious and systematic attention from the intellectuals and institutions of statecraft in India. In a sharp contrast to China's long-standing policy framework for overseas Chinese, which leverages the expatriate community for "national" ends, the Indian government has just begun mapping out the Indian settlements/communities abroad.

The first substantial migrations abroad were dictated and driven largely by indentured labor arrangements of the 19th century. It was against the backdrop of economic compulsions generated by colonialism that people of Indian origin began to migrate overseas in significant numbers in the 19th century and initially to the countries of Africa, Southeast Asia, Fiji and the Caribbean. This wave was triggered mainly by the enormous demand for cheap labor that arose in the wake of the abolition of slavery by the British in 1833-34. Forcefully engaged into the plantations of East and South Africa as well as the West and East Indies, these lower caste and class peasants and laborers largely escaped the attention of the Indian government and elite. Moreover, since in the countries of their residence they usually were far down in socio-political hierarchies, they rarely figured in the mental maps of a rather status conscious Indian elite. Some change in this regard was noticeable only after Gandhi organized the resistance in South Africa in the early years of the 20th century. The second wave of Indian migrations abroad occurred in the second half of the 20th century, with a steady outflow of some of India's best professionals to the developed countries of the West, and of India's skilled and semi-skilled labor in the wake of the oil boom in West Asia and the Gulf in the 1970s.

The moves made by the Indian government to upgrade the Indian Diaspora on its list of foreign policy priorities might also be seen as a response to the emerging contours and compulsions of the international geopolitical economy. It needs to be noted that the economic strategies of transnational groups represent a new source and force to reckon with in international finance and commerce. It needs to be explored further as to how, among specific groups, a sense of collectivism on a world-wide scale provides a key to their success in the new global economy. The potential influence of this kind of diaspora depends on its following characteristics: size; education/skills; income; and the activities in which it is engaged (skilled versus non-skilled labor; tradable sector versus non-tradable; hierarchy in the product cycle life—new industries versus mature industries).

Even though foreign direct investment (FDI) into India has been modest, non-resident Indian (NRI)-FDI has been remarkably limited. Total NRI investment out of the total FDI approved since January 1991 to December 2003 was around 3.5 percent. The highest shares have been the U.S. (20 %) and Mauritius (12 %). A state-wise comparison of NRI investment in India reveals one surprising feature. Despite Gujarati diaspora's size and wealth and entrepreneurial characteristics (and whatever its other effects on Gujarat), it has been quite chary of investing in Gujarat. For the time period 1991-2003, the state received Rs. 188 billion of foreign direct investment, of which the NRI share was a mere 4 percent. Gujarat has received just 7 percent of the NRI investment of Rs. 107 billion in the country. Andhra Pradesh and Maharashtra have received the highest NRI-FDI, followed by Karnataka, Delhi and Tamil Nadu (Table 3.1).

	No. of NRI Projects	Value of NRI Investment (Rs. Crores)	Total Foreign Direct Investment	Non-Resident FDI/Total FDI %
Andhra Pradesh	190	1905.8		
Maharashtra	273	1890.7	50333	3.7
Karnataka	163	1333	23970	5.6
Delhi	140	959.5	34636	2.8
Gujarat	88	756.5	18795	4.0
Tamil Nadu	192	683.3	24763	2.8

Source: Times of India February 4, 2004

Table 3.1: NRI-FDI into India

An often made comparison between Chinese and Indian Diasporas is that FDI from the former into China exceeds FDI from the latter into India by 20-25 folds to one. In the last decade, annual average FDI flows as a share of gross fixed capital formation into China has exceeded 10 percent, while in India's case it has barely been above 2 percent. Nearly 60 percent of Chinese FDI (from 1978 to 1999) came from three ethnically Chinese economies (ECEs)–Hong Kong, Macao and Taiwan.[21] As stated above, the diaspora's share in FDI in India has been under 4 percent. Most analysis on the economic effects of international migration and diasporas focuses on financial remittances. Yet equally important are the social remittances, namely the flow of ideas, technologies, theories, beliefs, world views, new ways of doing things, etc.

The High Level Committee on Indian Diaspora

With an officially estimated 20 million Indians living abroad as residents and citizens of other countries, the Indian Diaspora has come into its own. A High Level Committee on Indian Diaspora (to be cited hereafter as the HLC) was appointed by the Ministry of External Affairs in September 2000, with the approval of the then Prime Minister Atal Bihari Vajpayee to head the Bharatiya Janata Party (BJP)-led coalition government and recommend a broad and flexible policy framework after reviewing the status, needs and role of people of Indian origin (PIOs) and non-resident Indians (NRIs).

Formed under the Chairmanship of Dr. L. M. Singhvi, Member of Parliament and former High Commissioner of India to the United Kingdom, the HLC submitted its report to the Prime Minister in January 2002. This was the first time the government of India decided to undertake the task of recognizing the presence of twenty million strong Indian Diaspora and formulate new policies for building enduring linkages between India and the Indian Diaspora.

Before proceeding further, the author wishes to make a few points by way of clarification here. Given the constraints of time and space, the author's engagement with the report, which is replete with rich material and insights, is rather selective. For the purposes of the section that follows, the author has drawn upon various sections of the voluminous report of the Committee.[22] What the author wishes to illustrate in particular is the extraordinary complexity of the so-called "Indian" Diaspora, which the report of the HLC also refers to in parts.

The very fact that the HLC decided not to go into the issue of the Indian Diaspora in its immediate South Asian neighborhood, with the exception of Maldives, is also quite illustrative of the dilemma that is inherent perhaps in the very nature of the Indian Diaspora. The silence of the South Asian Association of Regional Cooperation (SAARC) countries in the report, with the exception of Maldives, speaks volumes of the wide-ranging implications of applying the notion of people of "Indian origins" within the post-colonial, post-partition South Asia.

Mapping Indian Diaspora: An Overview

According to the HCL, "the Indian Diaspora is unique as it

surpasses all others in its extraordinary diversity and global spread."[23] The term "diaspora" is defined by the Committee as follows:

> The term Diaspora is of Greek Origin. It referred originally, to a dispersion or scattering of the Jews beyond Israel, mainly in the 8th to the 6th centuries B.C. *It is now commonly used in a generic sense for communities of migrants living or scattered permanently in other countries, aware of its origins and identity and maintaining varying degrees of linkages with the mother country.* It is in this sense that the Committee uses the term Diaspora to refer to Indians who migrated to different parts of the world and have generally maintained their Indian identity (emphasis supplied).[24]

In the official understanding of the HLC, the term "Indian Diaspora" includes in its ambit both NRIs and PIOs. NRIs are Indian citizens, holding Indian passports and residing abroad for an indefinite period, whether for employment, or for carrying on any business or vocation or for any other propose. On the other hand, the term PIO is applied to a foreign citizen of Indian origin or descent. There is an underlying assumption throughout the report that, "since India achieved independence, overseas Indians have been returning to seek their roots and explore new avenues and sectors for mutually beneficial interaction, from investment, to transfer of skills and technology to outright philanthropy and charitable works."[25] There is at the same time an acknowledgement of the fact that barring some high profile names in the information technology and entertainment sectors abroad, the diaspora has been largely left out of the public sight and awareness. The Committee, one is told, is convinced that the reserves of good will among its diaspora are deeply entrenched and waiting to be tapped if the right policy framework and initiatives are taken by India. To quote the HLC,

> The Indian Diaspora has transformed the economies and has come to occupy a pride of place in the life of these countries. Its members are found as entrepreneurs, workers, traders, teachers, researchers, inventors, doctors, lawyers, engineers, managers and administrators. The success of the Indian Diaspora can be attributed to its traditional ethos, its cultural values and heritage, its educational aptitude and qualifications, and its capacity to harmonize and adapt. By playing a leading role in the global technological revolution, it has transformed India's image abroad. While it continues to flourish in different countries and in different walks of life, it continues to be rooted in ancient cultural heritage; at the same time, it is uplifted by India's prosperity and progress.[26]

It is now time to turn to a brief overview of the mapping of regional and country profiles of the Indian Diaspora by the HLC. Among the neighboring countries (the Maldives, Afghanistan, and Central Asia), there are an estimated 9,000 NRIs in the Maldives, out of an island population of 269,000, and only one Maldivian citizen of Indian origin. Against the background of migration over the last several centuries, mainly from the pre-partition Panjab, the size of the Indian community is said to have gone down from an estimated 45,000 in 1990 to 1,000 in 1996. The HCL also points out that during the Taliban regime there were serious threats to human security of the Sikh and Hindu minorities, and many were forced to flee the host country. As far as the Central Asian Republics (Kazakhstan, Uzbekistan, Turkmenistan, Tajikistan and Kyrgyzstan), the Indian community numbers 2,732 out of a total population of 55.5 million. The HLC is of the view that the Indian community in Central Asia is bound to increase in view of close economic and bilateral relations between the Central Asian countries and India.

As far as the Gulf Region is concerned, the Indian population is estimated at more than 3 million, almost all of them being NRIs, with more than half coming from the southern Indian region of Kerala. It needs to be noted that as much as 70 percent of the Indian population in the region consists of semi-skilled and unskilled workers, 20-30 percent consists of Indian professionals and white collar workers, and a small fraction is composed of domestic help. There is an acknowledgement of the fact by the HLC that the remittances from the Gulf, long recognized as a significant contribution to India's balance of payments, are mostly made by Indian workers in the first category. Whereas, following Operation Desert Storm the number of Indians in Iraq has been reduced to a handful, the Indian community in Libya is reported to have declined from almost 40,000 in mid-1980s to about 12,000 mainly due to an economic slow down. The HCL also underlines the fact that most of the countries in the region do not permit their Indian workers to obtain local citizenship regardless of their employment category, along with the vulnerability of the Indian community, especially semi-skilled and unskilled workers open to exploitation both at home and in the Gulf.

In various countries of Africa, including Mauritius and Reunion Island, a fairly significant presence of the Indian Diaspora can be found. While PIOs at over 220,000 constitute around 30 percent of Reunion's population, Mauritius is the only country where PIOs at over 700,000 constitute a majority at almost 70 percent of the population, which, as HLC points out, has enabled them to achieve political pre-eminence. While noting that the Indian Diaspora in South Africa numbers around a million, the HLC points out that the challenge before the Indian Diaspora is to remove the misperceptions about the community and joint the mainstream in nation-building. Limited Indian emigration to other parts of Africa took place mainly after the conclusion of agreements between the British government and the metropolitan countries for recruiting Indian indentured labor. Barring East and South Africa, Mozambique, Madagascar, Mauritius, and Reunion, the Indian presence in countries like Angola, Senegal, Ghana, Gambia, Namibia, Djibouti, Ethiopia, Eritrea, Sudan, etc. is comparatively limited or negligible.

In the discourse of the Indian Diaspora, another region of tremendous significance is Southeast Asia. This is also reflected to a significant extent, in India's Look East policy. According to the figures given by the HCL, the Indian community numbers 7,600 in Brunei, 55,000 in Indonesia, 1.67 million in Malaysia, possibly 2.9 million in Myanmar, 38,500 in the Philippines, 307,000 in Singapore, 85,000 in Thailand, and a very small number in Cambodia, Laos and Vietnam. To quote the HLC,

> The most unique feature of India's cultural interaction with Southeast Asia, which precedes the dawn of the Christian era, is that it has been entirely peaceful. Its imprint is visible even today in language and literature, religion and philosophy, art and architecture, of the whole of Indo-China, Myanmar and Southeast Asia. Large scale Indian emigration however took place only in the 19th and 20th centuries as a result of colonialism through the indenture or Kangani system, and also by 'free' emigration of traders, clerks, bureaucrats and professionals. Thousands of Indians were mobilized to fight in the Indian National Army (INA) in Malay and to contribute to the cause of Indian independence.[27]

In Israel, according to the figures furnished by the HLC, there are 45,000 PIO out of a population of 6.3 million. After living in India for over a thousand years, around 30,000 Indian Jews have migrated to Israel since the 1940s. The HCL notes that, "Though the younger generation born in Israel are loosing their Indian identity there is considerable interest in maintaining cultural links with India as they are aware that their ancestors never faced discrimination in India, unlike Jewish communities in other parts of the world."[28] Commenting on the Indian Diaspora in the Fiji Archipelago, the HLC noted with regret that, "the history of the still 340,000 strong Indian community in Fiji has been quite tragic. From the days of indentured labour, to the post-independence phase when jealousy of their economic status and political activism prompted several anti-India coups, the Indian community has been at the receiving end."[29]

The Indian Diaspora in North America

In Canada, the Indians constitute about 2.8 percent of a population of 30 million, with an annual average income nearly 20 percent higher than the national average. There is, however, an acknowledgement by the HLC of the reality that Indo-Canadians are organized on the basis of linguistic, regional, and other characteristics. Yet at the same time the growing political eminence of Indo-Canadians is said to be reflected in the increasing attention devoted to their concerns by the Canadian politicians.

However, it is the Indian-American community which numbers approximately 1.7 million that has earned the distinction of a model community. As the most rapidly growing Asian American group, the community is reported to possess the following impressive credentials: (a) a median income of U.S. $60,093, nearly double the median income of all American families; (b) 200,000 Indians are millionaires; (c) 58 percent of Indian-Americans over the age of 25 have a college degree; (d) 43.6 percent of Indian-Americans in the work force are employed as managers or professionals; (e) there are as many as 35,000 Indian-American physicians; (f) nearly 300,000 Indian-Americans work in high-tech industries; (g) 15 percent of Silicon Valley start-up firms are owned by Indian-Americans; (h) more than 5,000 Indian-Americans are on the faculties of American universities; and (i) 74,603 Indians are studying in the United States, making Indians the largest group of foreign students in the country.[30]

In India, the Indian-American community is now viewed as playing a major role in helping further India's foreign policy and security goals, as well as contributing towards its economic development. The Committee states:

> A section of financially powerful and politically well connected Indo-Americans has emerged during the last decade. They have effectively mobilised on issues

> ranging from the nuclear tests in 1998 to Kargil, played a crucial role in generating a favourable climate of opinion in Congress and defeating anti-India legislation there, and lobbied effectively on other issues of concern to the Indian community. They have also demonstrated willingness to contribute financially to Indian causes, such as relief for the Orissa cyclone and the Latur and Gujarat earthquakes, higher technical education and innumerable charitable causes...For the first time, India has a constituency in the US with real influence and status. The Indian community in the United States constitutes an invaluable asset in strengthening India's relationship with the world's only superpower.[31]

Global Perspectives of Other Diasporas: Lessons for India

One of the most interesting parts of the exercise undertaken by the High Level Committee on the Indian Diaspora is its approach to the study of other diasporas in order to derive "lessons" for India. The Committee studied in depth the Jewish, Polish, Lebanese, Italian, Filipino, Japanese, Korean, Chinese and the Irish Diasporas. Two diaspora models that appear to have impressed the HLC the most are the Jewish and the Chinese. The author quotes in parts from the Executive Summary of the report[32]

- Many countries, such as Italy, Poland, Israel, and Lebanon have granted the right of dual nationality to members of their Diaspora.

- Many countries with successful Diasporas have created viable structures for handling issues related to their Diaspora.

- Many Diasporas have contributed immeasurably to the post-war reconstruction efforts of the mother country such as the Jewish, Italian and Lebanese Diasporas. While commenting on the Jewish Diaspora's support for Israel, the Committee felt that its historical experience was suis generis and Israel's present requirements were also very different from India's. A telling example is that besides Israel's interest in strengthening links with its Diasporas, which it shares with all the other countries, one of Israel's foremost priorities in the large scale return and therefore 'immigration' of its two-thousand year old Diaspora, Israel being the only country to be entirely populated by its Diaspora rather than the other way round! ...*However the Committee felt that the contribution of the Diaspora to Israel in economic, political and cultural spheres contained important lessons for India. The activities of the Jewish lobbies outside Israel, particularly in the US congress, their extensive fund-raising abilities, large-scale funding for the scientific and technological development for Israel, their global networks which link Jewish associations and organizations worldwide as well as with the State of Israel, could serve as an example. The scheme of Israel Bonds, issued by the Government of Israel, to strengthen the national economy and infrastructure, could be adopted in the Indian context* (emphasis supplied).

- While the remittances sent home by the Lebanese Diaspora have played an important role in Lebanon's economy, the Philippines, which has a large emigrant blue-collar population, has passed legislation, created new institutions, boosted the strength of its overseas Missions and tightened its laws aimed at providing security to its overseas workers, which are very relevant for India.

- The Committee considered that another relevant example was that of the Chinese Diaspora, which still contributes 70% of all inward foreign direct investment into China, and attracts comparison because of the

> enormous contribution it has made to China's economic development.
>
> *The Committee concluded that while ethnicity was a factor in China's success in attracting investment from its overseas Chinese, economic imperatives including the booming Chinese economy, and sound government policies including flexible labour laws and efficient administrative procedures were the major factors responsible for this phenomenon.* The Committee noted that these incentives applied to all investors and there were no special incentives for the overseas Chinese. The Committee therefore strongly recommended to the Government of India –that if India wished to increase investment flows both from its Diasporas and other investors, it need to invest heavily in infrastructure, both social and physical, create a conducive operating environment for conducting business through administrative reforms, and implement the so-called generation reforms to increase the dynamism of the Indian economy (emphasis supplied).

Recommendations

In its interim report the High Level Committee on the Indian Diaspora has recommended to the government to respond to some of the significant issues that had figured in their discussions with the members of the diaspora communities. These include (a) charging a lower fee towards a PIO card but for a decreased validity of 10 years (rather than 20 years of validity for a fee of $ 1,000), (b) observation of *Pravasi Bharatiya Divas* on January 9th (the day Mahatma Gandhi returned to India from South Africa) of every year, in India and abroad, to recognize and appreciate the role of the Indian Diaspora in the promotion of India's interest, and (c) the institution of Pravasi Bharatiya Samman Awards for eminent PIOs and NRIs.

The HLC has examined the major issues pertaining to the Indian Diaspora, such as culture, education, media, economic development, health, science & technology, philanthropy, and dual citizenship, to recommend concrete steps to bring the Indian Diaspora closer to India for the first time in an institutionalized manner. In order to facilitate closer interaction between India and the Indian Diaspora and to continuously monitor it, the HLC has suggested setting up an autonomous and empowered body, similar to a planning commission, and also to constitute a Standing Committee of the Parliament.

The HLC report also suggests that the government of India as well as the state governments should try to remove all the obstacles for promoting philanthropic and voluntary or welfare activities of non-governmental organizations (NGOs) that the members of the Indian Diaspora wish to pursue in India. A very significant but controversial issue that came up for consideration before the HLC was that of dual citizenship. The HLC had encountered this demand particularly during their meetings with prominent members of the Indian community (*New Diaspora*) in North America and a few other advanced countries. They pleaded that the grant of dual citizenship will promote investments, trade, tourism, and philanthropic contributions in India. According to the Citizenship Act of 1955, an Indian forfeits his/her Indian citizenship when he/she acquires the citizenship of a foreign country. The HLC recommends the issuing of "dual citizenship" after taking appropriate safeguards pertaining to India's security concerns, in addition to carrying out necessary amendments in the Citizenship Act of 1955.

Deconstructing the Hindu Nationalist Strand of Indian Diaspora: Representations and Practices

The term *Hindutva* was coined by Vinayak Damodar Savarkar to both indicate and vindicate its distinctiveness from Hinduism. Hindutva to Savarkar was both the lifestyle and the destiny of a great race. It was not simply a term but an entire history, encompassing the religious, cultural and racial identity of the Hindus. The basic tenets of Hindutva were finally refined and propagated by Savarkar, who, in this sense, represented the high-water mark of ideology driven towards the establishment of a Hindu nation. The formation of the Arya Samaj in 1909, Hindu Mahasabha in 1915, Hindu Sanghathan in 1921-22, and finally the Rashtriya Swayamsevak Sangh (RSS) in 1925 and its political wing, the Jan Sangh in 1951, are "instances of giving the Hindu consolidation an organizational edge."[33] Yet very little of any consequence has been added to the core principles of the world view of Hindutva.

In the world view of Hindutva, there has been a serious and systematic construction of the Hindu identity in the service of Indian nationalism. The first and the most important feature of the Hindutva project remains the transformation of Hinduism into a regimented, codified, monochromatic order. There is little scope or space for diversity of opinion, practices, rituals, observances and individual choices. The Hindu nation is to be founded and united on the basis of racial and doctrinal purity. The understandings related to inclusions/ insiders and exclusions/outsiders of this unity however varied. Savarkar was willing to include the Sikhs, Jains and the Buddhists in his definition of Hindu, but Christians and Muslims could not qualify as Hindus since they potentially had "extraterritorial loyalties," and their "holy lands" were outside the territory of India.

According to Hansen,[34] Hindu nationalism shares the worship of strength, masculinity, and cultural purity. Savarkar believed in the idea of an "internal border," that is "the internalized individualization of nationhood." Accordingly, Hindutva is essentially a question of subjective feelings, loyalty, individual patriotism, a "will to nationhood."[35]

In the absence of such essential virtues, argued Savarkar, Hindus were likely to be dominated and exploited by alien faiths and/ or by more powerful forces. Such a discourse received further fillip at the hands of M.S. Golwalkar, "whose writings revolved around the question of construction of a cultural holism and national strength to negotiate and control the fragmenting impulses of modernity."[36]

Yet another element that drives the Hindutva world view relates to the manner in which the geographies of victimhood and threats are being written and placed at the very core of the "Hindu" imagi(nation). The term diaspora therefore sounds a special resonance in Hindutva discourse. The world that matters is divided into a coalition of friends and an alliance of foes. It is believed that threats to Hinduism and its purity could come in various guises and disguises: Westernization, pan-Islamism, missionaries, conversion, etc.

The Vishwa Hindu Parishad (VHP) remains firmly of the view that the Bharatiya Janata Party (BJP) should continue to "mobilise the Hindu vote bank" and form a Hindu Rashtra. The VHP has been quite vociferous in its call to unite "two hundred crore Buddhists and Hindus" of the world to form a "Vishal Hindu Front"–an anti-Christian and anti-Islamic front. It finds many similarities between the two religions and cultures as well as the laws. Buddha belongs to the Hindu pantheon of gods. Budh Gaya belonged to the Buddhists. He further added that Jains and Sikhs also belonged to the same Hindu culture. The VHP would, in addition to uniting the Buddhists, Hindus, Jains and Sikhs, also include Gypsies and ethnic faiths of other pre-Christian eras to create an "anti-imperialist" front. The VHP also perceives an international conspiracy of multinational corporations and the Christian missionaries in promoting consumer culture.

The critics of Hindutva continue to point out that the rewriting of history and the manipulation of memories are strategies integral to the project of controlling popular imaginations.[37] Yet it remains an incomplete project, challenged by a multitude of alternative imaginations. Hindutva's rewriting of history intentionally undermines the long standing patterns of peaceful coexistence. There were (and there are) aspects of life in which religion was an identifier but there were (and there are) also many other aspects in which more broad-bases cultural expression, evolving over time and through an admixture of various elements, gave an identity to social groups. There is no space whatsoever for such acknowledgments in the Hindutva discourse. Savarkar's writings, for example, are replete with images of the Muslims as aggressors, preserving Hindu Dharma and securing national honour and expressions such as "pratishodh" and "pratikar," which are synonyms for revenge, retribution and retaliation.

In India, Hindu nationalism has grown prodigiously from a dormant and apparently minor communal presence to being the party of the government over a short time. Despite loss of power at the Centre in recently held elections, the BJP continues to maintain its hold on a number of states of the Indian Union. The 1998 manifesto of the BJP said: "Our nationalist vision in not merely bound by the geographical or political identity of Bharat, but it is referred by our timeless cultural heritage, this cultural heritage which is central to all religions, regions and languages, is a civilizational identity and constitutes the cultural nationalism of India which is the core of Hindutva. This we believe is the identity of our ancient nation 'Bharatvarsh'..."[38]

The wide-ranging implications of "internet Hindutva" have also received critical scholarly attention in recent times. Rowena Robinson[39] has shown how a global Hindu electronic network links one to hundreds of sites on Hinduism, and how "these sites are 'virtually' battling it out with others –Islamic, Christian and so on—for souls". The RSS proudly displays its project of forging "the present day scattered elements of Hindu society into an organized and invincible force," whereas the VHP office in Delhi not only affiliates all VHP units abroad, it also works for the "affiliation of those institutions from foreign countries that have similar objects" and is resolved to encourage them and "give all assistance and help in their work."[40]

What is often overlooked is the fact that the Hindutva movement has reinforced tensions between Hindu and non-Hindu Indian-Americans and between Hindutvavadis and secular Hindus. It has been argued by Arvind Rajagopal,[41] who teaches media studies at New York University, that demographic factors too have contributed to the changing context for Hindtuva in the U.S., with the Indian-American population having more than doubled in each of the past two decades, growing to 1.7 million, or 1.9 million if those vouching for more than one race are included. Their growth rate during the 1990s was more than double the rate of growth of Asian-Americans as a whole for the period. The population is rapidly indigenising itself in generational terms: whereas in 1990, more than three-fourths of Asian-

Americans were foreign born, by 2000, the third and later generations already outnumbered the immigrants. On the whole, the population is educated and affluent, although the number of people in poverty is also fast growing, especially among female-headed households and the elderly. It has been pointed out by a number of observers that members of Hindu nationalist organizations in the United States often subdue their political rhetoric and concentrate on issues of cultural reproduction, presenting themselves as well-meaning guardians of Hindu values.

According to some analysts,

> If Hindu nationalists become accepted as the public voice for all people of Indian ancestry in the country, there could be a variety of consequences. The politicization of Indian Americans (largely through the Hindutva movement) has already brought about a significant shift in American foreign policy towards India and Pakistan, with the administration adopting a significantly more pro-India position than in the past (at least until the events of 9/11/2001). Tensions created within the Indian American community due to the efforts of Hindutva leaders to define and articulate 'Hinduness' but also 'Indianness' could spill over to wider society as all sides in the conflict (Hindu, Muslim, and Christian Indian Americans) are forging alliances with other American groups, leading to exacerbation of religious tensions within the United States and the development of competing ethnic blocks.[42]

To conclude this section, as Devesh Kapoor[43] puts it,

> ...it should be stressed that India's diaspora is inevitably a minority in the country of settlement. Both the Indian

> state and the diaspora from India's majority community must realize that the claims of protection of communities of Indian origin in their country of settlement are weakened if minorities in the countries of origin are not protected. One can not claim protection in one context while seemingly violating it in another context. This means that both the diaspora and the Indian government must handle their internal affairs with substantially greater care and circumspection.

Looking Ahead: Imperatives and Impediments before Diasporic Cosmopolitanism

The author's key intention in this paper has been to show how different meanings are being written into and read out of the term "Indian" Diaspora. Using insights from a critical geopolitical approach to the study of population flows and migrations, it has been argued that the (geo)politics of both space and time expressed through the notions such as "motherland" and "homeland" play a central role in making human-cultural mobility diasporic. In the case of post-colonial, post-partition India, the circulation/migration of Indians in different parts of the globe, including the Indian Ocean region, has gone diasporic rather recently. The "Indian" Diaspora, as has been argued, has two dominant strands at present.

The first strand relates to apparent secular, market-driven forces of a globalizing international geopolitical economy. This strand explains the setting up of the High Level Committee on the Indian Diaspora in August 2000 by the then National Democratic Alliance (NDA), a coalition government led by the BJP. The motivation behind the setting up of the Committee is a good example of how a particular kind of geographical knowledge about human mobility and population flows is being "officially" produced. While acknowledging the insights offered by the report of the HLC, the author has tried to show how places and peoples in the Indian Ocean region are mapped and "framed" by this joint venture in terms of state-centric desires, definitions and categories of the Indian Diaspora. It is not perhaps accidental that one of the most extensively used terms in the report is "motherland."

Rather than regret the exodus of its highly educated people, the establishment of this Committee provided an official acknowledgement by India of the potential advantages offered by this global and globalizing community of "flexible citizens." This non-resident community is now being perceived as an important component of a de-territorialized nation. Whereas groups such as the Global Organization of the People of Indian Origin continue to lobby various levels of the government of India to accord NRIs more official rights, from basic property protections to dual citizenship.

In terms of this apparent "secular" geopolitics of the Indian Diaspora, the non-resident Indian (NRI) is being perceived as a "displaced" global actor endowed with substantial economic prosperity that can be drawn into India through the "powerful" cultural attachment that "sons of the soil" are believed as well as expected to retain for their "motherland." Yet this grounded metaphorical attachment reveals an inconsistency between a global imaginary of a deeply territorial and nationalist idea of India and the often more powerful provincial-local affinity that emigrants might possess—for example, as *Panjabis*, *Gujaratis*. Theoretically speaking, the author submits that rather than seeing the "global" and the "local" as opposing scales, it might be more insightful to demonstrate how they operate in relation to each other on the one hand, and how processes of globalization (rather "glocalization") are likely to manifest themselves differently across diverse spatial and social contexts.

The second major strand of the "Indian" Diaspora which, of late, has been on the ascendance, relates to Hindutva going global. Indian migration across the globe has provided the right wing Hindu nationalist parties in India opportunities for securing sympathy, supporters and funds from this diaspora. This is arguably the most powerful "negative" impact that globalization has had on contemporary India with considerable implications for its bilateral and multilateral diplomacy and foreign policy. The money flowing back to India has been used to promote the interests of *Hindu Rashtra* or the Hindu

Nation, defined as a nation that privileges Hindu religious beliefs, values and customs to the exclusion of the rights of religious minorities such as the Muslims and Christians. The Indian Diaspora remains closely linked to India through arranged marriages, remittances and employment networks. These same connections can be used to promote a particular understanding of diaspora.

It has been argued that it is both feasible and desirable to speak of a "new" counter-hegemonic "multicultural" identity, in reference to individuals who have acquired the competence to "behave appropriately in a number of different arenas, and to switch codes as appropriate." Globalization has brought a reconfiguration of ethnic identities within advanced capitalist societies, enabling diasporas to feel "at home" in their places of settlement without abandoning their attachment to their homeland. However, the connections between these local "politics of recognition" are now globalized. Digital capitalism has made the imagination of a *global* Hindu Diasporic identity possible through the Internet in the same way as print capitalism made the imagination of a Hindu national identity possible in the colonial period. The continued (re)territorialization of much of the Hindu diasporic activity, however, limits the ability of the diaspora to act as a global political actor and address issues of cosmopolitanism.

Since it is possible to have both the peaceful and productive geographies of diasporas and a diaspora of hate, exclusion and assault, the international community could and should strive for shared spaces of diasporas, a truly cosmopolitan place where diasporic cultures are celebrated not only for their fusion of differences across different borders but also for coming together to create distinctive syncretic cultures. This in turn would require an acknowledgement of the fact that there is no such thing as the geographical knowledge of a diaspora(s) but several geographical knowledges. In the author's view, David Harvey [44] should be taken rather seriously when he points out,

> The supposed neutrality of geographical knowledge has at best proven to be a beguiling fiction and at worst a downright fraud. Geographical knowledges have always internalized strong ideological content...Geography has

> often cultivated parochialist and ethnocentric perspectives on that diversity. It has often been, and still is, captive to special interests and, hence, a formidable, through often covert, weapon in political and social struggle. It has been an active vehicle for the transmission of doctrines of racial, cultural, sexual, or national superiority. Cold War rhetoric, fears of 'orientalism', or some demonic 'other' that threatens the existing order have become pervasive and persuasive in relation to political action. Geographical information can be presented in such a way as to prey upon fears and feed hostility (the abuse of cartography is of particular note in this regard). The 'facts' of geography presented as 'facts of nature' have been used to justify imperialism, neo-colonialism, expansionism, and geopolitical strategies for dominance.

However, as Harvey also emphasizes, the "facts" of geography can also be used to promote humanitarianism and cosmopolitanism. In order to understand diaspora as a geopolitical problem, people need to overcome in the first place what a distinguished French political geographer, Yves Lacoste,[45] terms as, "lack of knowledge about conflicting conceptions, unexpressed mutual fears and above all the ignorance of those who, confident of their rights, are unaware or refuse to accept that an opposite opinion to their own might exist, in equally good faith." The space needed for dialogue(s) both within and among diasporas could easily be lost once the fears and the fantasies of religious fundamentalism of any kind are allowed a free hand in deciding the "rights" and "obligations" of communities in diaspora. Marketing diasporas for economic reasons, while using religion-informed cultural symbols, could also prove to be counter-productive in the long run.

It is worth pursuing the agenda of diasporas of cosmopolitanism; not a cosmopolitanism of an abstract kind based on a pseudo-scientific "view from nowhere" but a cosmopolitanism visualized and practiced through intercultural dialogue. It should, therefore, be possible to revisit and re-imagine the Indian Diaspora as having been formulated through different trajectories, in different landscapes, using symbols, memories and cultural artefacts that each group, both initial and subsequent, from all different regions/sub-regions of the sub-continent, brought with it when it moved into new landscapes. Herein lies an avenue for dialogue, adaptation and transformation among not only different diasporas (e.g., Indian, Chinese, Jewish, etc.), but also different strands within the Indian Diasporas. This holds the key to a comprehensive security of a wide-ranging, multifaceted, non-territorial labyrinth of human mobility and cultural flows.

The Diaspora as a Factor in U.S.-India Relations

Chapter 4

The Diaspora as a Factor in U.S.-India Relations

Arthur G. Rubinoff

Introduction

This chapter examines the impact that the Indo-American community has had on transforming the historic hostile bilateral relationship between Washington and New Delhi. It finds the role of Indians in the United States to be decisive in altering perceptions of decision-makers between two countries that had limited contact and conflicting interests. As Devesh Kapur suggests, any diaspora's ideational effects depends on its size, socio-economic characteristics and its access to points in the power structure in the country of origin.[1] In the first years of India's existence as an independent state when the Indian community in the United States was small and uneducated, its impact on foreign policy was negligible. In the mid-1980s, Myron Weiner speculated about whether the growing presence of the affluent Indian-American expatriate community in the United States would make a difference for bilateral relations.[2] As will be seen, the diaspora's influence in the United States has grown as its skills, education, income, and size have increased. It is apparent that the prosperous and demographically significant Indo-American community, typified by physicians and Silicon Valley computer technicians, has remarkably changed not only its image, but the perception of its home country in the United States. In a single generation the image of Indians in the United States and the subcontinent has been transformed from a malnourished skeleton in a filthy *dhoti* to a highly educated prosperous professional in a designer business suit who is a threat to American jobs—an impression reinforced by the impressive number of widely-read and acclaimed novels written in English by expatriates.

The diaspora serves as a reservoir of support for New Delhi in Washington. It has also played a major role in transforming Indian society by infusing new ideas—whether formally or informally—as well as economic, human, and social capital from the United States. Its entrepreneurial success in the United States has also influenced Indian policy makers as they undertook economic reforms, a reality recently acknowledged by Prime Minister and former Finance Minister Manmohan Singh on a recent visit to the United States.[3]

The Ambivalent Indo-American Relationship

Washington's actions attract greater attention in the course of bilateral relations because they impinge more on New Delhi's security and prosperity than vice-versa. This asymmetrical Indo-American relationship has a direct bearing on mutual perceptions. While Indians pay close attention to U.S. affairs, ignorance of India typifies American attitudes, and neglect has characterized the United States' policies toward a country that has not been regarded as economically significant. While the United States is India's leading foreign investor and trading partner, accounting for twenty percent of India's exports, these transactions amount to less than one percent of America's global trade and a negligible amount of U.S. foreign investment. The disparity of mutual importance, which had increased since the break-up of the Soviet Union, has made Indian officials—who have never been comfortable with the notion of a unipolar world—resentful of America's insensitivity.

It has been shown that individuals relate to international actors and their environment according to a set of relatively stable and durable thought patterns that translate into policy preferences.[4] The impressions Indian and American officials formed about each other's countries translated into policy.[5] As Harold Isaacs suggests, perceptions are particularly important in any foreign policy relationship where there is little shared history and "neither high politics nor high emotion,"[6] Mutually hostile perceptions have complicated relations between the world's two largest democracies and often impeded the resolution of outstanding issues. Due to their asymmetrical importance, bilateral relations have tended to focus on images rather than interests. Sulochana Raghavan Glazer and Nathan Glazer found that a surprising degree of emotionally weighted and corresponding ambivalent images—

including indifference, hostility, resentment, exasperation and disdain—characterized the relations between India and the United States.[7] According to former ambassador Chester Bowles, the corresponding ambivalent conceptions Indians have of the United States are quite different, but equally stereotyped from those the Americans have of India, since they have been shaped by similar factors. Writing in 1961 he found that, "India is inclined to look upon American foreign policy as negative, overly militaristic, and purely defensive against communism," while the United States saw a non-aligned India as unwilling to "stand up and be counted in a struggle between the forces of freedom and those of servitude."[8]

Historic Indian Perceptions

India has played a remarkably significant international role for a developing country with a large illiterate population. Public opinion has counted less than elite attitudes in the formation of foreign policy in India's parliamentary system.[9] The personality perceptions, attitudes, and beliefs of decision-makers shaped by education provide the ideological context and historical legacy in any foreign policy relationship.[10]

While international migration, education and return were characteristics of pre-independence India, that channel of migration was primarily with Great Britain the colonial power and not the United States. These Indian elite attitudes—which include Fabian socialism, Gandhism, Marxism and anti-Americanism[11]—were formulated by the British-educated founding generation. Mahatma Gandhi and Sarder Patel pursued their legal training there. A host of others, including Krishna Menon and many prominent bureaucrats, attended the London School of Economics (LSE) which ensured the lasting influence of Beatrice and Sidney Webb as well as Harold Laski on the Indian elite. Even B.R. Ambedkar, the untouchable leader who earned a Ph.D. from Columbia and drafted the Indian constitution, also studied at LSE. Others like Sardar Pratap Singh Kairon, and Lala Lajpath Rai, who studied in the United States, were exceptions, as was Jayprakash

Nararyan, whose socialism was reinforced at the University of Wisconsin and Ohio State during the depression.

Jawaharlal Nehru, who dominated the foreign policy apparatus and Parliament from 1947-64, was educated at Cambridge. Nehru considered American leaders condescending and, as a Marxist, deplored American materialism.[12] Nehru's policy of nonalignment with the great powers forged a wide-ranging consensus at home and provided prominence abroad. Little advantage, but a considerable loss of sovereignty, was seen by the majority of Indians in any formal ties to Washington. For the most part—with the exception of members of the pro-Western Swatantra party—Nehru's views on the United States were shared by his associates in the Congress Party and even exceeded by Hindu nationalist, socialist, and communist legislators.

There is a long-standing perception that the United States has consistently been reluctant to accord New Delhi great power status and constantly works against India's interests.[13] The transformation of the American image from the symbol of liberty, equality and democracy to an association with British imperialism in India was established during World War II.[14] Resentment still persists because China—not India—was granted a permanent seat on the United Nations Security Council in 1945. U.S.-Soviet competition and Indo-Pakistani rivalry aggravated Washington's bilateral ties with New Delhi. The U.S. alliance with Pakistan, formalized in 1954, has been the most prominent and continuing irritant in bilateral relations. The pact was widely viewed as an American intervention on the subcontinent that was explicitly directed against India rather than the Soviet Union.[15]

Nehru's daughter Indira Gandhi, who attended but never graduated from Oxford, had a more visceral antipathy towards the United States when she served as Prime Minister (1966-1977; 1980-1984). This sentiment was reinforced by Washington's insistence that India devalue its currency by fifty percent during the financial crisis of 1966, which the left parties depicted in a no-confidence motion as a "craven surrender" of India's economic independence to the United States.[16] The implicit justification for the state of emergency that she proclaimed in 1975 was that the CIA was trying to destabilize her government.

Legislators in both countries were particularly slow to abandon Cold War rhetoric after the disintegration of the Soviet Union. As late as the passage of the Brown Amendment of 1995, which weakened the prohibition on arms sales to Pakistan, there was a latent hostility that could consistently be tapped by New Delhi's opponents and supporters of Islamabad in Washington, while anti-Americanism was prevalent among elites in India.

The Indian Diaspora and the United States

The United States was late in discovering India. Prior to World War II, American contact, except for missionary activity with India, was nominal, and political and economic relations between the two countries were sporadic. As late as 1940, there were only around three thousand persons of Indian descent in the United States, and as a consequence, relations with their country of origin were of little domestic importance to either the general public or Congress. Under the circumstances, advocates for better relations such as J.J. Singh, the president of the India League of America, could make little progress in his attempt to secure backing from the Roosevelt administration for Indian independence.[17] Sympathetic to the anti-colonialism espoused by the Indian National Congress, Washington nevertheless felt it necessary to support its ally Great Britain, rather than the nationalist movement that was demanding independence from London.[18]

Early Patterns of Immigration

Even before New Delhi achieved independence, the barring of Indians and the denial of citizenship to them on the basis of race scarred America's relations with India.[19] The first wave of immigrants from South Asia who arrived in the United States in the 1890s was primarily agricultural laborers from the Punjab region who worked on farms in the Pacific Northwest and California. The latter often took Mexican wives.[20] No matter what their religious persuasion, all Indians were deemed "Hindus" and subjected to the widespread prejudice against Asians that prevailed in the first half of the 20th century. As a consequence, "the first and second generation of Indian leaders, including senior officials and bureaucrats....considered the United States a racist country comparable to South Africa in the way it treated minorities..."[21] Immigration from India for purposes of employment was completely barred under a 1917 statute, and in 1923 the Supreme Court ruled[22] that Indian nationals were ineligible for citizenship on the grounds that as "Hindus" they were not "white persons." After further restrictions banning Asians were applied by Congress in 1924, the Indian legislature retaliated in 1926 by passing the Indian Naturalization Act which denied Indian citizenship to nationals of any country that withheld the same privilege to Indians. Proposals for reform of the quota and naturalization provisions introduced by Claire Booth Luce (R-CN) and Emanuel Celler (D-NY) in 1945 were stalled by an anti-civil rights coalition of Republicans and southern Democrats. It required the active intervention of President Truman to secure passage of the immigration reform measure on July 2, 1946.[23] It would take the 1965 U.S. Immigration and Naturalization Act to reverse decades of discrimination and initiate preferential admission of skilled Asian professionals such as physicians. However, its impact on immigration would not be felt until the 1980s.[24] As will be shown, it would take another decade after that for Indian-Americans to become a factor in bilateral relations.

Year	Number
1910	2,544
1920	2,544
1930	3,130
1940	2,405
1950	2,398
1960	8,746
1970	13,149
1980	387,221
1990	815,447
2000	1,678,765

Table 4.1: Indian Americans in the United States by Decade

Historic American Perceptions

In the meantime, the relative lack of contact was responsible for uninformed condescending and critical perceptions of India transmitted by Christian missionaries.[25] As anthropologist Milton Singer suggests, these subjective images often reflect more about the psychology of the holder than about reality.[26] This was certainly true in the case of Mahatma Gandhi, who was alternatively depicted in the United States as a saint or a fraud.[27] Images of India in the United States projected by Katherine Mayo in 1927 were highly negative, as they pictured the country as characterized by fabulous opulence or pervasive poverty.[28]

These unflattering sentiments were developed and reinforced by a "self-indoctrinating" and circular information system that included school textbooks, the media, and academic writings which depicted India as a backward society.[29] A 1979 academic survey indicated that scholars continued to perceive South Asian countries as exclusively backward societies that neglected the foreign trade and industrial economies of the region.[30]

The Asia Society, in a review of some 300 school textbooks, found that the presentation of India was the most negative of all Asian countries.[31] According to a State Department analysis, American attitudes concerning India focused on disease, death, and illiteracy more than for any other place.[32]

As a result, public opinion surveys have consistently documented that most Americans have had misconceptions and negative feelings about India and Indians.[33] A 1928 poll found immigrants from India were regarded "as the most undesirable" of all newcomers living in the United States.[34]

American legislators and decision-makers are subject to the same impressions as the general public. It is the view of John Mellor that U.S. policy itself is the product of similar stereotypes that portray India "as poverty-stricken and helpless."[35] Certainly during the 1971 Bangladesh crisis, President Richard Nixon's tilt toward Pakistan "was influenced by his long-standing dislike for India and the Indians."[36] A similar sentiment is attributed to President Lyndon Johnson, who "regarded Indians as weak and indecisive."[37]

A former high Agency for International Development (AID) official who had been posted in New Delhi described "a majority" of key players in the White House, the State Department and Congress to be *ab initio*, anti-Indian.[38]

The American Congress is more likely to be representative of public attitudes than is the executive branch. Like other Americans, most congressmen get their news and impressions from the media.[39] The information they get about India is neither adequate nor accurate.[40] Even his service as Ambassador to New Delhi did not prevent Senator Daniel Patrick Moynihan, perhaps the most knowledgeable legislator of his time on the subject, from stating, "What does [India] export but communicable diseases?"[41] One of the most informed and thoughtful Congressmen, Lee Hamilton (D-IN), a chairman of a House Foreign Affairs subcommittee that dealt with South Asia and the Near East and later chairman of the full committee, was moved to exclaim in response to testimony describing India's circumstances, "I don't know that I have ever heard such a long list of difficulties, ills and problems and so little hope..."[42]

The complaint was raised that although India has one of the largest populations, most powerful military establishments and dynamic economies in the world, it has not been taken seriously by the United States.[43] Myron Weiner cogently explained the reasons why South Asia has until recently been accorded such a low priority in American thinking:

> Unlike the Middle East, Indonesia or Nigeria, it has no resources vital to the American economy. Unlike Latin America it is not a region with substantial American private investment. Its geo-political position raises no fundamental problems for American security....Unlike China...India has no deep cultural or historic ties with the United States, and unlike the countries of Western Europe, Israel and Greece, no significant segment of the American population originates from nor has an enduring association with

> the region. In short, none of the elements exist that attract the daily concerns of the president, Congress, the press, or the foreign policy publics.[44]

Implications for U.S. Policy

Relative to other areas of the world, the United States has neglected India despite the country's growing economic, political and strategic importance. Within both the executive and legislative branches, South Asia has had a low priority. American interests have been seen as limited in a region that was associated with problems rather than opportunities. Oriented towards Europe, the State Department until 1991 included South Asia with the Near East and resisted the creation of a separate bureau for the region. As a result, a deputy assistant secretary four levels removed from the Secretary of State handled relations with India. Under this arrangement, the "Near East received the lion's share of attention," and held six country directorates compared to two for South Asia, although the three-to-one population ratio was the inverse.[45] South Asia is also attached to the Near East in the National Security Council and the Central Intelligence Agency, causing regional issues to be handled intermittently by functional experts.[46]

The legislative scene is even more diffuse. During the Cold War the Senate Foreign Relations Committee concerned itself primarily with U.S.-Soviet issues and the Vietnam conflict and abrogated other responsibilities–which included South Asia–to subcommittee chairmen who showed an interest and desired a platform.[47] After a major reorganization of its subcommittees in 1970, the House of Representatives treated South Asia in a typically residual fashion and thereby reduced both continuity and expertise in that chamber. At times, South Asia has been paired with the Near East in the manner of the State Department, as a subcommittee of the House Foreign Affairs Committee, where Arab-Israeli and Iraqi matters overshadowed it. At other times it has been coupled with the Asia and the Pacific regions where it was dwarfed by concerns such as the Vietnam War and bilateral relations with China and Japan. As recently as the mid-1980s, only about five percent of the members of Congress had an interest in South Asia.[48] Given this situation, congressional concern about India is not constant. Legislative activity towards the region tends to manifest itself in amendments to related issues such as human rights and nuclear proliferation. When issues are peripheral to interest groups, political parties, and the congressional leadership, members have great discretion regarding their activities. This enables "marginals" to become involved in the foreign policy process as it relates to areas peripheral to the national interest. Hence "India bashers" such as Dan Burton (R-IN), Dana Rohrabacher (R-CA), and Robert Dornan (R-CA) have used the Foreign Affairs and Intelligence Committees as a platform to criticize New Delhi with impunity.[49]

The tendency toward neglect has implications for U.S. policy towards a region where American interests have been seen as limited. Hence, perceptions have, until recently, been more important than security interests in shaping U.S. policy towards South Asia.[50] Robert Dahl observed that perceptions about a policy in Washington tend to be "persistent, consistent and shared."[51] The most enduring factor in Washington's bilateral relations with New Delhi is the belief that India was on the wrong side of the two most important conflicts of the past century: World War II and the Cold War. Although millions of Indian soldiers served in the British Army, the Indian National Congress refused to support the war against the Axis powers so long as London would not promise independence. Prime Minister Jawaharlal Nehru was viewed as "clearly pro-Russian," and Indian nonalignment was seen as "a major obstacle to US efforts to rally and unite the free nations of Asia in the struggle against Soviet world domination."[52] While there is little institutional memory in Washington, these perceptions have remained consistent in the State Department and on Capitol Hill.[53]

Bilateral relations were rarely on an even keel, but tended instead to oscillate between high and low points. The high points were U.S. support for New Delhi during its 1962 border war with China, which coincided with the Cuban Missile Crisis, and U.S. relief programs that extended from the early 1950s into the next decade. The low points have been more numerous: differences that emerged during the Korean War, India's failure to sign the Japanese peace treaty, the inclusion of Pakistan in the American alliance system in 1954-55, the attempt by the United States to prevent India from using force in Goa in 1961, the U.S. decision to send the carrier Enterprise into the Bay of Bengal in 1971, and Indian resentment over the accrual of rupee currencies by the United States. Since New Delhi seldom agreed with Washington on issues like Afghanistan, foreign assistance to India was perceived as earning ingratitude and resentment rather than benefits for the United States, and Congressional appropriations subcommittees chaired by Otto Passman (D-LA) and Clarence Long (D-MD) only grudgingly provided it.[54] The situation of the Sikhs in the Punjab region and the ensuing civil war in Kashmir added a human rights dimension to bilateral relations that divided the expatriate community in the 1980s. Economic and nuclear issues are more recent irritants.

A Lag in Perceptions

The end of the Cold War—for the first time—provided anticipation that bilateral relations, freed from the historic shibboleths, would flourish. However, policy-makers' (especially legislators') beliefs are so deep-rooted that they have been slow to adjust to changing international circumstances. Even though Moscow was no longer regarded as a threat to Washington, hostility towards India lingered on Capitol Hill as late as the passage of the watershed Brown Amendment in 1995, which eased sanctions on Pakistan for Islamabad's nuclear program.[55] Anachronistic Cold War logic was resurrected to portray Pakistan as being a loyal partner of the United States, while India was depicted as being a client of Russia always taking positions contrary to American interests and branded "as the greatest source of instability in South Asia."[56] Predictably, the Brown Amendment's passage caused outrage in India and worsened relations with the United States. Parliamentarians from the parties on the left ridiculed the government of Prime Minister P. V. Narasimha Rao for pursuing what they regarded as a misguided policy of cooperation with the United States.[57] The setback to U.S.-Indian relations was signaled by a speech that Home Minister S. B. Chavan made in the Rajya Sabha on November 29, 1995. He claimed the selling of arms to Pakistan was indicative that the United States had "evil designs" on the subcontinent. His assertion that the United States was interested in acquiring a "foothold" in Kashmir was endorsed by the Bharatiya Janata Party opposition leader.[58] The fact that this unsubstantiated charge was widely endorsed throughout India without refutation is indicative of the persistence of obsolete perceptions. The passage of the Brown Amendment and the Indian parliament's reaction to it showed the delicate nature of the Indo-American relations. This legacy of mistrust has carried over to the conduct of the war on terrorism in Afghanistan, where the United States has had to delicately balance its improved relationship with India with its renewed commitment to Pakistan as a frontline state.

Changing Perceptions

Twenty years ago Surjit Mansingh found that few articulate persons in the Indian press or parliament were "pro-American,"[59] but that is no longer the case. Now there is concern that India has become too close with Washington because it is "over-invested in the United States." India's urban youth and burgeoning middle class have become Americanized through the globalization of the communications media. Hundreds of thousands of Indians have worked in the United States on H-1B visas. Thousands of have returned home—many who are employed in businesses engaged in the outsourcing of services. Once back in India they have become an important lobby for better relations with the United States.[60] In addition, "practically every educated or wealthy family in India has one or more members resident in America with vested interests in good relations with that country."[61] It is estimated that twenty five percent of the Indian elite has relatives living in the United States. The 74,603 Indians studying in the United States are the largest source of foreign students in the country.[62] Sixty percent of retired Indian generals have children studying abroad—half of them in the United States.

Even as vernacular politicians have replaced the earlier more sophisticated generation, the number of American-educated Indian legislators across the political spectrum is growing.[63] Reflecting increased cooperation between American and Indian legislators,[64] a recent parliamentary delegation included Milind Deora, son of veteran Mumbai Congress politician Murli Deora who earned a Bachelor of Science degree in Business Administration from Boston University; Sachin Pilot, son of the late Congress leader Rajesh Pilot who has an MBA from the University of Pennsylvania's Wharton School; B.J. Panada of the Biju Janata Dal, who majored in Scientific and Technical Communication from Michigan Tech; and the Bharatiya Janata Party's Manvendra Singh, son of former External Affairs Minister Jaswant Singh, who is an alumnus of Hampshire College.[65] Other prominent members of parliament (MPs) educated in the United States include Ajit Singh, son of former Prime Minister Charan Singh, who actually became a U.S. citizen before renouncing his American citizenship in order to return to India and run for parliament, and of course, Palaniappan Chidambaram, Finance Minister in the United Front government in 1996 and again in the Congress-led government in 2004, who earned a Harvard MBA. Children of prominent politicians who have studied in the United States include Congress leader Sonia Gandhi's son Rahul, who studied at Harvard, as did Dayanidhi Maran, the son of former Industries Minister Murasoli Maran of the Dravida Munnettra Kazhagam (DMK); Jyotridaya Scindia, the son of the late Madhav Rao Scindia, who earned an MBA at Stanford; and Dushyant Singh, the son of Vasundhara Raje, who attended Boston University. While an education in the United States does not guarantee support for Washington's policies, it does impart an understanding and transmission of American values and culture. Students, as well as an increasing number of other immigrants to America, serve as a bridge between the two countries.

The new Indian elites that have emerged in both countries have had a significant impact on Indo-American relations. Indian economists have routinely been educated abroad and worked at institutions such as the World Bank and International Monetary Fund. Many did not return home after completing their education. British-trained economists tended to endorse the command economy model. Some of the initial dissenters from the state-dominated economic strategy were economists who tended to locate in the United States, such as Jagdish Bhagwati at Columbia University and T.N. Srinivasvan of Yale. In recent years they have been reinforced by a new generation of American-educated scholars who have returned to India and assumed positions of influence. These include Arun Shourie, whose dissertation at Syracuse was critical of India's licensing regimes; Rakesh Mohan and Suman Bery, two Princeton-trained economists who both headed the National Council of Applied Economic Research (NCAER); S. Venkitararamanan, a champion of liberalization who did his doctoral work at Carnegie Mellon and was a member of the Indian Administrative Service (IAS); and Vijay Kelkar, who earned a Ph.D. at Berkeley before becoming finance secretary.[66] Others have moved from India to the American financial sector. Jayant Sinha, son of former Finance and Foreign Minister Yashwant Sinha, joined Citibank in New York before moving to Bear Sterns, and then Lehman Brothers. It is believed his endorsement of free enterprise affected the evolution of his father's economic thinking.[67]

After the demise of the Soviet Union, ethnic politics became more important in Washington. Since New Delhi's belated adoption of a free market economy, India's hundreds of millions of consumers have "attracted the attention of both Wall Street and Main Street" as well as the U.S. Congress.[68] American legislators have finally realized that India's 1991 economic liberalization can yield domestic dividends. Economic opportunity has for the first time figured in congressional thinking about India. Legislators, who once avoided the region,[69] now regularly visit the commercial centers of Mumbai (Bombay) and India's silicone valley in Bangalore, as well as the capital, Delhi.[70] PepsiCo and General Electric, which have major investments in India, have become important lobbyists for that country in Washington. As American investment in India increases, so too has New Delhi's influence in Washington, thanks to the activity of the U.S.-India Business Council and the India Interest Group lobby. At a time when ethnic politics have trumped nuclear proliferation, Indian interest groups have replicated the tactics of the Israeli lobbies in Washington[71] and in recent years have held a number of joint functions with Jewish groups on Capitol Hill.[72]

The Changing Face of the Indo-American Community

New Delhi's position in Washington has especially been bolstered by the political activity of the over 1.7 million Indian-Americans (according to the 2000 census)—up from 387,000 in 1980—who reside in the United States (See Figure 4.1). Fifty three percent were born in India—a declining majority of whom came from Gujarat—while the rest migrated from diasporic communities in England, Africa, the Caribbean, and Pakistan.[73]

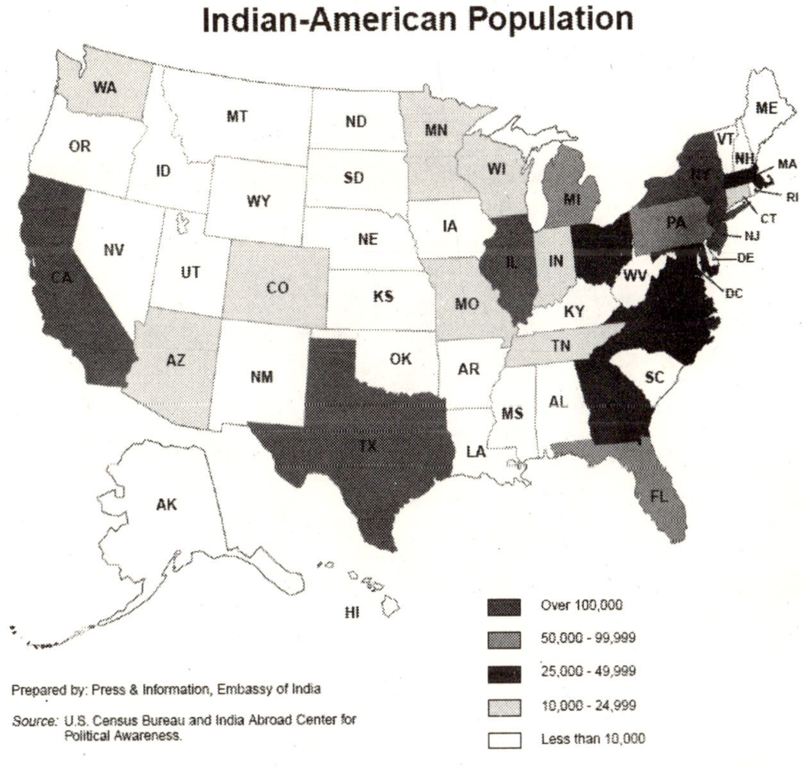

Figure 4.1: Indian-American Population of the United States

While their influence is diluted by Khalistani and Kashmiri separatists and a Pakistani-American community that is one-tenth the size, it is growing nonetheless. Their annual growth rate of 7.6 percent– or 38 percent in five years to a total of 2.3 million in 2005–makes the community the fastest growing ethnic group in the country.[74] Many own small businesses, including thirty seven percent of all hotel rooms in the United States.[75] The educational achievement and economic status of this upwardly mobile community has succeeded in changing the perception of Indians in the United States (See Figure 4.2). Indian-Americans have a median income nearly fifty percent higher than the average American–$60,093 compared to the national average of $38,885.[76] Moreover, they have the smallest number of people living below the poverty line (less than six percent). The community, which includes 200,000 millionaires,[77] has a higher per capita income, and a

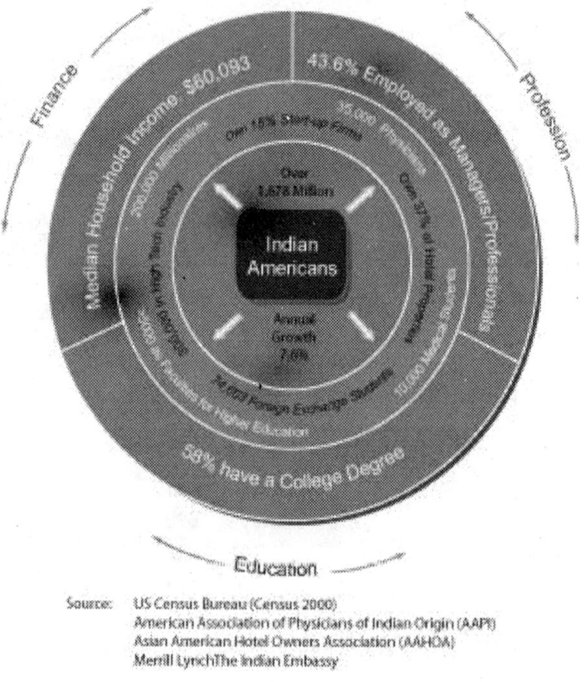

Figure 4.2: Indian-American Education, Employment & Income Status

larger percentage of its workforce (forty six percent) holds a managerial or professional position than any other group except Japanese-Americans in the United States.[78] Fifty eight percent of adults have college degrees (triple the number of whites in America and twenty times the number of Indians in India) and 5,000 are academics, many in elite business schools. The community has an especially high representation of doctors (35,000), engineers, scientists, architects and computer technologists (300,000). They account for fifteen percent of all high-tech startups in the Silicon Valley.[79] Among their success stories are Vinod Khosla, co-founder of Sun Microsystems; Sabeer Bhatia the creator of Hotmail; and billionaire Gururaj Deshpande.[80] Others have achieved prominent influence at Citibank, U.S. Air, and United Airlines.

These demographic and economic factors have translated into political influence in both countries. Highly paid Indo-American professionals, derisively characterized by their opponents as the "chapatti lobby," are politically active–especially in the major urban-industrial states of California and the Northeast and Midwest, as well as Texas. Their outreach through such groups as the Indian American Forum for Political Education (IAFPE) which has 28 chapters across the United States and the Indian American Political Advocacy Council (IAPAC) translates into political and financial clout.[81] The American Association of Physicians of Indian Origin was instrumental in lifting restrictions against foreign-trained doctors practicing in the United States. Indian-Americans raised four million dollars on behalf of political candidates in the 1992 election; six years later this figure had almost doubled to seven million dollars.[82] President Bill Clinton managed to raise over a million dollars for the Democratic National Committee at a single event in 2000.[83] Under the circumstances, both Republicans and Democrats have attempted to mobilize the community's resources.[84]

Members of Congress see little downside, and have many reasons to be attentive to the community's concerns.[85] The Indian American Friendship Council attracted nearly forty lawmakers to a July 1999 function in Washington which featured speeches by House

Minority Leader Richard Gephardt, House International Relations Committee chair, Benjamin Gilman, and Doug Bereuter, the chairman of the House subcommittee that dealt with Asia. The India Abroad Center for Political Awareness regularly runs summer sessions for congressional interns, an activity that has led to the placement of more than three dozen staffers of Indian origin on the Hill.

This growing influence of the Indian-American community[86] is reflected in the strength of the Caucus of India and Indian-Americans in the House of Representatives, which claims 163 members and makes it the largest country caucus on the Hill in the 108th Congress (2003-05). The caucus was founded by Frank Pallone (D-NJ), whose district had a significant population of Indian-Americans, and Bill McCollum (F-FL), who was critical of Pakistan's record on narcotics and terrorism after India's champion Stephen Solarz (D-NY) left Congress in 1993. The positions of the bipartisan[87] caucus on South Asian and related matters, such as immigration, family reunification, and civil rights issues, must be taken into account by an administration which regards its numbers as a mixed blessing and a threat to executive control of foreign policy. The sale of wheat and aircraft were more instrumental than the Caucus in lifting sanctions against New Delhi after the 1998 nuclear tests.[88] The author's research indicates that its strength and accomplishments are exaggerated. The Caucus' principal activities are feel-good resolutions praising India's democracy and contrasting New Delhi's political system with the authoritarian military dictatorship in Pakistan. Nevertheless, the Caucus–despite its rivalries[89]–has for the first time provided India "with an institutional base of support on Capitol Hill."[90] It has done so by enlisting floor speakers, lining up votes, and placing material in the *Congressional Record.* Whereas a generation ago, supporters of India such as Stephen Solarz and Charles Percy had difficulty in finding colleagues and community activists to advance New Delhi's interests, the Caucus has been instrumental in negating the influence of Pakistan and defeating Dan Burton's annual amendments to slash assistance to India.

The example of the House Caucus was not lost on the Senate. In March 2004, a 35 member "Friends of India" grouping was formed in the Senate in conjunction with the Indian Embassy, the first such country-focused grouping in the history of that body—a development made easier by the departure of legislators with a broader agenda than ethnic politics, such as the late Daniel Patrick Moynihan and John Glenn. Co-chaired by John Cornyn (R-TX) and Hilary Rodham Clinton (D-NY), its membership includes Senate Majority Leader Bill Frist (R-TN), Senate Minority Leader Tom Daschle (D-SD), Judiciary Committee Chair Orrin Hatch (R-UT), Finance Committee Chair Charles Grassley (R-IA), Appropriations Chair Thad Cochran (R-MS), and other influential senators such as Joe Lieberman (D-CN) and Edward Kennedy (D-MA).[91]

The wealthy non-resident Indian (NRI) community in the United States has also become a magnet for Indian politicians engaged in fund-raising for their own elections.[92] Indian finance ministers of all political persuasions regularly approach NRIs—always an important source of remittances—to invest in their country of origin.

The net result of these diverse developments has been a remarkable turnaround in congressional attitudes toward India and U.S.-Indian ties[93] That was evident in the role the Indo-American community played in garnering legislative support for the nuclear agreement reached by New Delhi and Washington in 2005.[94] "The transformation of congressional attitudes from indifference or deep-seated hostility to their current positive state on Capitol Hill confirms the necessity for a foreign country to have a strong domestic base of support in the American political system if it intends to be influential in Washington."[95] It reinforces the administration's disposition for improved ties with India in light of the threat of global Islamic terrorism after 9-11-2001 and the prospect of the challenge presented by China. Yet, even though the image of Indians in the United States has been dramatically and positively transformed, the delicate nature of bilateral relations remains inhibited from achieving partnership by their residual pattern of ambiguity and mistrust. This wariness is evidenced by India's unhappiness with America's renewed commitment to Pakistan as a frontline state, and American anxiety over outsourcing service jobs to highly-educated, but lower-paid Indians. The irony of the evolution of the Indo-American relationship was not lost on Congressman Gary Ackerman. He bemoaned what he called "India bashing," arguing that "for years we told the Indians they were too aligned with the Soviet Union, they were too socialist; they had to free their economy and be entrepreneurial. Now that India is free and entrepreneurial, we are telling them you are coming on too strong."[96] Ironically, because of outsourcing, few Indians will be migrating to the United States.

The Indian Diaspora in Britain: Political Interventionism & Diaspora Activism

Chapter 5

The Indian Diaspora in Britain: Political Interventionism & Diaspora Activism

Asaf Hussain

Introduction[2]

The population from India has had a global migration history. Since 1834 Indians have migrated to widespread places in the world. The British during their colonial rule in India had taken Indians to their African colonies, where they formed part of an indenture system.[1] This system, which operated in colonial times, has been considered to be another name for slavery.[2] Although "in India, crossing the seas was prohibited by the sacred Hindu scriptures," in spite of this restriction, mass migration resulted in "nearly 20 million [people] settled in 70 countries."[3] The colonization of India opened the doors for new migration opportunities and Indians availed themselves of it. Some, like Dadabhai Naoroji, even became a Member of Parliament (MP) in 1892, while the British Indian Army fought in Britain's imperial wars, and forty Victoria Crosses were awarded to its soldiers between 1912 and 1947.[4]

Mainstream economic migration of Indians to the UK started taking place during the 1950s. The new states of India and Pakistan were then suffering from fragile economies and manpower exports were beneficial to them. On the other hand, Britain was desperate to receive manpower from its former colonies for its own development. Over the decades, many migrant groups settled in Britain, but the Indian migrant group became one of the most important non-European groups settled in Britain. Firstly, they were highly developed culturally and satisfied the needs of their community. Secondly, they made important contributions to Britain in economic terms. Thirdly, the Indian migrants also made significant monetary contributions to the economy of India. These were mainly economic reasons, but they were instrumental in embedding Indian migrants within British society.

This paper will explore two questions. First, how have Indian migrants raised themselves into becoming the significant minority in a closed culture still characterised by the colonial syndrome? Second, how have successive Indian governments tried to utilize this significant minority?

Diaspora and Development

Diasporas from various countries that settled in the Western countries have become very important groups because of their levels of development. These levels of development can be judged in three ways. First, this can emanate from the composition of the group and the extent of their labour/self-sufficiency. This division of labour relates to how much they can satisfy the needs of their communities–as they want it. From this angle, one can categorize their level of development as "high" or "low." Second, if the level of development is high then such diasporas will have more access and influence within their country of migration (COM). If the diaspora cannot exercise any influence in their COM, this represents a low development of the diaspora itself. Third, if their level of development is high then these diasporas can also attract the attention of the governments of their country of origin (COO). They therefore become useful in helping to achieve the agenda of their COO.

According to the above criteria of diaspora developments, the Indian Diaspora, which had begun to migrate from India after 1947 to Britain, did not at first bring about real achievements. The situation changed in the 1980s, and there was a reason for this. The Indian Diaspora had come mainly from villages and individuals worked as labourers in industrial factories and other low-paid areas of employment. However, in the 1970s Indians also arrived from the former African colonies of Britain. They were not poverty-ridden but well-educated, middle-class Hindu (as well as Muslim and Sikh) professionals and businessmen from Uganda, Tanzania, Kenya and Malawi. They were second-generation migrants, with the first generation having gone from India to Africa. They had worked with the British colonial authorities and established their trustworthiness with them, but had not identified with the African population at all. In the post-independence period, the Africanization policies of the new African states resented the Indian presence because of their high levels of economic development and the social distance which existed between the two groups.

The Indian population in Britain, according to the statistics of 1999–2000, is over 942,000. Some 40 percent of the population lives around London. Other segments of the population are based in the East Midlands and Manchester. The predominant group in the second migration was mainly Hindu Gujaratis who settled in the urban areas of Britain "particularly in Leicester and north London. They came as whole family units, often sending a single member first to establish a base and make links with extended family members already in residence. Once settled they began to reproduce organizations and practices familiar to them from their time in Africa."[5]

The second migration brought a "major change in the development of Hinduism in Britain" along with "experience and skills relevant to community development and the formation of religious institutions."[6] This led to the establishment of many Hindu temples, community organizations and charitable trusts to safeguard their religion and culture. Many of these organizations, like the Confederation of Gujarati Organizations, Maharastra Manda, Punjabi Unity Forum, Hindu Cultural Society, etc. were generally known as community organizations. Yet the Indian migrants could not be considered as a monolithic community as there were many "divergent trends" among them.[7] Their different histories of migration and different ethnicities separated them even in their settlement in Britain. For example, a

> number of Hindus of Gujarati origins were settled in the area Balham and Tooting, a significant number of Hindu Punjabis were settled in Southall... Each one had a different history. Furthermore, among the Gujaratis in Balham, 'community' refers to a linguistic

> commonality among those in that geographic area. For the Punjabis in Southall, linguistic commonality combines with residential concentration and shared religious activities so that 'community' is truly evident socially and geographically.[8]

However, it must be said that whatever their differences, they did have one thing in common: they were proud of their COO–India.

With time, as their economic conditions improved, their social networks expanded, and they were quick to learn how to use the resources of the public service facilities like town halls and other public premises for their festivals.[9] While some of these organizations were opened privately by various groups, the Indian High Commission also supported the spread of Indian culture in Britain by opening the Nehru Centre, which held talks, exhibitions, cultural evenings and a number of other activities to raise the image of India. On an individual level, the achievement of the Indians themselves was commendable. In Britain, there were some 30 Indian professors in various universities engaged in disciplines like computer sciences, engineering, biochemistry, aerospace, etc. as well as numerous medical doctors and nurses.

Unlocking Closed Cultures

British culture was a closed culture, not an open one. This may come as a surprise to many, for its policies of accepting large numbers of migrants and supplying them with passports and citizenship was unlike other European countries, and was indicative of an open policy. This was an open policy for economic reasons, but this did not mean that Britain had opened up its culture to migrants. Conversely, the migrants had come for economic reasons, not to change their culture. The reason why British culture was closed was a legacy of the colonial syndrome. Though by the 1960s, when decolonization began, by no means did all British people endorse colonialism, the colonial syndrome remained part of British culture because many still considered earlier British colonial history as a great achievement. The colonial syndrome continued to manifest itself within the British societal context in two ways: firstly, through the politics of exclusion relating to racism, and secondly through the politics of closure relating to the identity of "Britishness."

The politics of exclusion emanated from colonialism. Many justified the colonial period with the rationalization of the "white man's burden," that the British had acquired colonies in order to bring civilization to them. The assumption was that the people of such cultures were inferior and did not possess any civilization, while Britain was doing them a favour by imposing its rule. This led to the creation of a white/black dichotomy within British society. This obviously created a system of exclusion of non-whites through racial discrimination. Racism had not been eradicated from British society before the 1960s because decolonization had not taken place. Racism in British society operated at the individual, institutional and structural level. Indians and other migrant groups suffered discrimination, in spite of the Race Relations Acts and other regulations trying to enforce equal opportunities. British governments have seemed to lack a strong political will to eradicate racism, and the racist card (in particular, stopping immigration) has always been featured to a greater or lesser extent as an issue of national elections.

The politics of closure on the other hand raised another issue: what is "Britishness?" Could the Indian migrant community become part of "Britishness?" This was a much more complex problem of the British context than racism. There was no doubt that the English, Scottish, Welsh and Irish were part of Britishness, but what about the South Asians, Chinese, Africans, African-Caribbeans, Somalis, etc? This question obviously bothered some segments of British society. Technically one was British by possessing a British passport. That was not the problem. The problem was whether or not one was British through the acquisition of a common culture of "Britishness."

Intellectual arguments from the liberal and conservative schools of British nationalism could not find a solution. Parekh contrasted the two schools of nationalism prevalent in Britain: conservative and liberal nationalists. Conservative nationalists related to territory, common language, culture, blood ties and history. They regarded "the integrity of the nation as the highest political value" and felt "deeply uneasy about the presence of outsiders."[10]

Socialists and liberals, on the other hand, argued like the conservatives that unity of the nation was the prime objective and that citizens cannot be united only by the laws, obligations, rights and duties imposed by the state. Citizens should be united on a "strong sense of national identity" which could be related to history and common tradition. This kind of liberalism made room for ethnic minorities in the national identity by allowing them the right to their cultures, while stipulating that

> immigrants should acquire 'those traits that make up national character' or at least the 'essential elements of national character'. Since for Miller, 'National Character' includes a shared view of the past, tastes, sensibilities and so on, it must be taken to mean that immigrants should be required to acquire these" and that "'immigrants' must abandon values and ways of behaving that are in stark conflict with those of the community as a whole.[11]

The tragedy was that such schools of thought were part of the politics of closure in which migrants were offered little or no choice. British culture was confused and did not know how to accommodate the South Asians; it was contradictory. The strategy advocated by the liberals was to take the assimilationist approach. They thought that society could become the "melting pot" in which their majority would dominate and exert pressure on, for example, the Hindus to become assimilated into their culture. Realizing the failure of the assimilation theories, the policy-makers began to accommodate them through a new theory, namely the "salad bowl" approach. This implied that every "vegetable/salad ingredient" could maintain its own identity. British society was soon being labelled as a multicultural society. Multiculturalism was a way of living in accordance with one's own culture amidst other cultures. One culture did not need to have any linkage with any other culture. This policy has now been considered to have backfired, for serious questions have been raised as to the loyalties of the migrant British groups. Most of the groups have sought their identities within their religions and/or their countries of origins.

Extending Diaspora Spaces

The failure of the British government to purge the colonial syndrome left many migrants in a dilemma. They held British passports and enjoyed a number of benefits including voting rights, etc., but they had a problem relating to the country of adoption. Since they could not consider themselves truly British without "Britishness," how could they redefine themselves? The impact of the colonial syndrome should not be underrated. It disillusioned the younger generation who were British-born and who started searching for new identities. This changed their identities from being migrants into becoming a diaspora.

Many studies have loosely used the term "diaspora" to label each and every migrant group. However, the term does have specific connotation in relation to the Jews, who gave it a specific meaning. For the Jews, the term "diaspora" applied to the period of their dispersal which resulted from the persecution by the Romans after the second destruction of their temple in Jerusalem in 70 CE. They rooted their identities into their religion and followed their religious culture wherever they were settled. Being Jewish gave them an identity and focussed their minds on the land of Israel that they had lost. Migrant groups may often want to integrate or assimilate into the COM. The diaspora group, on the other hand, may accept integration, but its concern will always be with the COO. The Indians also strongly identified with India. For the Jews, Israel was their sacred land mentioned in the Bible while for the Indians, Bharat was the land of their gods and goddesses.

There is no doubt that diasporas are "deterritorialized" and "transnational," but Vertovec in his study of the Indian migrant group made the observation that migrants can develop what he labelled as "diaspora consciousness."[12]

> Diaspora consciousness is a particular kind of awareness said to be generated among contemporary trans-national communities... Its particularity is described as being marked by various dimensions of dual or paradoxical nature. This nature is constituted negatively by experiences of discrimination and exclusion and positively by identification with a historical heritage (such an Indian civilization).[13]

This diaspora consciousness produced the diaspora conscious Indian migrants (DCIM) who acted as ambassadors and agents of their countries of origin. Those who had suffered from an identity crisis from the politics of exclusion and closure found refuge in their COO. The DCIMs projected the image of India and safeguarded the younger generation's identity, rooting it in the Indian culture. The older generation had been concerned about the identities of the younger generation. The first step that they took to safeguard these identities was the establishment of Hindu temples and many other organizations which started mushrooming all over Britain. Knott observed that the younger generation, with little or no links with India, still had "an awareness of some aspects of their families' religious practices and participation in festivals and a knowledge of stories about Krishna, Rama, Ganesh and the goddesses."[14]

Britain as has been explained was a closed culture. There had to be a strategy for how to penetrate it. This was done through the Indian culture. The more skilfully the cultural instrument was used, the more the Indian community made inroads into a closed culture and the result was that the culture and image of India was increasingly appreciated. The more their culture was experienced by the original indigenous British, the more it raised the image of India.

Indian culture penetrated British society in a number of ways. First, as many temples were built in Britain, they opened their doors to the British public (unlike the mosques). The temple had an office staff which made it easy for anyone to contact them to arrange visits from school children and other organisations. Second, the festivals of

Hinduism celebrated by the temples were open to anyone. Some of the festivals like Diwali were celebrated in such a public manner that the British public living near it could not have avoided partaking in it. In many cases civic dignitaries were invited to partake in such festivals. Diwali was also celebrated in the House of Commons with many members of the Indian community present.

Third, the most effective way of cultural penetration was through the development of food-consuming markets in Britain. It also particularly appealed to many vegetarians and vegans in British culture. Thousands of Indian restaurants had popularised Indian foods all over Britain. This had been an effective cultural instrument in a way that no other South Asian country such as Pakistan, Sri Lanka, Nepal, etc, seems to have developed (though many restaurant staff people are Bangladeshi in origin). Indian cultural hegemony asserted control over all other South Asian foods. For example, thousands of years of Muslim rule in India left its impact on South Asian food and dishes like mughalai kormas, biryanis, pillaus, kebabs, koftans, etc. that were of meat origin with Turkish, Afghan and Iranian origins.

Fourth, the Indian world of fashions penetrated British culture as well. Not only did some British women wear saris, dupattas, shalwar khamis, but some from the younger generation had pricked their noses so as to wear nats (nose rings) or tried henna decorations on their hands.

Fifth, Indian films had created a version of Bollywood in Britain. Not only have many of their film scenes been shot in British locations by film producers but some British stars have wanted to act in Bollywood films. The headquarters of Bollywood was at Leicester and many Indian stars had visited this city. There were also many theatre companies projecting Indian themes. Some of the prominent names were Tara Arts, South Asian Arts, Akademi, South Asian Diaspora Literature and Arts Archive, Hungama Productions, Priya Pawar, Kali Theatre Company, Vaya Naidu and Company, South Asian Dance Alliance, and Surdhwani.

Sixth, classical Indian music has had a lot of influence in Britain. Great musical artists like Ravi Shankar, the best Sitar player in India, have made their mark on Britain. A Pakistani Qawal led by the lead singer Nusrat Fateh Ali Khan started becoming popular in Britain, but his premature death ended the affair. The Punjabi dance Bhangra and its music had become very popular in Britain. Also, the younger generation of British-born musical stars had made recordings of songs integrating Western and Indian music. Some of these productions had a profound impact upon artists in Britain, as Sir Andrew Lloyd Webber produced a stage musical called *Bombay Dreams* (2002).[15]

Seventh, most of the above aspects of the culture had made successful penetrations into the closed culture. They had received strong support from radio and TV stations operating from the major cities in Britain. Furthermore, linkages had been made by Indians with national radio and TV stations like the BBC to project Asian music through their radio stations. Hindu businessmen had established their own MATV station operating from Leicester. It not only projected Indian movies every day, but all kinds of social, political, cultural programmes imported from India. There were some eleven radio and TV stations which operated under various names like Sunrise Radio, Zee TV, Asia 1 TV, MATV, Sabras Radio, Radio XL, Apna TV, Namaste TV, etc. All of them project Indian songs and Indian news and aspects of the Indian culture. Apart from this, there were a number of ethnic publications which were popularly read among the migrant Indians like *India Weekly*, *Gurajat Samachar*, *Garavi Gujrat*, *India Home and Abroad*, *Amar Deep*, *Southall Gazette*, *Asian Affairs*, etc.

While these aspects of culture had strongly reinforced the Indian culture, some talented British Indians have made their mark on British national programs. Their programs have not only engaged British celebrities but also British audiences. For example, *The Kumars at No. 10* has been a very popular entertainment program. Many talented Indian stars became well known in Britain. According to one report,

> a growing number of British actors are flying to Bollywood instead of Hollywood as Indian directors try to woo audiences with 'crossover films' that appeal to international markets. Over the next few months,

> four films made by prominent directors will be released with British stars... the trend has been reinforced by the success of Gurinder Chadha's *Bend it like Beckham*, Nira Nair's *Monsoon Wedding* and Ashutosh Gowariker's *Lagaan*, nominated for a best foreign film Oscar in 2002."[16]

Bollywood also made films which subtly penetrated into British traditions and twisted them skilfully into its own successes. For example, the celebrated early nineteenth-century English novelist Jane Austin's novel *Pride and Prejudice* was transformed by Gurinder Chadha, an Indian film-maker, into *Bride and Prejudice* (2004) in order to attract British crowds in Britain. Well-reviewed and well-received or not, there was no doubt that such "cross-over" cultural activities marked a considerable achievement in penetrating the British market. Stars like Amitabh Bachchan, Shabani Azmi, and Gulshan Grover pulled large crowds and boosted not only the image of Bollywood but also India. Some film-makers made nostalgic films of Indo-British colonial and decolonization experiences, such as the most famous Richard Attenborough's *Gandhi* (1982).[17] There were many Indian groups who had made yoga and Indian dance popular in Britain. One major group was Bharatya Vidya Bhavan, whose purpose was to encourage and propagate the understanding of Indian art and culture. Its objectives were to become a centre of learning in the UK for Indian culture. It not only trained teachers in the subject but also provided venues of visiting Indian artists to various centres in Britain. It also staged dramas in both the Indian and English languages and also performed classical Indian dances. This was just one of the organizations. The global presence of Indians was acclaimed by some academics as a process of "ongoing and developing civilization" for "culture is seen as the motor of civilization."[18]

It is one thing to create cultural spaces within a closed culture. It is another thing to extend it into other levels. To maintain it, one had to play by the rules of the British game, which meant laying the foundations of cultural space within the British culture. This could only be done if economic space was also created. Britain was a capitalist society and the stronger the economics of the community, the greater the influence it could wield. The second migration had changed by becoming well educated.

They were of two categories. There were businessmen or professionals, but having settled in Britain they had created economic spaces. In general then, the Indian Diaspora could be divided into three categories. To start from the third tier which was the lowest level, the majority were retail traders comprised of shop owners who operated on a small-scale and had corner shops, grocery stores, Indian sweets shops, etc. On the second tier, there were a number of businessmen who had created a strong middle class. They owned jewellery shops, fashion shops, Indian restaurants, travel agencies, etc. On the top level, that is, the first tier, there were multi-millionaires. Some were steel magnates like Lakshmi Mittal, while others were into oil, banking and telecom areas like the Hinduja brothers, Shrichand and Gopichand. Others like Lord Paul were in the Caparo Group, or in the hotel business like Jasminder Singh, or brewery business like Manubhai Madhvani or into electronics like Gulu Lalvani. Some of these millionaires were as young as 21 years old, as was the case of Reuben Singh. Altogether, some 450 major South Asian businessmen existed in Britain. Among the Chambers of Commerce and industry, which existed in almost every major British city, there were Asian chapters of it in which the majority were Indian businessman. The economic spaces they had established were used to create cultural and political spaces. One separate category, also part of the Indian Diaspora but not included in the business sector, were the professionals: doctors, dentists, accountants, lawyers, engineers and academics. Each had a professional body which the Indians might seek to influence, while academics exerted influence within their university institutions.

While all these categories operated from Britain, many of them had business connections with India. Indian businessman from India too had made their connections with Britain. Some 125 companies had opened their offices in London and were investing in the UK and doing a flourishing trade. Some of the company organizations considered important were the Indian Development Group (UK),

Indian Development Fund, Confederation of Indian Organizations, India Group, and Indian Forum.

According to Chandrashekhar Bhat, these Indian elites attracted the attention of the Indian government during the 1970s for Indian development programmes. They were labelled as non-resident Indians (NRIs). In order to attract their money, financial schemes were set up, like the Resurgent India Bonds which "tapped $4.2 billion in 1998."[19] During the 1990s, the migrant Indian community in Britain was mobilized in a number of ways and there is no doubt that this action created rich dividends for India. According to the latest report, in 2003 the Indian community sent £10 billion to India.[20] This was a significant amount and it indicates a number of facts about the Indian community in Britain. Firstly, that the community in general was more affluent than any other immigrant community. Secondly, that they were seriously interested in the development of their country and sent such large amounts of money to India. As some of the members of the Indian migrant community became more affluent, the Indian government began to take a serious interest in them as they could be used as an economic instrument to serve the interests of the Indian government. They "were encouraged to invest in India through certain attractive schemes as much as they were welcomed to launch industrial enterprises along with the transfer of technology."[21] Yet the NRIs were in reality a selective category of "middle-class elite families" who comprised "highly skilled groups of professionals, scientists, doctors and engineers."[22]

Later the Indian government must have reconsidered the scheme as overly selective and concluded that it had to be expanded. This kind of interest by the Indian government in its overseas Indian migrants increased, and in 1999 a mass-scale mobilization of a category of migrants known as the People of Indian Origin (PIOs) took place. A PIO Card was created by the Ministry of Home Affairs in March 1999 "to reinforce the emotional bonds of Indians who have made other countries their homes, but who now have a yearning to renew their ties with the land of their origin. Persons of Indian origin up to the fourth generation settled anywhere in the world" were all available to register as PIOs.[23] Furthermore, the PIO Card holders were given many facilities in India to buy and dispose immovable properties and obtain admission for their children in schools. Also, they were given concessions that they would not require visas to go to India if their stay did not exceed more than 180 days. It is estimated that the NRI population is about 6.7 million and the PIOs around 15 million worldwide.[24] The Indian government was expecting to get them all to register for the PIO Card, which would open various facilities for them.

The ambitions of the Indian companies were not merely to sell their products or services, but to capture the global market and to leave India's mark as a global power in economic terms. One report commented that

> India's top companies are already building a niche in global markets, selling high-tech products and services at keen prices. Helped by a highly skilled but modestly paid workforce, India's engineering, pharmaceutical and technology firms are giving rivals such as IBM a run for their money on their home turf... business to business is where India is already making waves, in particular in software services where companies like West India Produce (WIPRO) have become a major competitor with U.S. companies like General Electric, Cisco Systems and Alcatel. [25]

Another company is Alfosys, which even exports India's software, and its clients have been Boeing, Cisco Systems, Dell, Toshiba, and Visa International. A third company, Tata Consultancy Services, which is a branch of the Tata group, has also made its presence felt in Europe. Also, pharmaceutical companies like Randaxy Laboratories were producing drugs and selling them at cut prices.[26]

Some Indian companies that recognized the affluence of the Indian migrants had also begun to target them. One of the largest Indian companies owned by Subrata Roy is Sahara India Parivar. It is in the lime light not only because it owns TV stations, a bank, an airline, real estate and employs 700,000 people, but because it has top film stars on its books which attracts attention. This company is planning to market "hoopla and showbiz that will be the key to selling Sahara to expat Indians... it is all good publicity for the Sahara development's satellite towns, shopping malls and gated luxury leisure complexes catering to India's burgeoning middle class."[27]

The growing middle classes in India have become a significant factor that attracted the attention of political parties. The growth of the Indian middle classes has been strengthened by the return of some of the Indian migrants. Where once there was a "brain drain" from India, in contemporary times there is a "brain gain" with Indians heading back for their homeland. According to one report,

> an entire generation of Indians saw the West as the land of opportunity. They left their homeland in their thousands and transformed themselves from poor economic migrants to successful businessman and professionals. But India's booming economy and promises of an affluent lifestyle are drawing increasing numbers of Indians living in America and Britain back to their roots. The reverse migration that began as a trickle in the late 1990s is now large enough to suggest a 'brain gain' for India... There are an estimated 35,000 returned non-resident Indians living in the city of Bangalore alone. Attracted by a booming economy, Indians who have amassed professional experience and savings from their years in the West, can afford a luxury lifestyle when they return to their cultural roots.[28]

This kind of brain gain has not happened in other neighbouring countries in South Asia, where there are only brain drains. According to the Economic Councillor of the Indian High Commission in London,

> the trend seems to affect the more non-Westernised first generation in this country, the ones who came here at a point in their life for higher education or as executives, they settle down for a while and then they

> return. It is not as relevant to the second and third generation or truly westernized Indians. This group has far too many links here in Britain to find it attractive enough to move... I am aware of some people who have gone back. It has either been for better career opportunities or the pursuit of an entrepreneurial venture after making some money here. Some have ventured on to business opportunities in India but have not necessarily moved lock, stock and barrel. There are also people from here who have gone and invested in outsourcing industries in India. There are certainly more and more people including British-based Indians who are venturing into businesses there. Just because some are choosing to make the most of opportunities in India does not mean there are any less here. Lots of Indians can hold decent jobs here. It is a lifestyle and business issue. As a top-notch executive, the salary level available in India now promises a better lifestyle than here in Britain.[29]

The effect of this brain gain has been that India's middle classes have become stronger. Indians are not returning for religious reasons, but for economic, social, and cultural reasons. It makes them feel more at home than living in Britain. The DCIMs have done an excellent job in creating *cultural and economic spaces* for themselves within the British context.

The predominant instrument used was to make political contacts and DCIMs to cultivate those contacts carefully, which led to the creation of political spaces for themselves and the COO. Within the British political context, this was necessary because it could change the image of India and facilitate trade and other Indian national interests in Britain. This strategy was undertaken with two agendas in mind. One was the realization that having influence and lobbies in the COM could facilitate one's economic projects. The other was that it was prompted by Indian Embassy officials whose task was to spread the influence of India through networking. This task could be achieved by the Indian Diaspora, some of whose members were businessman and local city councillors who were in touch with local MPs because of their political party affiliations. It could also be one of the tasks of community leaders.

However, the story of the younger generation was different. The political awareness of the younger generation of South Asian migrants in general increased in Britain. There were reasons why this level of political awareness rose. One important reason was because the

> presence of National Front and other anti-immigrant candidates in elections has increased their awareness of the political issues, and contributed towards an increasing degree of political mobilization and, indeed, participation in elections in order to counter the anti-immigrant propaganda. This is also the response of the major political parties. These parties have not only felt the need to take steps to involve Asians in their activities and campaigns but have openly sought their votes in various elections [since] 1974....[30]

Apart from awareness among the Indian younger generation, the most practical way of becoming influential, which was often used by Indian businessmen, was by making large donations to political parties. Mr Lakshmi Mittal donated two million pounds to the Labour party. Previously, he had donated £125,000. According to White "when the first gift was revealed a year later it was linked to the fact that Tony Blair had written to the Prime Minister of Romania shortly afterwards, backing Mr Mittal's efforts to take over a steel plant in that country."[31] This was a powerful way of wielding political influence in British politics.

Growing political awareness had different effects on the diaspora groups in Britain. Among the Indian migrants, the importance of political influence was not considered to be a job of the Embassy of India only. The DCIM worked effectively to benefit their country of origin by creating a positive image of India. Such images influenced the opinions of employers and opened the doors of the job market for non-Muslim Indians rather than Muslims, who from the 1990s were feared as potential terrorists. Politically, the Indians established themselves within the main political parties at both a local and national level. Within the local City Councils, there were some 250–300 Councillors elected from various political parties, which led them to form a British Indian Councillors Association. Many British cities also had from time to time a Lord Mayor of Indian origin. Most of the councillors were at first drawn to the Labour Party, but subsequently their presence was noticeable in both the Conservative and Liberal Democratic Parties. Some of the political parties were dependent on their constituencies for Indian votes. Such MPs were strong supporters of the Indians in Britain. Two political parties (Labour and the Liberal Democrats) formed a Friends of India parliamentary group. Apart from this group, there was also a British Indian Parliamentary Association which transcended party lines and met regularly to discuss India's concerns, and was known as the Curry Club.

Some four Indians themselves were members of the British House of Commons. There were eleven members of the House of Lords, and some of them were very prominent like Lord Parekh and Lord Dholakia. The latter was the first Indian to become the Chairman of the Liberal Democrat Party. With such an impressive presence in British politics, it is not surprising that the lobby for India was strong and could be used to help the political, economic, and security interests of India. Some Members of the House of Lords like Lord Swaraj Paul headed the Indo-British Round Table, which was a pro-India lobby group working closely with the Indian High Commission and taking care of the interests of India. Other Indians occupied very important positions in all three British national political parties.

One must wonder that while all these spaces were created, had the Indian Diaspora launched on some conspiratorial plan? There was no such plan. The reason why the Indian Diaspora progressed was because it had a diaspora philosophy that had two aspects. Firstly, the Indians were proud of their culture and were ready to spread it anywhere. Secondly, the Indians had a strong identity as Indians. This emerged from their COO. The great majority have strong nationalistic feelings for their country and its culture. Even if some Indians were secular, their identities were well rooted into their COO. Equipped with their diaspora philosophy then, it was not a problem to construct cultural, economic and political spaces in the COM. Although their COM was a closed culture, the Indian strategy was to penetrate it through culture, which they did.

There were two other factors which facilitated this success. India had a very positive view of its diaspora, and the Indian embassy and its diplomats were always there to give the diaspora direction. The Indian government had realised the role their migrants could play for India. The Indian embassy had close relations with the leaders of the diaspora in Britain. Prime Minister Nehru was interested in overseas Indians, but his vision and advice for the diaspora was clear: they should be "the best citizens of the country of their adoption."[32] This did not imply that they should become westernized and forget their Indian identity. On the contrary, he wanted them to be ambassadors of India by being the best Indian nationalists. As the diaspora developed economically, later Indian governments were more concerned with the amount of money that the Indian Diasporas could remit home to facilitate economic development. Both these perspectives were common to other South Asian states as well. The Indian Diaspora had made its impact upon British society as stated above through the creation of the spaces within it. But the second reason for its success was that the British government knew that India had a population which by the turn of the millennium would exceed one billion people. For the British, India was a huge consumer market for selling their goods. Trade relations between the two countries accordingly were very strong.

Politics of Indian Identities

The strategy of the Indian Diaspora for building cultural, economic and political spaces within British society has been effective. It had not only successfully penetrated British society, but had also created a positive image of India. Yet under the surface there were problems. These problems had always been there and had emanated from caste divisions rather than sectarianism or secularism. However, since the love for India was stronger, it had held them together as 'Indians," but the problem came to the surface in India when there was a clash between the political parties and their ideologies. The Congress had a secular ideology considering every citizen as Indian, but the Bharatiya Janata Party (BJP) party had a fundamentalist Hindu ideology. The Hindu fundamentalist movement had become powerful during the 1990s and begun to spread its influence in Indian politics. It opposed secular India and secular Hindus, who accused its supporters of making political capital out of the religion. The BJP started redefining who was a Hindu through the ideology of *Hindutva* and tried to change the nature of Indian society.

The *Sangh Parivar*, the umbrella organization for Hindu fundamentalism, also realized the importance of the Indian Diaspora and sought to penetrate it. When its political party, the BJP, came to power in 1988 as part of a governing alliance, the perspective of the Indian government changed. It recognized the importance of the financial strength of the diaspora and wanted to use it for political party funding purposes. It had begun to extend its tentacles into the British Indian Diaspora.

To achieve this end, the Indian government set up a Committee on the Indian Diaspora (CID) in September 2000 which was headed by a BJP MP, Dr L. M. Singhvi.[33] He had been a very successful High Commissioner to Britain and also held the rank of a cabinet minister. The CID was expected to explore both the NRIs and PIOs in terms of their "aspirations, attitudes, requirements, strengths and weaknesses" and "expectations from India."[34]

Apart from the above-mentioned objectives, it would be naïve to think that there was no hidden agenda. The real purpose of the CID was to explore the possibility of mobilizing the migrant diaspora into serving the purposes of the *Sangh Parivar*. The BJP-led government was perhaps the first government of India to take seriously the task of changing and mobilizing the attitude of Indian migrants. One aspect of the agenda was the conversion of vulnerable targets from Diaspora Conscious Indian Migrants (DCIM) to Diaspora Conscious Hindu Migrants (DCHM), which was linked to the BJP's domestic policy of cultural homogenization.

The ideology of *Hindutva* was alien to Hinduism. It was an extreme nationalist ideology which had no roots within traditional Hinduism. The thinker who articulated this brand of Hindu fundamentalism was V. D. Savakar (1883–1966), who published in 1923 a book entitled *Hindutva: Who is a Hindu?* Savarkar defined the Hindu nation on the basis of being the Aryan race. To him, the "Hindu identity was formed by the commingling of the blood of the Aryans with the people they encountered."[35]

Extreme nationalist Hindus like K. B. Hedgewar, who founded the Rashtriya Swayamsevak Sangh (RSS) in 1925, had read Savakar's book, and the two planned the formation of a youth cadre. RSS recruits dressed with khaki shorts and white shirts became the contingent of Hanuman with a saffron coloured flag.

In 1940, M.S Golwalkar took over from Hedgewar. He authored a book entitled *We, Our Nation Defined* in 1931 and wrote that

> the foreign races in Hindustan must either adopt the Hindu culture and language, must learn to respect and hold in reverence Hindu religion, must entertain no idea but those of the glorification of the Hindu race and culture, i.e. of the Hindu nation and must lose their separate existence to merge in the Hindu race, or may stay in the country, wholly subordinated to the Hindu nation, claiming nothing, deserving no privileges, far less any preferential treatment–not even citizen's rights.[36]

As the RSS developed and expanded it had a number of other organizations which all became linked and came to be known as *Sangh Parivar* (family of right-wing organizations). S. P. Mookerjee founded the Bharatiya Jana Sangh in 1951, which changed its name to the Bharatiya Janata Party (BJP) in 1979. However, the BJP strongly supported the fundamentalist Hindu nationalism and became the political face of the *Sangh Parivar*. Another organization was opened in 1966 named the Vishva Hindu Parishad (VHP), which started to counter the spread of secularism in India. It considered that all other home-grown faiths like Buddhism, Jainism and Sikhism were part of the banyan tree, which implied that they were all Hindu in origin.

The Hindu caste system was comprised of four castes: the Brahmins were the priestly caste and desired to hold all the power amongst themselves. The other three castes were the Kshatriyas (the administrative caste), the Vaisyas (the tillers of the soil) and the Sudrsa (the untouchables), who did not enjoy the same status as the Brahmins. It is not surprising to note that "most scholars... agree that this religion is notoriously difficult to define... what the word 'Hinduism' stands for, in essence, is Brahmanism. This become clear when once we strip it of its multiple layers of accumulated accretions from within the larger Indian tradition."[37]

However, while Hinduism may be tolerant, Brahmanism was never tolerant. The founders of *Hindutva* ideology were Brahmins. According to Robinson, *Hindutva* had two forms because it

> splits itself into a project of violent retribution and a project of cultural affirmation... the two strands intertwine in schemes to destroy the Muslim or Christian monuments and to unearth or rebuild temple structures that really or allegedly lie beneath. But, for the most part, the projects can exist side by side without most people understanding the insidious and dangerous linkages between them.[38]

Lele considered these two aspects of *Hindutva* as

> two faces of Brahmanism. Together they constitute the two basic features... consent as benign face and coercion as the malignant one. These two faces of Brahmanism have always coexisted and continue to do so today within what we now call Hinduism. As to which one becomes more visible and when, is determined by the context and the way in which active social agents respond to it. The instruments of

> dominance and power remain normally hidden behind an aura of legitimacy.[39]

Lele's argument is correct and he further reinforces it by writing that

> the *Sangh Parivar* must stage frequent spectacular and symbolic acts such as *rathayatras*, *yagnas*, mosque demolitions, temple constructions and anti-minority riots in order to keep that attention deflected... what is being affirmed in the name of Hinduism, as their cultural heritage, by those outside India, is a complex and confused web of practices and beliefs whose relevance can only make sense through a thorough exploration of the context in which this new awakening has occurred.[40]

As stated earlier, the *Sangh Parivar* and its various branches had realized the strategic importance of the diaspora in Britain long before the BJP came to power. They had a very peculiar mandate: to transform Indian identities into Hindu identities among those who belonged to Hinduism. The first strategy was to project "cultural and national affirmation encapsulated in various elements" so as to attract "a large section of the middle class Hindus resident within and outside India."[41] For the DCIMs of the Hindu faith, there was no conflict in working in Britain for *Janam Bhumi* (birth place), *Karma Bhumi* (place of work) and *Matru Bhumi* (ancestral land) as they did not conflict with each other.[42] There was no problem with this identity.

The problem arose when *Hindutva* asserted

> the primacy and priority of Hindu identity within and outside India. It would be myopic to view such identity merely as an expression of primordial affinity. Rather it entails a creation of a wholly new social and political identity using religious community as its base and employing a new religious discourse and practice through a network of newly created organizations.[43]

In this definition then, the DCIMs with their new *Hindutva* identity became its new adherents in Britain.

Yet the Indian Diaspora, as stated earlier, was not monolithic but divided into various sects in religious terms and class in economic terms. The *Sangh Parivar* had to transcend these barriers. According to Bhatt and Mukta,

> the strength of the *Hindutva* movement lies in its ability to draw in large numbers of people who are not upper caste or middle class both in India and the diaspora. While members of the Indian upper castes and emergent middle classes have undoubtedly provided the intellectual leadership of the *Hindutva* movement, both within India and outside, there are important signs of previously stigmatized groups rising in social status through the espousal of *Hindutva* ideology. In India, for example, very poor migrant workers have been implicated in violence against Muslim communities. In Britain, there is evidence that working class individuals from a traditional leather-working community in Leeds became leading members of the Hindu Swayamsevak Sangh.[44]

The *Sangh Parivar* wanted expatriate Hindus to

> constitute a source of power not just to India but also to the Hindu nation. They were the spokesman for Hindu India abroad and partners in the country's efforts to become a major player. BJP mouthpiece *The Organiser* (21-1-2001) quoted the Indian Prime minister saying 'we do not merely seek investment from Hindu organizations and asset transfer. What we seek is a broader relationship, a partnership, a partnership among all children of mother India'. BJP election manifestoes have often stressed the importance of NRIs

> and accorded high priority to the protection of their interests.[45]

As stated earlier, most of the temples and other Hindu organizations in Britain were opened with the support of the Hindu working classes and the Gujarati community. However, when the *Sangh Parivar* approached them, the first in undertaking this new *Hindutva* identity were the Hindu Gujaratis, particularly from East Africa. According to Tikekar, the

> predominance of the East African Gujaratis among the British Hindus has been also an important factor in this process. They acquired a sense of a 'superior race' as they constituted an intermediate class under the British rule in East Africa. They regard Gujarat as the most modern and dynamic part of India. All this leads to an extreme defensiveness about events in Gujarat and the rise of fascism, so that criticizing the VHP is seen as tantamount to criticizing Gujaratis. They came to Britain fortified with their experience of organizing Bharatiya Swayansevak Sangh (BSS) – the African incarnation of RSS.[46]

They were strong in their support of HSS and VHP in Britain and had almost 60 *shakas* (branches) all over Britain. They produced a publication called *Sangh Sandeesh* which reported many activities in Britain of the Hindus as well as other news of interest. They had another organization by the name of Virat Hindu Sammelan, which opened in 1989 and was sponsored by the HSS and VHP, and had connections with 300 other organizations. The message of the Sammelan

> was predominantly of all Hindu unity, an attempt to transcend internal differences and the construction of a unifying and global platform for Hindus. It provided an opportunity to bring together different political strands in support of the newly invented ritual of

> *shilanyas* in India. It is interesting to note that the Sammelan received support from the British MPs of all political persuasions–and complimentary messages right from Buckingham Palace and 10 Downing Street and officials from the British establishment.[47]

From this, one can deduce the high level of networking of the HSS and the VHP in Britain.

The VHP (UK) claimed to represent the entire Hindu population in Britain. There was a reason for this. British multicultural society offered it the freedom to do so and it could penetrate other European countries freely. It held its fifth European conference in Frankfurt and some 1,200 delegates attended. It had some forty branches in the region and produced its own publication known as *Vishwa Hindu*. However, in Britain it claimed to have contacts with 550 organisations and affiliations with some 350 organisations.[48] This gave them not only credibility but also authority. This facilitated their secret agenda of transforming identities from being Indian into becoming Hindu.

The Reaction of the Diaspora

Diaspora activism in favour of conversion from being Indians into becoming Hindus, as well as opposition to this, was tremendous in Britain. If the BJP government had divided the diaspora, those alienated would not have accepted it peacefully. It was their reactions which started bringing out the exposure of the BJP government and its *Hindutva* ideology as well as the violent massacres in Gujarat in 2002. Many secular Hindus who were supporters of the Congress Party also protested because they did not want to change their identities. It seems likely that only those who had some kind of resentment against Muslims were more vulnerable to changing their identities. Also groups like Human Rights Watch and the Concerned Citizens' Tribunal produced powerful reports which were widely circulated in Britain.

The overall effect of this was that the perfect image which had been built over the years began to become tarnished.

Some Muslim organisations wrote a detailed report entitled *In Bad Faith: British Charity and Hindu Extremism* which exposed how the Hindu Swayamsevak Sangh UK, Vishwa Hindu Parishad UK and Kalyan Ashram Trust UK misused funds and the UK to support Hindu extremism in India.[49] The challenge before the new Congress-led Indian government in 2004 was to reverse the change in the identity of the diaspora, returning from Hindu fundamentalism to Indian nationalism while uniting the diaspora. The diaspora had become divided as the Muslims, Sikhs, Buddhists, Jains, Parsis, etc., had their own great civilizations in India and could not relate to India as the holy land of gods and goddesses. Yet they certainly could relate to it on the basis of nationalism. It is too early to predict how the new Congress-led government will handle these challenges. However, during his recent visit to the UK, the Indian Prime Minister, Manmohan Singh, made clear his views about the Indian Diaspora.

He considered the diasporas of Britain a "bridge between their adopted land and India" and stated that "the country took 'pride in their achievements'."[50] Therefore, the strategy was not to accuse any segment of the Indian Diaspora of disloyalty to India. British Prime Minister Tony Blair also reinforced Manmohan's views by commenting that the 1.5 million people of Indian origin in Britain are "at the heart of our relationship" (that is, the relationship between Britain and India) for "their cultural values contribute significantly towards making Britain the vibrant, dynamic society that it is today. They are a vital bond between our two communities."[51] This will lessen, but not eradicate, the differences between the DCIMs and the DCHMs. The objective of the Indian Prime Minister's visit to Britain was to persuade the British Prime Minister to support India's attempt to become a permanent member of the UN Security Council. This was agreed to by Tony Blair, who stated that "India is a country of 1.2 billion people. For India not to be represented on the Security Council is, I think, something that is not in tune with the modern times in which we live."[52] This ploy of Manmohan Singh also placed the responsibility on the shoulders of the Indian Diaspora to lobby the British government to strongly support India's desire. No one from the diaspora would oppose this and the aim was to bring Indians, regardless of political or religious persuasion, together to achieve this aim.

Conclusion

The study of the Indian Diaspora is very useful as a model for the development of diaspora studies. It can yield many useful lessons for studying other diasporas. This is not to say that the Indian Diaspora is the perfect model. However, despite certain flaws, it has been a model which other diasporas have had to follow to become a significant force in British life. There is no doubt that the diasporic development of Indians has a status value in Britain. They have earned this status through their own efforts and initiative to change the context still infected with the colonial syndrome. The second migration was very helpful for achieving this. Any country which has a diaspora that has earned the kind of status gained by expatriot Indians in Britain has to be proud of it.

Part Three
The Diaspora in China's Security Strategy

Diasporas in China's Security Strategy

Chapter 6

Diasporas in China's Security Strategy

Bertil Lintner*

Introduction

While exact figures are not available, Western intelligence officials believe that perhaps as many as two million people from the People's Republic of China, or PRC, have migrated legally and illegally since 1978. They estimate that 30,000-40,000 a year go to the United States–the preferred destination–and the same number to the rest of the world. This is the third time in China's history that such a massive exodus has taken place. The first wave came after the fall of the Ming Dynasty in 1644 and consisted mainly of non-Mandarin speaking southerners who opposed the Manchu seizure of power in Beijing. These migrants established overseas Chinese communities all over Southeast Asia. The next wave came after the Taiping rebellion and other upheavals in the mid- and late-19th century as the Manchu Qing Dynasty crumbled and warlords tore the country into lawless fiefdoms. Not only did the migrants–again mainly from the southern coastal provinces–swell the existing Chinese communities in Southeast Asia, but newly invented steamships took them to North America, Australia and the Pacific.

This time, the migrants come from all over China. Better overland routes have led to a steady movement of people, primarily from the southern province of Yunnan, but also from Sichuan and Guangdong, to northern Thailand, Burma, Laos and Cambodia. Further field, from the Russian Far East to the Pacific Islands, new Chinese migrants are making their presence felt. Whole families are also being smuggled into South Africa, where Chinese gangs operate under the guise of student organizations. Over the past two decades, even Japan, with its strict immigration laws and controls, has seen a massive influx of Chinese migrants. In Europe, thousands of Chinese

* This paper is part of a larger research project conducted under the auspices of the John D. and Catherine T. MacArthur Foundation.

have settled in Hungary—which now has a significant Asian population—and in France and the United Kingdom.

Contrary to common beliefs, most of these migrants are not escaping from poverty or fleeing political persecution. Many come from the richest parts of China, and pay fortunes to be smuggled to foreign countries. Few of them show any interest in politics in their new host countries. Rather, it is the dream of an even better life abroad that fuels the third wave of Chinese migration. While China is developing fast economically, expectations have also risen, and many seem to believe that those can best be fulfilled abroad. With better communications and more information from the outside world reaching China, Chinese migration has become globalized, and it is already beginning to change traditional demographic patterns in places such as the Russian Far East and the Pacific region. Apart from the smaller groups of dissident students and intellectuals, the new migrants are not hostile to the Chinese government. On the contrary, as was shown in worldwide demonstrations by groups of overseas Chinese protesting the embassy bombing in Belgrade in May 1999, many remain patriotic and identify themselves with the "motherland."

As Russian researcher Igor Saveliev of Japan's Niigata University has pointed out, "as a sending country, the PRC pursues policies of enhancing ties with overseas Chinese"—old as well as new migrants—to attract remittances and investment. At the same time, Saveliev states, "the PRC government's growing interest in migrants' activities overseas is frequently expressed in diplomatic missions' attempts to gather them in embassies and consulates by organizing various events."[1] According to Pal Nyiri, a Hungarian sinologist, "increasing migration from China and resurgent Chinese nationalism overseas is clearly linked to the PRC's great power aspirations."[2]

China's official policy towards migration was expressed by the Shanghai New Migrants Research Project Team as early as 1995:

> Since reform and opening, people who have left mainland China to reside broad (called 'new migrants' for short) have continuously become more numerous. They are currently rising as an important force within

> overseas Chinese and ethnic Chinese communities. In the future, they will become a backbone of forces friendly to us in America and some other developed Western countries. Strengthening new migrant work has important realistic meaning and deep-going, far-reaching significance for promoting our country's modernizing construction, implementing the unification of the motherland, expanding our country's influence and developing our country's relations with the countries of residence.[3]

It is obvious that the Chinese authorities, while pledging to cooperate with the West to stem the flow of illegal migrants, are also actively encouraging migration. There are three main reasons for this policy:

1. To ease population pressure and alleviate unemployment in China. Migration serves as an important social safety valve in a country which has a "floating" population of anywhere between 30 and 100 million people.
2. Remittances from overseas Chinese–old as well as new migrants–are a significant contribution to the Chinese economy. In the Fujian province especially, entire towns and villages depend on remittances from abroad.
3. Large Chinese communities abroad give the Chinese authorities friendly footholds in the countries where the migrants have settled.

The third reason is no doubt the most controversial, and could cause conflicts in some countries with a growing ethnic Chinese population. To quote Pal Nyiri,

> ideas of deliberate 'demographic expansion' by China as well as revived fifth-column theories–seeing overseas Chinese as a political pawn that can be mobilized by

> the Chinese government in international conflicts—are on the rise in various quarters: among politicians in the Russian Far East, journalists in Southeast Asia, and sometimes in the US media, as in the recent spying case of Chinese-American physicist Wen Ho Lee.[4]

In the late 1990s, a string of revelations of Chinese industrial espionage in the United States had a severe impact on America's racial relations, and threatened to undermine the high level of acceptability that the Chinese-Americans have managed to achieve following decades of discrimination. Frank Ching, a Hong Kong-born Chinese-American wrote in 1999:

> ... virtually every Chinese is tarred—visitors, students, diplomats and business representatives. All are suspected of spying. Similarly, it is suggested that there are no legitimate Chinese companies—every one is considered to be a front for the Chinese military or some intelligence agency. It assumes that every member of every Chinese delegation is on an intelligence mission, as is every Chinese student.[5]

The anti-Asian hysteria has echoes of World War II, when every Japanese living in the United States was considered a spy, and nearly all of them were rounded up and interned in camps throughout the war. Thus, it is important to deal with this issue delicately so as not to foster racist sentiments, but Chinese migration to a number of countries and areas has had an impact that could have far-reaching demographic as well as political consequences.

The Russian Far East

As a result of Josef Stalin's purges in the 1930s, the Russian Far Eastern city of Vladivostok—which was predominantly Chinese—was until recently the only major port in the Pacific Rim without a

Chinese community. Since the collapse of the Soviet Union, however, Chinese merchants have come across the border to sell clothes, tools, toys, watches and other cheap consumer goods in a sprawling new market in one of the city's eastern suburbs. There is still no Chinatown as such in Vladivostok. The new immigrants are scattered in the suburbs or they are concentrated in other far eastern towns such as Urrurijsk and Blogoveshchensk, and in the smaller township of Pogranichnyi, where they now outnumber the European population.

Not all of them have entered Russia illegally. There is an acute shortage of labor in the Russian Far East, and at any one time there are 10,000-12,000 Chinese contract workers in the area, invited by Russian companies or working for Chinese-owned enterprises. Even according to Russian sources, they are preferred to local workers because they "are highly organized and disciplined at work. As compared with local inhabitants, they do not drink and do not demand any immediate payments except some obligatory minimum."[6]

The problem of actual illegal migration—and the organized cross-border crime that has followed in its wake—is far greater and was deemed important enough to be highlighted in a joint declaration by Russian president Vladimir Putin and his Chinese counterpart Hu Jintao that was signed on May 27, 2003. Russia and China agreed to create a joint working group to curb the uncontrolled movement of people across the border. Facing racial prejudice and the threat of deportation, many choose—or are forced—to work for ethnic Chinese organized groups, the so-called Triads, which are spreading their influence over the Russian Far East.

The rise in illegal migration and organized crime have fueled racist attitudes towards all Chinese, even ordinary businessmen who are actually victimized by the Triads through their protection—or, more precisely, extortion—rackets. Some sources, however, argue that the prevailing perception that Chinese migrants are coming like a "tidal wave" is grossly exaggerated. In a paper presented at San Diego State University in January 2001, Russian academic Mikhail Alexseev emphasized that Chinese migration to the Russian Far East is not remotely similar to the Chinese presence in New York, San Francisco, or even Moscow.[7]

Yet threat perceptions are nevertheless important conditioners of local attitudes. After all, there are some 100 million people in China's northeastern region, while the total population of Russia's Far Eastern Federal District–an area two-thirds the size of the United States–is not more than seven million, so the pressure is there. Even if the number of newly arrived migrants from China does not exceed 200,000, or a mere 3 percent of the total population–a figure often mentioned in the Russian press–many locals see it as a trend and believe that in another decade or two the numbers could be much higher.

Russia's Far East may be too poor–and the climate too harsh–to attract huge numbers of migrant workers, who are better off at home in China. However, there is plenty of land, and thousands of Chinese farmers have settled in the border areas, where they grow vegetables and other crops. More importantly, business opportunities abound, especially in the booming underground economy. Although it may be a trickle rather than a flood, Vitaly Nomokonov, director of the Center for the Study of Organized Crime at the Far Eastern State University's Law Institute in Vladivostok, calls the movement of people across the border "unstoppable" and said that the authorities must make sure it does not "damage Russia's national interests."[8]

Economically, the Russian Far East is already becoming integrated with China. Chinese gangs control many of the casinos in the region (there are more than a dozen gaming establishments in and around Vladivostok), Chinese restaurants, and even some Russian hotels and eateries. The Far East has always been a stronghold for Russian organized crime, but many of the leaders of the indigenous Russian crime groups that previously dominated the region have been killed in turf wars, while others have gone out of business or died in mysterious circumstances. Now, many small-time Russian gangsters work for Chinese syndicates, either as contacts for local business deals or as security guards at the casinos. The most powerful crime lord in the Russian Far East is no longer a Russian godfather, but a Chinese man from across the border: Lao Da, "Elder Brother", alias Li Dechuan and Liang Chuannan.[9] His three gangs–The Wolves, The Snakes and The Mad Dogs–have effectively outmaneuvered the old Russian godfathers and now control local gambling, tourism operations, and prostitution. They smuggle everything from fish (a very lucrative business in the Russian Far East) to illegal migrants, and regularly extort protection money from local Chinese as well as Russian business people.

Over the past few years, the networks of the Chinese underground banking system—which handles more money transactions in China and in overseas Chinese communities than are sent through official banks—have also reached the Russian Far East. This flow of black money costs the government millions of rubles every year in lost revenue.[10]

The relationship between the local Russian criminals who remain in business and new Chinese crime bosses such as Lao Da is not clear, but it seems that the Chinese are far better organized and, therefore, have the upper hand. How well-connected in high places he and his colleagues are is also difficult to determine, but enforcing the law—and curbing corruption within the police and local government—has never been easy in this remote corner of Russia. In late 2002, the police actually arrested Lao Da and about a dozen of his associates, but the case collapsed and not one was brought to court.[11] Typically, out of a total of 151 bribery cases filed in 2001 and 2002 in the Far East, only 20 made it to court—and, in the end, only one of the suspects received a prison sentence.[12] The central Russian authorities, far away in Moscow, are slowly losing both political and economic control over the Far East.

It is uncertain how the Chinese authorities view this development, but Lao Da seems to have no problem traveling back and forth across the border to visit his hometown of Shenyang in China's Liaoning province, where he is equally well-connected. This may be explained in the context of corruption, but it should also be remembered that Vladivostok and other cities in the Russian Far East were built on land conquered by the Russians from the Chinese in the 19th century. Russian sovereignty over all territories north of the Amur River was recognized by the Chinese authorities under the treaties of Aigun and Tianjin in 1858, but with strong opposition from the Emperor at the time, Xianfeng of the Qing Dynasty. Given modern China's general attitude toward the "unequal treaties" of the 19th century, it is not far-fetched to assume that many Chinese consider large tracts of the Russian Far East lawfully theirs. A formal annexation of the Russian Far East may not be possible, but as Chinese migration into the area continues–and Chinese businessmen of all stripes tighten their grip on the local economy–Moscow's ability to exercise effective control over its most remote federal district is bound to become more tenuous.

Southeast Asia

For centuries, Southeast Asia has been receiving wave after wave of Chinese migrants looking for greener pastures. However, while in the past the migrants tended to assimilate fairly well into their new communities, the new arrivals are not like their predecessors who spoke regional dialects, exhibited little nationalism, and identified mainly with the localities from which they came. The recent arrivals–and over the past decade, large numbers of Chinese have moved into Burma, Laos, northern Thailand and Cambodia–speak Mandarin and tend to identify with China as a whole. According to Andrew Forbes, a sinologist based in the northern Thai city of Chiang Mai: "They're much more patriotic and loyal to the motherland ... the new-wave Chinese are very different from those who migrated in the past. They have grown up in a country that has been far more unified than before. There's now a different sense ... of being Chinese."[13]

There is no direct evidence that Beijing is trying to use the more nationalistic new migrants to spread its influence. Their impact appears to be primarily economic through new shops and businesses in the area. Yet because of their increasing numbers, they have begun to encounter age-old resentment that people often feel towards new immigrants. In economically ravaged places like Burma and Cambodia, for example, the Chinese newcomers are blamed for depriving the locals of jobs and business opportunities.

At the same time, China's growing political and economic clout has given the recent arrivals greater confidence and assertiveness. This sense of national pride is one factor that could provoke tensions between recent migrants and not only the indigenous local population but also older settlers who fear that it will re-ignite latent animosity or reinforce longstanding suspicions towards ethnic Chinese communities in their adopted countries. In Cambodia's capital Phnom Penh, for instance, about 300 Chinese gathered outside the U.S. embassy in May 1999 to protest against the bombing of the Chinese Embassy in Belgrade. A smaller gathering of ethnic Chinese Cambodians then held a counter-demonstration, heckling the protesters. "You are not our brothers," one of them yelled. "Your people killed my people during Pol Pot time." Cambodia's Chinese suffered badly during the 1975-79 Khmer Rouge regime, which was backed by Beijing.[14]

The total Chinese population of Cambodia is estimated at 350,000, of whom 200,000 live in Phnom Penh—and most of them are recent arrivals. Old communities have been joined by doctors, dentists and businessmen from Shanghai, architects from Taiwan, and investors from Malaysia and Singapore. Since 1990, a major resurgence of Chinese culture has also occurred, and the largest and most prestigious Chinese school in Phnom Penh, *Duanhua,* now has more than 10,000 pupils. This makes it the largest Chinese school in any country where Chinese is not one of the official languages.[15]

Since 1999, China's overall influence in Cambodia has increased dramatically. In February that year, Prime Minister Hun Sen—a former ally of Vietnam—paid an official visit to China and won praise from the leadership in Beijing for shutting down Taiwan's liaison office in Phnom Penh in the aftermath of his July 1997 coup against his then Co-Prime Minister, Prince Norodom Ranariddh, who had invited the Taiwanese in.[16] At a time when the Western countries were concerned about the deteriorating human rights situation in Cambodia and re-evaluating their aid programs in the country, China extended a U.S. $200 million interest-free loan and U.S. $18.3 million in foreign assistance guarantees. Since then, Chinese investment in Cambodia has also increased markedly, and Hun Sen—a former foe—has become one of China's most trusted allies in Southeast Asia.

The situation is somewhat similar in Burma. While Western countries shun the country's military junta for its abysmal human rights record, China opened its border with Burma in the late 1980s. The flourishing trade that has come in its wake has led to an influx of

Chinese into northern Burma that is so massive that it threatens the demographic balance of the area. When a person in the northern Burmese city of Mandalay dies, his or her death is not reported to the authorities. Instead, the person's relatives send his or her identity card to a broker in Ruili or some other town across Burma's northern border with China's Yunnan province. There, the identification papers are sold to anyone willing to pay the price.[17] The Chinese buyer's photo is substituted on the card, and he or she can then move to Mandalay as a Burmese citizen.

In this way, thousands of Yunnanese have settled in towns in northern Burma, bought property and set up businesses, often in partnership with local Chinese from Kokang, a district in northeastern Burma that always has been inhabited by the Chinese of Yunnanese extraction. They now pervade commercial life in Mandalay, including the trade in precious stones, jade and narcotics. The presence of almost unlimited amounts of drug money, which has to be laundered, has pushed up prices of real estate beyond the means of most ordinary Burmese. Not surprisingly, this new wave of Chinese migration has indeed re-ignited old anti-Chinese sentiments among many Burmese, feelings reflected in cartoons and short stories in local Mandalay publications.[18] The possibility of a repeat of the anti-Chinese riots, which rocked the capital Rangoon in 1967, cannot be ruled out if the immigration continues unabated.

Politically, Burma has emerged as one of China's closest allies in the region, perhaps even more so than Cambodia. When the West imposed an arms embargo on Burma after mass killings of pro-democracy demonstrators in 1988, China moved in and supplied the new junta with weapons, tanks, military aircraft and naval vessels. China's arms sales to Burma over the past 15 years total U.S. $1.2-1.4 billion, and it is doubtful whether the Burmese junta would have survived without the backing from China. Economic ties between the two countries are also close, and they function mostly to China's benefit. The newly-established businessmen in Mandalay and elsewhere do not keep their earnings in unreliable Burmese banks; the funds are deposited across the border in China.

The Chinese communities in Burma maintain close business links with China, and loyalties to the "motherland" are demonstrated by articles in *Mian Dien Hua Bao (Burmese Morning Post)*, a relatively new Chinese-language newsweekly published in Rangoon. Significantly, this is the only newspaper in Burma that is published in a language other than Burmese or English. Burma's own ethnic minorities, of whom there are many, are not allowed to print newspapers in their languages.

The Pacific

The first Chinese to settle in the Pacific came as carpenters and cooks aboard ships that came to the islands in search of sandalwood in the 19th century. Many set up shops and trading stations in islands such as Fiji, Tahiti, the New Hebrides (now Vanuatu), New Guinea and the Solomons. For more than a century, that was not a concern. On the contrary, had it not been for the Chinese shopkeepers and traders, there would not have been much commerce at all. That began to change when in the late 1980s Tonga began to sell passports as a means of raising badly needed revenue for the resource-starved Polynesian kingdom. The idea came from a Hong Kong-based American investment adviser, Jesse Bogdanoff, who made a deal with Taufa'ahau Tupou IV, the King of Tonga, and most of the customers were Hong Kong Chinese. Britain had just signed an agreement with China for the return of Hong Kong, and a new category of British passports had been introduced for most residents of the territory. They were "overseas dependents," which meant that they had no right of abode in Britain, and the new passports were of dubious value even as ordinary travel documents. For U.S. $33,000, someone who was otherwise "stateless" could become a "Tongan Protected Person" and carry a Tongan passport.

The scheme turned out to be a scam—most of the money ended up in one of Bogdanoff's investment companies and not in Tonga's state coffers. Yet it nevertheless inspired other small Pacific island states to follow suit. Following the independence of the Marshall Islands in 1990, the new republic established diplomatic relations with the PRC. Under the agreement with the former administrative power, the United

States, citizens of the Marshall Islands had the right to reside and work in the United States. The Marshall Islands embassy in Beijing then began to sell passports for U.S. $25,000 apiece to Chinese—who were then able to move to the United States. It is estimated that more than 1,500 Marshall Islands passports were sold before the scheme was stopped in 1999 after pressure from the United States.[19] By then, the Marshall Islands had also shifted recognition to the Republic of China, or Taiwan, again a move motivated by the need to make money for a country with no arable land and few natural resources. Taiwan effectively "buys" recognition from some of the smallest and poorest island states to enhance its legitimacy as an independent nation.

The passport-for-sale issue nevertheless put both Tonga and the Marshall Islands on the PRC's map, and it led to a—by island standards—significant migration to those countries. In Tonga, Chinese set up grocery stores which forced many locals out of business. In the Marshall Islands, Chinese migrants opened restaurants, karaoke bars and other small businesses. Chinese garment workers have been hired to work in factories in Fiji, where Chinese migrants also are beginning to replace the Indian minority as a business community since many Fijian-Indians were forced to leave following ethnic unrest and military coups in the late 1980s.

Even more significantly, the Northem Mariana Islands—which chose to become a U.S. commonwealth rather than an independent state when the Trust Territory of the Pacific Islands was dismantled in the 1980s—has made it a policy to hire workers from China and some other Asian countries. Under the agreement with the United States, the CNMI (the Commonwealth of the Northern Mariana Islands) controls its own labor laws and immigration. Consequently, the CNMI government stated that the minimum wage in the territory should be U.S. $3.05 per hour instead of the U.S. standard of U.S. $5.50. It also opened the gates for foreign labor. As a result, no less than 28 garment factories with more than 15,000 low-paid workers were established in the CNMI—and the goods could then be sent to the United States duty-free as the CNMI was a U.S. territory. This arrangement has been severely criticized by U.S. law makers—among them Rep. George Miller, who has been trying to fully extend U.S. immigration's reach along with U.S. labor laws to the CNMI–but it also put the territory on the PRC's map.

Apart from the garment factories–and assistance from the United States–the CNMI's only other major income comes from tourism. These days, many tourists come from the PRC, and one of the main attractions is a huge casino on the island of Tinian. In April 2004, direct flights began from Shanghai to the main CNMI island of Saipan, from where the tourists continued to Tinian. Like all other foreign visitors, the Chinese are not required to have U.S. visas to enter the CNMI for stays up to 30 days. U.S. immigration authorities have warned that this arrangement and the easy entry into the CNMI for foreign workers serve as a loophole for illegal migrants to enter the United States. From the CNMI, illegal migrants are smuggled by boat to the nearby island of Guam, which is within the U.S. immigration area. Once there, they can apply for asylum, and the case would have to be processed by a U.S. court. In October 2004, U.S. authorities uncovered a syndicate that smuggled illegal migrants to the United States, and the scheme involved the use of Saipan as a springboard to Guam and the United States mainland.[20]

Chinese migration into the Pacific has been paralleled by the PRC expanding its influence over a region that has long been regarded as America's home turf. According to Benjamin Reilly, a senior lecturer at the Australian National University in Canberra, the long-term aim of this expansion is to challenge "the United States as the prime power in the Pacific ... it can no longer be taken for granted that Oceania will remain a relatively benign 'American Lake'."[21] Another motive, of course, is to undermine Taiwan's efforts to get official diplomatic support for "the Republic of China" from the island states in the Pacific. The PRC has funded government buildings in Vanuatu and Samoa, and it paid for the construction of the venue for the 2003 South Pacific Games in the Fijian capital Suva. According to Reilly, Chinese aid disbursements have moved from near zero to being one of the largest in the region in only a few years. China's aid to the Pacific's largest state, Papua New Guinea, is now second only to that of the former colonial power, Australia.[22] The PRC also provides military assistance to the few Pacific countries that maintain military forces–Fiji, Papua

New Guinea, Tonga and Vanuatu—which clearly indicates that it has long-term strategic interests in the region.

The PRC's interest in Tonga proves this point. For years, Tonga was Taiwan's staunchest ally in the Pacific. However, in 1998, Tonga shifted recognition to Beijing. Its king received a red-carpet welcome in Beijing along with promises of aid. Even more importantly, Wu Quanshu and Wei Fulin, deputy chiefs of the General Staff of the Chinese People's Liberation Army, visited Tonga in 2000 and 2001 respectively. Tonga may be tiny—no more than 100,000 people live on 700 square kilometers of land—but it is strategically located in the middle of the Pacific Ocean.

The number of new Chinese settlers on the Pacific Islands may not be significant in a global context, but migration to these small states with their tiny populations has upset traditional ethnic and economic patterns. In Fiji, the trade union movement has condemned the hiring of hundreds of Chinese garment workers and complained that the influx of Chinese migrants has "depressed wages, work conditions and employment opportunities,"[23] In 1998, Tongan pro-democracy advocate Akilisi Pohiva asserted that Chinese migrants were causing "economic, political, social and moral problems," and in late 2000, several hundred Chinese shopkeepers and their families were expelled from the country "for their own protection."[24]

Reilly argues that such tensions between Chinese and indigenous population groups are unlikely to dissipate, especially as more Chinese nationals venture into the Pacific with unclear or dubious immigration status. Yet the tiny Pacific States may also be incapable of stemming the flow of Chinese migrants—or unwilling to turn down generous offers of aid from the PRC—in which case the Pacific Ocean, in the long-term, may well become a Chinese instead of an American lake. Also in the longer-term, it seems inevitable that the PRC's interests in the region will clash with those of the United States.

Conclusion

The massive Chinese migration to other parts of the world, which began in the late 1970s when the PRC relaxed its restrictions on foreign travel, is likely to upset demographic balances in vulnerable areas like the Russian Far East, the Pacific Islands and northern Burma. However, it is an unstoppable movement, partly because of population pressures inside the PRC—and the PRC government's policy of encouraging such migration because the new Chinese Diasporas play a vital part in the PRC's aspirations to become a great power. In the long term, this could lead to problems of different natures. For Russia, it could mean the "loss"—in reality if not in name—of its huge Far Eastern District. For the United States, it seems inevitable that a clash of interests is going to take place in the Pacific Ocean. With China likely to overtake Japan as the leading Asian power in the Asia-Pacific within the next few decades, Chinese migration and the role of Chinese Diasporas in the region are issues that warrant careful studies. It may not be a deliberate deployment of a "fifth column," but, as Pal Nyiri points out, "a case of local political will and migratory *fait accompli*, of which Beijing is simply taking advantage".[25]

China & the Chinese Diaspora in the Philippines

Chapter 7

China & the Chinese Diaspora in the Philippines[1]

Aileen S.P. Baviera[2]

Chinese Diaspora as a Security Problem: Perceptions in Southeast Asia

Thinking about the role of the "Chinese Diaspora" in terms of Southeast Asian security and China's security strategy in Southeast Asia, one cannot help but be brought back in time to the 1950s and 1960s. China then represented a triumphant revolutionary society bursting with passion for the communist cause, patriotism at its peak following the end of civil war, while nearly all of Southeast Asia consisted of young, post-colonial nation-states wracked by internal socio-political conflicts, which included ethnic division, communist insurgencies, or—for Indonesia and Malaysia—a considerable overlap of the two. It was in this context that the ethnic Chinese in multicultural and multiracial Southeast Asia came to be suspected by the indigenous ethnic majorities as a communist "fifth column," out to undermine the governments of their countries of residence and to promote the aspirations and objectives of the Chinese "motherland" instead.

In Indonesia, Suharto's New Order regime portrayed the ethnic Chinese minority as "the third side of a triangular threat together with the People's Republic of China and the PKI (Partai Komunis Indonesia)."[3] Such suspicions of China and the ethnic Chinese persisted even after the PKI had waned. In Malaysia, with the Chinese at about 30% of the population and most of the local communists being of ethnic Chinese origin, the government was very concerned about the potential influence of China over this group, which may have led to Malaysia's pragmatic attitude towards China that has been in effect since the 1960s.[4]

From the 1980s up to the present, following the opening of China's economy to foreign trade and investments, Southeast Asia's ethnic Chinese again became suspect as to their allegiance when many of them, having become affluent in their adopted countries, began to send money back to their home villages and provinces, as well as ventured into mainland industries with their investments. Among the natives of Southeast Asia, suspicion was fed by resentment and envy of the conspicuous economic success by the ethnic Chinese, apprehension of China's growing economic influence, and alarm at the possible consequences of the interface of the two. This was grounded on the fact that much of direct foreign investment (DFI) in China since its opening up has come from "Chinese overseas," overwhelmingly from Taiwan, Hong Kong and Macau, but also from Southeast Asia. In some Southeast Asian countries, there were attempts to discourage such transfer of funds and outflow of capital. In the Philippines, investments by Chinese Filipinos in China were described in the press as "capital flight" and even as downright "unpatriotic"[5] rather than being taken simply as migrant remittances to their hometowns or foreign investment opportunities.

In 1991, the Singapore Chinese Chamber of Commerce and Industry organized an international convention of World Chinese Entrepreneurs which Lee Kwan Yew addressed and emphasized the importance of links among the ethnic Chinese. Lee noted that "as Chinese, we are affected by the future of China," and suggested that China's modernization would benefit from the experience of "Chinese overseas," namely the examples set out by Hong Kong, Taiwan and Singapore.[6]

Similarly, new discourses on East Asian development traced the success of ethnic Chinese-dominated economies in part to racial and cultural attributes, and included intensive networks among them. However, the idea of encouraging networks based on an exclusivist ethnic group ruffled feathers in multiracial Southeast Asia. When talk of a "Greater China" or a "Great China Economic Zone" (*Da Zhonghua Jingji Quan*) came into vogue, this raised so many eyebrows across Southeast Asia that the Beijing government itself had to downplay the proposition, even though Hong Kong and Taiwan scholars in particular seemed very enamored by the concept.[7]

By the time of the second conference of World Chinese Entrepreneurs two years after the first one, Lee had become much more sensitive to Singapore's neighbors and warned that increasing investments by overseas Chinese in China could affect race relations in some member countries of the Association of South East Asian Nations (ASEAN). He noted that if relations turned sour between China and any Southeast Asian country, those ethnic Chinese who had invested in China would be accused of disloyalty.[8] His main argument, however, was that the ethnic Chinese can serve as a bridge between two dynamic parties – attracting Southeast Asian capital to invest in China and mainland Chinese capital to invest in Southeast Asia.

Moreover, in the 1990s, as China continued to grow not only in economic wealth but also—as a consequence—in political influence and military power, a "China threat theory" emerged in global and Asia-Pacific academic and policy circles. Many Western media sources highlighted China's advances in military modernization and strategic doctrine, irredentist ambitions vis-à-vis Taiwan and the South China Sea islands, as well as its growing assertiveness in foreign policy. China's reaction to the "China threat theory" was the counter-accusation that the West was fanning the idea in order to deliberately keep China back and limit its economic and political influence. Nonetheless, in this environment other nations became more conscious of the possible risks to their security that the large and embedded presence of ethnic Chinese might represent. In the North American experience, this was punctuated by highly-publicized cases where certain individuals were alleged to have engaged in espionage and made illegal contributions to political campaigns in the United States.[9]

What do these patterns of perceptions and mistrust towards Chinese populations outside of China illustrate? Possibly, from the perspective of the ethnic Chinese, they illustrate the continued perception that they are still a "foreign" or "alien" presence in their adopted countries, making them vulnerable to criticism and pressure from different groups, particularly in periods of economic crisis. Yet from the perspective of the local indigenous population, and in particular the majority cultural group and economic elites, the mistrust may be partly attributed to fear of challenges to their own culture, values, and resources that may arise from the ubiquitous and culturally cohesive ethnic Chinese, especially those that may have strong ties to an emerging power such as China.

This paper examines the phenomenon of the Chinese Diaspora in Southeast Asia, with particular emphasis on the Philippines, towards an assessment of whether or not the diaspora plays a significant role in the "security strategy" of China.

Basically, the answer to this question lies in an understanding of (1) what is meant by "the Chinese Diaspora" and "the ethnic Chinese," (2) the history of migration and the evolution of Chinese presence, (3) migrant Chinese relations with the government of their country of residence, and (4) the nature of migrant Chinese ties with China through the years. The paper argues that based on these considerations, the ethnic Chinese minorities in the region have not been and are not likely to be useful as *significant* instruments for the *deliberate* advancement of China's security goals and interests in Southeast Asia, especially if security is understood here in its traditional (realist) sense of a great power China seeking political supremacy in the region, or even military parity with or advantage over other great powers.

It is more plausible to argue that the contributions of Southeast Asia's ethnic Chinese to China have been in the aspects of economic security rather than military security, and perhaps even human security – through direct contributions to their relatives and hometowns and villages, and to a much lesser scale direct investments in the local economies of said hometowns and home provinces (with the exception of Singapore, whose investments were not mainly tied to hometowns or pre-existing local linkages but were more policy-driven).[10] If China's "security strategy" is then defined as framed by its desire to become an "advanced socialist state" or in terms of "comprehensive security," then certainly it may be said that the ethnic Chinese of Southeast Asia have had a significant role, although the impact was greater felt at the local rather than at the national dimension.

At the same time, these propositions do not exclude the possibility that certain individuals, families, business interests, or organizations may have played a direct or indirect role in covertly or overtly, deliberately or inadvertently, influencing decision makers in Southeast Asia towards certain policies that again, directly or indirectly, favor China's security goals. This may be particularly true for those with strong economic ties and political connections to the central government or key ministries in Beijing. It would also not be surprising if China—like any other great power—occasionally relies on its nationals, compatriots or former citizens to provide political and economic assessments on the country in question. In very open societies such as the Philippines, ethnic Chinese who freely move among the elites would certainly be well-placed to serve as listening posts, if indeed they were under the influence of China. Yet the irony of the situation of the ethnic Chinese is that those who are best-placed to serve China presumably because of their own influence and access to information are those who have already integrated with the mainstream societies in their adopted countries and are therefore, as noted by Fitzgerald, "least likely to respond to appeals or instructions from Beijing."[11] Granted that there are such occurrences, by their very nature they are not well-documented other than through anecdotal reports; thus their impact will be difficult to prove.

A Brief History of the Diaspora and the Evolution of Chinese Identity in Southeast Asia

Chinese immigration to Southeast Asia started as early as the 12th century, and had become very important by the 15th century. Many of the early Chinese settlers and traders intermarried and eventually became assimilated with the local population. In the Philippines, the Spanish colonial administration was very much oriented towards trade with China, which opened the way for new migrants, particularly traders from the Fujian province, to come to the islands. Yet discrimination against the Chinese was very strong under Spanish rule. Many of the prejudices currently held by Filipinos against Chinese can be traced to this nearly 400-year long period of history. The Chinese were occasionally segregated and expelled from the rest of the population. Due to Spanish abuses, there were intermittent Chinese insurrections followed by massacres by Spanish soldiers which led to the dwindling of migrant populations. However, Spain acknowledged the important role of the Chinese in the colonial economy, particularly as a source of tax revenue, and eventually allowed the migrant population to grow and establish its own institutions. When the Americans in turn became the country's colonizers, they restricted new immigration in order to prevent the Chinese from using the Philippines as a gateway to America. This policy was relaxed only in 1937 when women, children, and some intellectuals were admitted to the Philippines as refugees following the Japanese invasion of China.[12] Prior to this, there were already few full-blooded Chinese in the Philippines, as the men had previously been forced to marry locals.

The late 19th to early 20th century saw great political upheavals occurring in China, and news from the home front inspired patriotism and philanthropy among the overseas Chinese who mobilized themselves during the struggles against Western imperialism, the anti-Japanese resistance, and the civil war between Kuomintang and Chinese communists. It was in this light that strong links between the Chinese communists and communist movements in Malaya, Thailand, and Indonesia began to flourish.[13] However, the Chinese who had started to do well in the Philippines, as in the rest of Southeast Asia, were mainly more concerned with helping families back in their hometowns in coping with their immediate economic, social and cultural needs, rather than with returning to or investing in China itself as the economic situation in China was simply not stable then.[14]

Immigration to Southeast Asia was again almost completely interrupted after the communist victory in 1949, which made the native-born or Southeast Asia-born Chinese predominant in the region. This loss of direct or continuous contact with China until the 1970s meant disruption in political and cultural links, which subsequently led to a tendency by the Chinese communities to gravitate to Hong Kong and, in some cases, Taiwan.[15]

Post-war migration to the Philippines consisted mainly of children of Philippine Chinese parents who had returned to China, but who were born and raised in Hong Kong after their families again left China in the 1950s.[16]

No new migration in significant numbers had occurred since 1949, until China itself eventually relaxed policies restricting the movement of its people in the 1990s. However, they became undocumented aliens because of strict Philippine immigration policies against the Chinese. These new arrivals, to a certain extent, helped to strengthen the China orientation of the Philippine Chinese community because they were more familiar with the situation in China, but for the large part they were also treated as "others," often in a non-accepting way, by those who had already become acculturated and integrated. Only this year has the Philippine government decided to relax visa requirements for the People's Republic of China (PRC), mainly to attract tourists.

This diaspora that has occurred over many centuries, responding to push as well as pull factors, has resulted in the multitude of "overseas Chinese identities" co-existing or sometimes overlapping today, and different levels of "Chineseness," as roughly illustrated in the table below.

Nomenclature[i]	Who they are	Orientation
Zhongguo ren	Chinese from the mainland as well as from Hong Kong, Macau, and Taiwan.	Full identification is with China (discounting pro-independence Taiwanese).
Huaqiao or "sojourner" Overseas Chinese, or sometimes referred to as the more generic "Chinese overseas"	Usually first generation migrants who hope to return eventually; they hold Chinese citizenship. (Also within China is a category of "domestic overseas Chinese," i.e., *huaqiao* who had returned to China after 1949, among them students, nationalists and their families).	Main identification is with China; live in Chinatown. (As returned overseas Chinese, they were "welcomed" but suspected of bourgeois ideology. Persecuted during the Cultural Revolution, many were disillusioned and tried to leave.)
Huaren or "ethnic Chinese" • *totok* of Indonesia • *sinkeh* of Malaysia • *tsino/intsik* of Philippines	Second-generation migrants, i.e., SEA-born; may have been naturalized as Southeast Asian citizens.	Well-versed in Chinese culture and have some Chinese education but have decided to remain in Southeast Asia; live in or near Chinatown.
Huayi or "people of Chinese descent"	Third generation migrants; either of pure or mixed parentage. By self-identification, includes *Tsinoys* or *Tsinong Pinoy* in Philippines.	They often see China as a foreign country; have little or no Chinese education, do not speak the language but may still observe major cultural practices; live outside Chinatown and attend non-Chinese schools.
Highly-acculturated Chinese	By self-identification, includes *peranakan of Java & peninsular Malaysia; baba or Straits Chinese; Sino-Thai; "Filipino" (na may dugong intsik).*	Little or no self-identification as Chinese; often do not speak Chinese and do not even consider themselves part of a diaspora.
Other identity markers	Provincial versus metropolitan Chinese China-born vs. local-born Full-blooded Chinese vs. *mestizo*	In the Philippines, ethnic Chinese in provinces tend to be more at ease with Filipinos, and join both Chinese and local Filipino civic organizations. Some go into local politics but not the bureaucracy, and maintain residence in Chinese community to preserve business advantages.[ii]

[i] See Suryadinata, 2, 4-5, and various other sources.

[ii] Chinben See, 328.

Table 7.1: Differences in Overseas Chinese Identities

For many second- as well as third-generation Southeast Asia-born ethnic Chinese, they hardly consider themselves connected to any country other than that of their birth in terms of political allegiance, primary social and cultural values and relationships, and present economic interests. There is some objection to being called "overseas Chinese" because their identities are not defined in relation to their being "overseas" or away from China, since they already consider their adopted countries as home. They would thus prefer to be considered as cultural minorities of the Philippines, where they make up only about 1.5% of the population (or Indonesia at under 3%, but for Malaysia's 30% ethnic Chinese it may be another matter) rather than as part of a "Chinese Diaspora."[19] If they were to leave Southeast Asia to take up permanent residency elsewhere, the destination is not likely to be China but rather North America or Australasia.

In terms of orientation, the first-generation migrants tended to gravitate towards either of two types: the "nationalists" (those who identified either with China or Taiwan) and the "traditionalists" (those who had no particular ties to either China or Taiwan, but were basically concerned with the politics and issues of the ethnic Chinese community).[20] With the passage of generations, migrant communities were transformed from being more "nationalist" to more "traditionalist."

Wang Gungwu observes that unlike the Chinese in America, Europe and Australasia, who were mainly *huaqiao* (i.e., recent immigrants with passports and traveling papers issued by Beijing, Taipei or Hong Kong-Macao) and who may still have strong "patriotic" sentiments, the Southeast Asian Chinese were mostly locally born, homogenous in place of origin, wealthier than their counterparts in other regions, and many—having gone through the nationalist movements in Southeast Asia of the late colonial period— "understood the new realities" or were fully committed to being loyal to their adopted countries.[21]

The nature of the Chinese community organizations also reveals much about their changing orientation. In a 1988 study comparing Southeast Asian Chinese and North American Chinese, Edgar

Wickberg made the observation that in Southeast Asia there continued to be a proliferation of clan and district associations (which were declining in North America), and a continuation of community-wide 'umbrella' associations (which existed only in a nominal form in North America),[22] the former indicating the much greater influence of local ties to hometowns than ties to the Chinese nation-state as a whole, and the latter indicating an almost parochial preoccupation with internal community affairs rather than relations with the larger national or international community. The exception to this in Southeast Asia was Singapore, where associations tend to be built around common professions. In the Philippines, the proliferation of associations has also been partly attributed to the competition for power and prestige among community leaders, demonstrating that rather than being cohesive as they may appear to the outsider, the ethnic Chinese are deeply divided and factional. [23]

Chinese community associations in the Philippines include the Federation of Filipino Chinese Chambers of Commerce and Industry (FFCCCI) (originally anti-communist and pro-Taiwan, but later opened up towards Beijing for economic rather than politico-ideological reasons), the much less influential Filipino-Chinese Business Club (a pro-Kuomintang (KMT) faction) and the Filipino-Chinese Amity Club (an old pro-Beijing group). There are also pyramids of clan and hometown associations under the Grand Family Association, school organizations, and benevolent societies, but the Kuomintang cultural organizations as well as anti-communist leagues of earlier years have become defunct.[24] These informal organizations helped created an "order" that helped make the businesses run by ethnic Chinese competitive in an environment where the formal legal and administrative structures are relatively underdeveloped,[25] but otherwise the success of the ethnic Chinese owed little to either China or Taiwan. On the contrary, it was the successful ethnic Chinese communities in Southeast Asia and the Philippines who contributed significantly to socio-economic development of both China and Taiwan.

Factors that Affect the Potential Strategic Role of Chinese Diasporas in the Philippines

There are political, economic, as well as cultural factors that prevent the Chinese in the Philippines, whether *huaqiao, huaren, huayi, or tsinoy*, from playing a bigger role in advancing China's security goals. These can also be traced to the history of ethnic Chinese presence in the country.

Political Factors

1. China's Basic Non-interventionist Policy and Discrimination Against Overseas Chinese Since 1949

Prior to the establishment of diplomatic relations, most Chinese community organizations had links to the Kuomintang in Taiwan. The Kuomintang relied greatly on support from the overseas Chinese as a source of legitimacy, and therefore played a very active role in their affairs in the Philippines, such as by lobbying with the Philippine government on issues of their citizenship, propagation of Chinese education and culture, and economic discrimination. The KMT, like the Qing Dynasty before it, had encouraged chauvinism and loyalty by Chinese overseas.[26] After Manila switched recognition to Beijing, these links were not transferred automatically to the People's Republic of China, as Beijing's "overseas Chinese" policy was the exact opposite of the Kuomintang's. Beijing officially maintained a one-citizenship policy and advised citizens to "be loyal to the Philippines," although Beijing frequently reminded them of their "roots and consanguinal ties" to China.[27]

Other policies of the Chinese Communist Party (CCP) towards overseas Chinese did not exactly encourage political loyalty. While the party did invite support for the anti-Japanese struggle and its own conflict with the KMT before 1949, after the communist victory the CCP became internally preoccupied. In the1950s, "overseas Chinese" were represented in the National People's Congress (just as during the Republic, they were allowed to sit in the Provisional National Parliament in Nanking), but this representation was more symbolic than substantive, as it consisted of China-based or returned overseas Chinese and was mainly concerned with issues affecting returnees.[28] Moreover, a decision was made in 1956 to make "overseas Chinese work" subordinate to foreign policy.[29] The implication was that any dealings between China and Southeast Asian Chinese should be consistent with and under the general framework of Chinese foreign policy vis-à-vis that country.

During the ultra-leftist Cultural Revolution, within China there was even great antipathy against overseas Chinese who were seen to be bourgeois "capitalist-roaders." Their situation had become so difficult for returned overseas Chinese that they began to leave during the Cultural Revolution until the 1980s. They were barred from joining the Communist Party, Army, Youth League, top universities and important agencies. They were considered reactionaries, and did not lose their identity as "overseas Chinese" even when in China. Fitzgerald also cites a Cultural Revolution report which exhorted cadres of the Overseas Chinese Affairs Office to "interfere with the Chinese abroad as little as possible."

It was already under reform-oriented Deng Xiaoping's watch when clearer objectives for overseas Chinese policy were enunciated. This policy included: (1) reduce, if not stop, the departure of "domestic overseas Chinese intellectuals;" (2) attract ethnic Chinese professionals to participate in the modernization of China; (3) secure more remittances and investments from the ethnic Chinese (especially after isolation by the West following events at Tiananmen in 1989); and (4) encourage them to be a bridge in unifying mainland and Taiwan.[30]

Beijing thus began to value the Chinese abroad for two roles they could play: the first in helping the modernization of China, and the second in preventing any support for Taiwan's breakaway. Apparently, no role was envisioned or encouraged with respect to foreign relations between China and Southeast Asia; on the contrary, the call to "subordinate overseas Chinese policy to foreign policy" precisely indicated Beijing's desire to keep the connection between these two issues clearly delineated, and not to allow the ethnic Chinese question to get in the way of its foreign policy goals.

2. Strong Kuomintang Influence Among Philippine Chinese from 1949-1975

The mere fact that diplomatic relations between Manila and Beijing were suspended from 1949 to 1975 meant that in general, it was very difficult for China to maintain contact with ethnic Chinese communities in the Philippines. Some Philippine Chinese managed to sustain links that had been forged before 1949, such as the Wah Chi World War II veterans (an all-ethnic Chinese guerilla group) and the Amity Club. They contributed in some way to the establishment of diplomatic relations by translating news and publishing information about "new China" in the Philippines and setting up a Hong Kong-based hostel, transport services, and cultural exchange programs to facilitate travel between China and the Philippines.

Many of the Wah Chi veterans, who might have been expected to be more politically loyal to China than the younger or Philippine-born Chinese, were disappointed when after the establishment of diplomatic relations, the Beijing government turned its attention mainly to the wealthy ethnic Chinese businessmen and "taipans," and ignored their own important historical role which had brought together the Filipinos and mainland Chinese in the anti-Japanese struggle.[31]

On the other hand, the Kuomintang had extensive links with the ethnic Chinese throughout this period, tolerated by successive Philippine administrations in the name of a common anti-communist ideology. Thus, by the time of the establishment of diplomatic ties between Manila and Beijing, China's relations with the ethnic Chinese had a very low base, the main problem being the entrenched influence of the Kuomintang.

The KMT actively intervened in the most influential Chinese community institutions – the schools, Chinese language newspapers, the FFCCCI, and other organizations. There were even KMT members among the Philippine Chinese who were elected into the KMT Central Committee. Kuomintang influence was most felt in the way a parallel Chinese education system was allowed to exist in the Philippines, with the curriculum, textbooks and teacher-training directly under their control until the 1970s.

In contrast, the PRC embassy in Manila after 1975 compared to the Republic of China (ROC) official mission before 1975, took a generally pragmatic and passive attitude towards the Philippine Chinese. While the embassy would respond to requests for assistance on matters of education or to invitations from pro-mainland groups to grace anniversary celebrations, it did not initiate much contact. Over time, embassy relations with the ethnic Chinese improved, possibly due to increasing familiarization with each other, increased interest by ethnic Chinese in economic and cultural linkages with China, cordial relations between the two governments which helped mitigate the sensitivity of the Philippine government to PRC-ethnic Chinese links, and the waning influence of the Kuomintang (see Table 7.2).[32]

Policies toward Philippine Chinese in the 1950s	Kuomintang	Communist Party of China (Gongchandang)
Citizenship	Encouraged Chinese citizenship; Jus sanguinis.	Acknowledged problems caused by dual citizenship but seemed to accept jus sanguinis.
Jurisdiction	Claimed jurisdiction over Chinese abroad as a right and responsibility (case: Yuyitung brithers).	Some strong public statements but no action to support; objective was to undermine KMT influence rather than that of host country.
Issues and concerns re: Chinese community	Promotion of education and culture, remittances, legal protection, appeals to patriotism. Lobbied against Retail Trade Nationalization Act and Filipinization of Chinese schools	Same as KMT but in addition, support for socialist modernization and non-recognition of Taiwan.
Education	Controlled Chinese schools through teachers and curriculum.	Extended assistance in textbooks.
Political membership	Allowed membership in KMT by overseas Chinese.	Only PRC citizens can join PRC organizations. Philippine Chinese who were appointed members of the CPPCC as overseas Chinese representatives were PRC citizens. During GPCR, condemned as bourgeois.
Relation of overseas Chinese to foreign policy	Maintained "colonial" ties with overseas Chinese; at times jeopardizing foreign relations.	"Overseas Chinese policy should serve foreign policy;" encouraged OCs to be loyal and respect the laws of host country.

Table 7.2: Comparing Taiwan and Beijing Policies toward Philippine Chinese

3. Mass Naturalization Law and Philippine Efforts to Integrate the Chinese

Prior to the establishment of diplomatic relations with Beijing in 1975, the Marcos government offered mass naturalization of citizenship to Chinese Filipinos, many of whom were previously considered stateless. For many *huaren* and *huayi* who had known no other country but the Philippines, this resolved the last obstacle to their identification and political allegiance as Filipinos.

The Filipinization of Chinese schools also came in 1973, a move that was meant to hasten integration as well as to prevent possible attempts by Chinese communists to use the schools for "communist indoctrination."[33] Fitzgerald, however, notes that if the CCP had any interest in influencing the Chinese schools in Southeast Asia even prior to diplomatic relations, it was most likely with the overwhelming motive of dislodging the KMT from Southeast Asia more than any other motive.[34]

Meanwhile, as integration was encouraged, Manila adopted a very strict immigration policy against the entry of new Chinese migrants.

4. Political Insecurity and Passiveness of Ethnic Chinese

Colonial policies of isolation and decades of economic and political discrimination took a toll on the sense of political efficacy of the Philippine Chinese. In order to feel secure, it had become their habit to assume a very low political profile but to be very astute in developing political connections. Come election time, when candidates for the highest positions would invariably approach them for financial backing, they were more likely than not to extend support to the main opposing camps rather than just one, although not necessarily on an equal basis. That way, whoever emerged the victor would feel indebted to them.

Small ethnic Chinese business establishments would often display pictures of the proprietor together with prominent political figures in their places of work, to show off their social status as well as for protection against extortionist tax collectors or health inspectors. More than anything, they were concerned about protecting their economic interests. The Philippine Chinese also shied away from becoming too politically active, especially given the often volatile state of politics in the country. Some made the mistake of openly supporting the corrupt president Joseph Estrada, who was later ousted by a popular revolt of the middle class, which once more led to criticism of the ethnic Chinese as a group.

Another indication of insecurity is that many older Chinese are even critical of newer organizations such as the pro-integration Kaisa Para sa Kaunlaran, whose younger members sometimes assert positions on national issues, in contrast to focusing on purely community affairs. Those who do become confident enough to engage in politics are likely to be those who have fully acculturated, and they do so usually by running for positions in local government (e.g., as district, town or city officials), rather than seeking to be in executive or legislative bodies where they would be more strategically placed to influence policy.

5. Underground Communist Movement in the Philippines

The communist insurgency in the Philippines, by now the longest running in the region, may also have had an effect on China's relations with the Philippine Chinese.

Compared to Indonesia, Malaysia, or even Thailand, where the ethnic Chinese constituted a significant percentage of the underground communist movements, the Chinese in the Philippines did not play a significant role in the establishment and subsequent growth of the Maoist (and erstwhile pro-China) Communist Party of the Philippines. They were neither a major conduit nor target for Beijing's support along fraternal ideological lines.

It seemed more likely that the Philippine Chinese avoided excessive identification with China, particularly during the Cultural Revolution period, because that would make them more suspect as being linked with the local communist movement. Anti-communist policies as well as the presence of KMT supporters in the community also checked any opportunities for CCP representatives to organize among the ethnic Chinese.[35]

There were documented instances of the CCP extending some political and material support to the Maoist New People's Army during the 1970s, but this was believed to have ended when China embarked on its economic reforms in the 1980s and as the Philippines itself went through post-martial law democratic transition.

Cultural Factors

1. Low Level of Education of Elites

China's closest links with the Southeast Asian and Philippines Chinese are with first-generation migrants who have become very successful entrepreneurs and industry leaders in their adopted countries. Many of them have had no formal education, or received only a few years of education on the mainland prior to migration in the early 20th century, and therefore do not read or write well in Chinese. It is the second-generation migrants who have had better education opportunities–sometimes in China, Taiwan, or Hong Kong–and are able to read and write in Chinese.[36] Even then, relatively few ethnic Chinese in Southeast Asia, with the exception of Singapore, speak Mandarin.[37]

One observation that has been made is that despite their wealth, the top rung Chinese economic elites in the Philippines are not well-educated enough to play a strategic or influential role in terms of shaping either Chinese policy towards their host country or the host country policy towards China. With few exceptions, their ties to China are also largely concentrated on parochial attachments to their home village or province. This may be one reason why the main thrust of PRC policy towards the ethnic Chinese has been to attract investments, rather than to encourage them to play a role in foreign policy. On the other hand, for the local Chinese their main interest in maintaining ties with the PRC was for private profit and personal prestige within the Chinese community.[38]

This is evident in the fact that the biggest Chinese business federation–the above-mentioned FFCCCI–unlike its counterpart the Philippine Chamber of Commerce and Industry, is unable to issue policy statements or even take positions on vital issues affecting their own members. Moreover, when the Federation hosts a delegation from the mainland, it links them up mostly with members of the Chinese community, rather than the mainstream industry players or political leaders. In that sense, they are not very effective as a bridge between the two countries and can thus play only a minimal role in advancing China's goals. Yet this may also mean they are unable to function significantly in articulating Philippine economic and political interests to the Chinese government, even if the Philippine government has a stronger claim on their loyalty.

The Philippine government does on occasion press such claims on their allegiance– such as when then president Fidel Ramos brought the six wealthiest Chinese-Filipino business tycoons or "taipans" with him during a state visit to China in April 1993. While in Beijing, Ramos announced that the six had agreed to form a consortium to invest in major infrastructure projects in the Philippines, which signaled to his Chinese hosts and to the "taipans" that their loyalty should be to the Philippines, while at the same time signaled his intention to use the ethnic Chinese as a bridge in improving relations between China and the Philippines.[39]

2. Filipinization of Chinese Schools in 1973

The Filipinization of Chinese schools led to a decline in the traditional linkages between the ethnic Chinese and Taiwan. In the mid-1980s, there were as many as 140 Chinese schools all over the country. From 1949 until 1975, these schools were under the direct influence of the Kuomintang, with the content of instruction left to the Taiwan government until the 1960s. Wickberg describes the tightly-knit structure of Chinese school associations in the Philippines as "like the dream of an early Kuomintang theorist of mass organizations."[40]

With Filipinization, Chinese language instruction was reduced to 100 minutes a day, and the curriculum came under Philippine government regulation. The schools had to open their doors to non-ethnic Chinese, which was a major impetus for integration. However, because of the interface between the schools and many other cultural organizations, interest in cultural ties with other Chinese peoples remained strong, so that there was also enthusiasm for restoring links with the "homeland" upon the switch of diplomatic recognition.[41]

In addition to the Filipinization of the Chinese schools, factors that may have greatly facilitated integration of Philippine-born Chinese include the fact that the Filipino culture is itself a melting pot and therefore readily accommodates even new elements of Chinese culture, the tolerant philosophy of Catholic religion practiced by the great majority of Filipinos, and democratic politics in the Philippines which encourages pluralism and diversity. Of added interest is that even in Muslim communities in the southern Philippines there is a very high degree of acculturation by earlier migrants, and acceptance of a dominant Chinese role in the local economies, with none of the strong anti-Chinese emotions displayed in other Muslim-dominated countries of Southeast Asia.

3. Factionalism Within the Community

The factionalism within the Chinese community in the Philippines has been described as unprecedented in Southeast Asia, originally arising from various groups taking different sides in the China-Taiwan dispute, but eventually deteriorating into simple rivalries for power and prestige.[42] Ang See demonstrates this by noting that of five Chinese language dailies, two are pro-Beijing, two are pro-Taipei, and one is neutral. There were two rival factions in the volunteer fire brigades, and some family associations were also split into two factions. The Chambers of Commerce, literary groups, music clubs, and some schools also have defined leanings. Although at present, this is true mainly for the first generation Chinese, they still happen to hold the key leadership positions and wield influence over the community.[43]

Such factionalism must also have deterred the Beijing government from cultivating more active links with the Philippine Chinese, as it was careful not to be criticized by the pro-Taiwan Chinese, for fear of driving them further into the other camp.

Economic Factors

1. China's Investment Boom Coincided with Economic and Political Crisis in the Philippines

By the time China improved its investment climate in the early 1980s, the Philippines was moving into a serious economic and political crisis and few among the ethnic Chinese entrepreneurs were capable of expanding into the Chinese market in a big way.

The development of Xiamen as a special economic zone, however, attracted many investors, particularly in the 1990s when a wave of kidnappings in Manila targeting wealthy Chinese drove many to send their children to study in China and put up some investments there. However, as with other Southeast Asian Chinese, most preferred small-scale, local operations whereby they could enjoy more flexibility, fewer restrictions, and better incentives by dealing with local authorities instead of ministries or the provincial-level bureaucracy.[44]

Since the economic ties were to local authorities who knew or cared little of China's strategic foreign policy objectives, it is doubtful if there were serious attempts by the Chinese side to use the Chinese Filipinos who had economic stakes in China to influence Philippine policy at the highest levels.

2. Chinese Exports Directly Compete with Chinese Filipino Businesses

Ironically, while the Chinese Filipinos were perceived as potential bridges to facilitate economic cooperation between China and the Philippines, many of them were engaged in manufacturing industries in the Philippines and therefore were the first to suffer direct competition from China-made imports. Chinese Filipinos have been known to take the lead in a "Buy Filipino Movement" formed in tandem with other protectionist organizations during the height of the Asian financial crisis, mainly targeted against the uncontrolled entry of Chinese products which they could not compete with.

3. Poor Links and Networks with Other Chinese Communities in Southeast Asia

While no systematic studies have been performed on the issue, an insider to the community reveals that any perception of links between the Chinese Filipino business community and counterparts in Southeast Asia would be ungrounded, as the most serious occasion for networking to take place would be through the occasional same-surname reunions.

Conclusions

There is a huge gap between perception and reality of the ethnic Chinese situation in SEA, including the Philippines. The Chinese Diaspora is now composed of mainly second- or third-generation individuals who identify more with their host country than with China. In the Philippines, they are in fact well-integrated but are still perceived as an "alien" minority by many in times of economic crisis, when their loyalty becomes more suspect.

The growth of Chinese power has encouraged more patriotism among the Chinese, but the main motivation for links with China is still economic. Moreover, historically and at present, there are political, cultural, and economic impediments to the ethnic Chinese becoming instrumental to the promotion of China's security strategy for Southeast Asia.

Are the Philippines, however, typical of Southeast Asia? The Philippines may not be typical of the Southeast Asian experience with ethnic Chinese, although there are significant commonalities.

Each diaspora has its own story that is worth listening to and worth understanding.

Sources

1. Baginda, Abdul Razak, "Malaysian Perceptions of China: From Hostility to Cordiality" in Herbert Yee and Ian Storey, eds. The China Threat: Perceptions, Myths and Reality (London: RoutledgeCurzon, 2002), 227-247.

2. Carino, Theresa Chong, Political Leadership and the Federation of Filipino-Chinese Chambers of Commerce and Industry: Continuity and Change (1954-1994). Dissertation at CSSP, 1995.

3. Carino, Theresa Chong, "The ethnic Chinese, the Philippine Economy, and China" in Leo Suryadinata, ed. Southeast Asian Chinese and China: the Politico-Economic Dimension (Singapore: Times Academic press, 1995, 216- 229.

4. East Asia Analytical Unit, Department of Foreign Affairs and Trade. Overseas Chinese Business Networks in Asia, 1995.

5. Fitzgerald, Stephen, China and the Overseas Chinese: A Study of Peking's Changing Policy 1949-1970. (Cambridge University Press, 1972).

6. Gungwu, Wang, "The Southeast Asian Chinese and the development of China", in Leo Suryadinata, ed. Southeast Asian Chinese and China: the Politico-Economic Dimension (Singapore: Times Academic press, 1995), 12-30.

7. Hill, Ann Maxwell, Merchants and Migrants: Ethnicity and Trade among Yunnanese Chinese in Southeast Asia (New Haven, Connecticut: Yale University Southeast Asian Studies, 1998).

8. Hing, Lee Kam, "The Political Position pf the Chinese in Post-independence Malaysia" in The Chinese Diaspora: Selected Essays, ed. Wang Ling-chi and Wang Gungwu (Singapore: Times Academic press, 1998).

9. Hodder, Rupert, Merchant Princes of the East: Cultural delusions, Economic Success and the overseas Chinese in Southeast Asia. (Chichester/New York/Brisbane/Toronto/ Singapore: John Wiley & Sons, 1996).

10. Huang, Yen-ching, Community and Politics: The Chinese in Colonial Singapore and Malaya (Tiumes Academic press, 1995).

11. Interview with Go Bon Juan.

12. Lim, Benito, "A History of Philippine-China Relations" in Aileen San Pablo-Baviera and Lydia N. Yu-Jose, eds. Philippine external Relations: A centennial Vista (Manila: Foreign Service Institute, 1998), 201-275.

13. See, Chinben, "Chinese Organizations and Ethnic Identity in the Philippines" in Jennifer Cushman and Wang Gungwu, eds. Changing Identities of the Southeast Asian Chinese since World War II (Hong Kong: Hong Kong University Press, 1988), 319-334.

14. See, Teresita Ang, "The Ethnic Chinese as Filipinos" in Leo Suryadinata, ed. Ethnic Chinese as Southeast Asians (Singapore: ISEAS, 1997) – Leo 2, 158-210.

15. Sukma, Rizal, "Indonesia's Perceptions of China: The Domestic Bases of Persistent Ambiguity" in Herbert Yee and Ian Storey, eds. The China Threat: Perceptions, Myths and Reality (London: RoutledgeCurzon, 2002), 181-204.

16. Suryadinata, Leo, "China's Economic Modernization and the Ethnic Chinese in ASEAN: A Preliminary Study" in Leo Suryadinata, ed. Southeast Asian Chinese and China: the Politico-Economic Dimension (Singapore: Times Academic press, 1995), 193-215.

17. Suryadinata, Leo, ed. Ethnic Chinese as Southeast Asians (Singapore: ISEAS, 1997) - Leo 2.

18. Wickberg, Edgar, "Chinese organizations and Ethnicity in Southeast Asia and North America since 1945: A Comparative Analysis" in Jennifer Cushman and Wang Gungwu, eds. Changing Identities of the Southeast Asian Chinese since World War II (Hong Kong: Hong Kong University Press, 1988), 303-318.

Economic Security & Chinese Migration to the Russian Far East

Chapter 8

Economic Security & Chinese Migration to the Russian Far East

Elizabeth Wishnick

Introduction

Over the past decade, Russian and Chinese leaders have succeeded in putting the history of past conflicts behind them and forging a partnership based on common foreign policy and economic interests. Nevertheless, adverse demographic and economic trends in the Russian Far East have prompted Russian officials on the national and regional levels, as well as public levels in these areas, to describe Chinese migration as a threat to the integrity of the Russian state. For China, however, migration is conceived as an economic security issue, and Chinese leaders and scholars consistently downplay Russian concerns over the potential geopolitical consequences of Chinese migration to the Russian Far East. This paper examines the interrelationship among globalization, migration, and economic security, and focuses on the political, economic, and social factors promoting Chinese migration to the Russian Far East.

Globalization, Migration, and Economic Security

The process of globalization transforms social relations and transactions by "generating transcontinental or interregional flows and networks of activity, interaction, and the exercise of power."[1] Globalization has uneven distributive effects, however, and not all communities have the same degree of access to or involvement in global networks.[2] Instead of promoting integration, globalization may also serve to highlight economic disparities within countries and accentuate areas of conflict among them. This is because, as James Rosenau asserts, globalization is a complex process that may lead to fragmentation as well as integration, or even to both simultaneously, a dynamic he terms "fragmegration."[3]

Rosenau further notes that globalization may not be the dominant force in a particular community and points to the equal importance of processes of localization. Global migration flows, for example, may promote a global division of labor, but localization may give rise to calls for protectionist economic measures by "resistant locals."[4] Saskia Sassen argues conversely that the process of migration itself exemplifies the tension between globalization and localization, as migrants represent localized elements, remaining rooted in networks and retaining their ties to their home communities, while taking up residence in cities where elites view themselves as cosmopolitan or global.[5]

Despite the rapid expansion of global and interregional labor flows, nation-states still play an important role in regulating migration, particularly since global governance in this area is relatively undeveloped.[6] Typically receiving states seek to limit migration, though this is very difficult, and regulation, to be effective, needs to be combined with labor policy.[7] Communities have different reactions to migrant labor flows: some may seek to regularize illegal migration to minimize associated social problems, while others opt for punitive measures to deter would-be illegals from entering and competing with locals for jobs.[8] While migrants may create jobs by opening new businesses, for example, recipient communities may perceive the newcomers as a threat to their livelihoods. Sending states, on the other hand, focus on increasing access to employment opportunities and the rights of migrant workers, especially family reunification. Thus migration may raise economic security concerns for both sending and receiving states.[9]

Economic security is a component of human security, a concept that emerged from the late Cold War era debates about the interconnection between development and national security. The 1994 UN Human Development Program elaborated a broad conception of human security, which included economic security (basic income), food security (access to food), health security (freedom from disease), environmental security (a non-degraded ecosystem), personal security (protection from physical violence and threats), community security (ability to pursue one's cultural identity), and political security (basic rights and freedoms). Although the concept of human security has been criticized for its excessive breadth, the main contribution of this approach has been to highlight the importance of the security of people and to shift the level of analysis in security studies from the nation-state to the individual.[10] Despite the efforts of political scientists to create distinct analytical categories, some phenomena, such as migration flows, defy such neat categorization. Migration may adversely affect the security of individuals (both of migrants and individuals in receiving states), communities (migrants' home communities and host societies), and states (through conflict between the migrants' home country and the host country.)[11]

Globalization and China

For China, globalization (*quanqiuhua*) is a relatively new concept, dating back to September 1996 when Foreign Minister Qian Qichen referred to it in his State of the World message as a new trend promoting greater international cooperation.[12] In Chinese usage, it has a purely economic meaning and refers to the increasing proliferation of global economic flows of goods, capital, and technology. While Western commentary focuses on the retreat of the state confronted with globalizing dynamics, Chinese scholars take the opposite stance, arguing that globalization enhances the need for state intervention, and that the state retains the capacity to regulate these flows (though not without some difficulty).[13] In effect the Chinese state is trying to "manage" globalization by trying to take advantage of opportunities to advance China's development, while controlling the direction of economic change and seeking to limit negative consequences, such as the accentuation of regional disparities.[14]

Instead of highlighting the denationalization of economic activity, Chinese discussions of globalization call attention to a network structure underlying globalization of economic flows.[15] This is partly self-descriptive, since Chinese business networks in East Asia have created a distinctive form of globalization in the region, rooted in the proliferation of small and medium-sized firms, family ties, and other personal relationships based on personal connections and mutual benefit (*guanxi*).[16] Some of the Russian concerns about Chinese migration patterns stem from the fear that opening Russian borders to Chinese labor cooperation is paving the way for the institutionalization of Chinese migrant networks within Russia that are established to serve the needs of the Chinese economy, to Russia's detriment.[17]

Chinese Labor Migration to the Russian Far East: Push and Pull Factors

Russian concerns about Chinese illegal immigration today are fueled by a perception of demographic pressure from China. By 2004, the Russian Far East had a population of 6.68 million that inhabited a territory of more than 6.2 million square kilometers, compared to 107 million Chinese who lived in the three Northeastern provinces (Heilongjiang, Jilin, and Liaoning) with a territory of 1.9 million square kilometers.

Due to the high cost of living and underemployment, the Russian Far East lost 7 percent of its population by the mid-1990s. Although the northern regions of the Russian Far East experienced the most substantial outflows, the population of Primorskii Krai and Khabarovskii Krai declined by 1.5 percent and 3.3 percent respectively.[18]

Province	Total Population	Natural Growth Rate
Heilongjiang	38,130,000	2.54%
Jilin	26,990,000	3.19%
Liaoning	42,030,000	1.34%
Total	107,150,000	

Source: China Statistical Yearbook (Beijing: China Statistics Press, 2003), p. 98.

Table 8.1: Population of the Chinese Northeast in 2002

While the Chinese Northeast is relatively less populated than central and southern China, it has been disproportionately affected by adverse economic trends. These three provinces hold just 8% of China's population, but receive 22% of the country's poverty relief.[19] Thus, according to Hu Angang, a renowned Chinese economist, layoffs from state-owned enterprises in the northeastern provinces are nearly twice the national average of 18.3%: 31.3% in Heilongjiang, 31.9% in Jilin, and 37.3% in Liaoning.[20] Considering that workers in state owned enterprises (SOE) account for more than 73% of industrial labor in the Chinese Northeast, the region faces severe unemployment and underemployment problems.[21] Moreover, food-producing regions such as Heilongjiang have also been adversely affected by China's entry into the World Trade Organization (WTO), as the province's key soy crop now faces competition.[22] Even prior to Chinese entry into the WTO, farmers saw continually diminishing revenues as prices for their products dropped by 22% from 1997-2000.[23]

With the number of new entrants into the urban workforce not peaking until 2005, Chinese Labor Minister Zhang Zuoji characterized the employment situation in the Northeast as "very grim."[24] It is very difficult to find accurate unemployment statistics, since they measure the number of jobless but do not include the large number of laid off (*xia gang*) workers, who, while still on the books, are not working and may not receive salaries or other benefits.

Looking at the issue from the other direction, Table 8.2 below shows the number of fully employed staff and workers in the three Northeastern capitals: Harbin, Changchun, and Shenyang. Beijing, Shanghai, and Guangzhou are included for comparative purposes to highlight the relatively lower levels of full-time employment in the Chinese Northeast. Guangzhou and Changchun have similar population figures, but the southern capital has nearly double the number of fully employed workers. While Harbin has three million more people than Guangzhou, the two have similar numbers of fully employed workers. Shenyang has half the population of Shanghai, but one-third the number of fully employed. There are more than two million more people in Beijing than in Harbin, but the Chinese capital has more than double the number of fully employed. Although one out of four Beijing residents is fully employed, approximately one out of every five in Harbin has a full-time job, and nearly one in seven for Changchun and Shenyang.

City (2002)	Total population	Number of Fully Employed Staff and Workers (2002)
Beijing	11.36 million	4.35 million
Changchun	7.12 million	910,000
Guangzhou	7.2 million	1.7 million
Harbin	9.48 million	1.73 million
Shanghai	13.34	2.92 million
Shenyang	6.88 million	1.1 million

Source: *China Statistical Yearbook* (Beijing: China Statistics Press, 2003), pp. 390-91.

Table 8.2: Full-time Employment in Selected Provincial Capitals

The author's July 2004 survey of 250 Chinese workers in Harbin (40) and three border cities in Heilongjiang province, Suifenhe (90), Dongning (60) and Heihe (60) who worked in the Russian Far East shows that unemployment was the primary factor that motivated respondents to seek employment there.

I was unemployed	49.2% (123)
My work unit sent me there	21.6% (54)
I was looking for a better job	16% (40)
The standard of living is higher in Russia	5.2% (13)
To marry a Russian	2.8% (7)
To become a Russian citizen	1.6% (4)
To emigrate to a third country	1.6% (4)
To buy property in Russia	1.2% (3)
To become a permanent resident of Russia	0.8% (2)

Table 8.3: Why Did You Go to the Russian Far East to Work?

Decreasing industrial employment opportunities in the Northeast and inadequate government compensation have already led to large-scale strikes. From March to April 2002, thousands of laid off (*xia gang*) workers in three Northeastern cities, namely Liaoyang (Liaoning province), Daqing (Heilongjiang province), and Fushun (Liaoning province), took to the streets to protest non-payment of wages and benefits.[25] Recognizing the economic situation as a threat to social stability, Chinese leaders now assert that revitalizing the Northeast is a key priority. After the strikes Prime Minister Wen Jiabao visited Daqing and Fuxun, and in early 2004 the Chinese leadership announced a new program to rejuvenate the northeastern industrial base, targeting key sectors.[26] At this writing, it remains unclear what impact the new program will have on the Chinese Northeast's substantial structural economic problems.

Chinese who work in the Russian Far East disproportionately come from the Chinese Northeast, primarily from the Heilongjiang province (62.4% of respondents from the July 2004 survey, compared to 18% from Jilin, 17.2% from Liaoning, and 4% from Inner Mongolia, with 2.4% from other parts of China). Of the 250 surveyed, 76.4% rated their experience as either satisfactory (56%), positive overall despite problems (14%), or very positive (6.4%). Respondents rated good living conditions (37.6%) and salary (25.6%) as the most positive aspects of their experience in the Russian Far East.

The next two tables disclose the income of Chinese workers in RFE and their occupation.

Less than 1,000	3.6% (9)
1,000-3,000	36.4% (91)
3,000-5,000	37.2% (93)
5,000-8,000	6.8% (17)
8,000-10,000	0.4% (1)
More than 10,000	14.4% (36)
No answer	1.2% (3)

Table 8.4: What Was Your Monthly Salary in the Russian Far East? (in Chinese Yuan)

In particular, workers in construction, the restaurant business, and trade can earn significantly more money in the Russian Far East than at home.[27] Considering that China's minimum wage does not exceed 600 yuan per month,[28] most Chinese workers in the Russian Far East reported a much higher income, with 37.2% earning more than five times the Chinese minimum, and 14.4% exceeding that baseline tenfold.

Individual Trader	47.6% (119)
Businessperson	15.6% (39)
Construction worker	13.6% (34)
Restaurant worker	8.4% (21)
Forestry worker	4.4% (11)
Official	4% (10)
Student	2.4% (6)
Farmer	0.8% (2)
Other	3.2% (8)

Table 8.5: What Was Your Occupation?

Migration and the Security of the Russian Far East

Chinese policy-makers support legal labor cooperation with Russia because they contend that it takes advantage of the natural economic complementarities (*hubuxing*) between the two countries– Russia has land and resources, but suffers from a shortage of workers, while China lacks land and resources but has an oversupply of labor. Nevertheless, Chinese officials consistently deny Russian allegations that China is promoting illegal migration. During Jiang Zemin's first visit to Moscow in September 1994 at the height of Russian concern regarding Chinese migration to Russia, the Chinese leader defended China's policies in the border regions and stated that he hoped that Russia "would protect the legitimate rights and interests of Chinese citizens who are engaged in normal trade and other activities. Jiang stated his opposition to illegal migration and attributed concerns over the issue to the inadequate preparation on both sides to the opening of the border." [29] The Chinese leader noted that he and Russian President Boris Yeltsin had agreed to continue to develop regional cooperation despite these problems, "rather than giving up eating for fear of choking, as the Chinese saying goes."[30]

Despite reassurance by Jiang and subsequent efforts by other Chinese officials, Russian policy-makers on the national and regional level have continued to raise the Chinese migration issue. In reflection of its continuing importance to Sino-Russian bilateral relations, the July 2001 Agreement on Good Neighborliness, Friendship, and Cooperation between the Russian Federation and the People's Republic of China pledged that the two countries would combat illegal migration, promote stability in their border regions, and develop mutual trust in their regional relations.[31] Nevertheless, Chinese officials and scholars have sought to downplay Russian security concerns about the migration question.

Fueled by wildly inaccurate "guesstimates" of the numbers of Chinese in Russia, demographic determinism is a regular feature of Russian policy and scholarly analyses of China-Russia relations. Both national and regional media continually publish vastly inflated numbers of Chinese migrants in Russia–ranging from several hundred thousand to five million. According to estimates from a leading Russian specialist on Chinese migration, as of 2000 there were 250,000-450,000 Chinese in Russia, which included approximately 20,000-25,000 in Moscow and a maximum of 20,000 in each of two of the border regions, Khabarovsk Krai and in Primorskii Krai.[32]

In a March 23, 2004 article in *Izvestiia*, Sergei Prikhodko, the Russian president's deputy chief of administration stated that there are now no more than 150,000 to 200,000 Chinese living in Russia on a permanent basis and that the most recent census found an even smaller number–35,000. Prikhodko stated unequivocally that "there is no basis for saying that the government of the People's Republic of China (PRC) 'promotes' its citizens to resettle in Russia, especially not illegally."[33] The Russian Interior Ministry also supports this view–according to regional data, in 1994 just 64 percent of foreign visitors (predominantly Chinese) to Primorskii Krai left the region within the time allotted by their visas, but from 1997 to 2000, more than 99 percent left on schedule.[34]

Chinese officials and scholars on both the national and regional level question the motives of Russia in viewing Chinese migration to the Russian Far East as a threat. Chinese officials deny that Chinese migration constitutes a real problem either for Russia or Sino-Russian relations.[35] Many Chinese scholars attribute Russian concerns over Chinese migrants to the popularity of "China threat" views in the Russian Far East, particularly during gubernatorial elections.[36] According to one regional expert, Russian allegations of Chinese expansionism in the region stems from trends within Russia, such as nationalism, Eurocentrism, and concern with Russia's weak position in the Northeast Asian balance of economic power.[37] Reflecting some Chinese concern over the consequences of the post-9/11 improvement in Russian-American relations, another scholar attributed the continued Russian securitization of the migration issue to the influence of the discussion of the "China threat" in the U.S. According to this analysis, American "China threat" views were then transplanted to Russia and refocused on the imbalance in population between China and Russia, China's territorial claims, the lack of democracy in China, and the historical tendency for the most populous countries to be expansionist.[38] Other scholars are prepared to go only so far as to admit a problem of trust in Sino-Russian regional relations that is owed to the history of their border relations.[39]

Apart from rebutting Russian claims that Chinese migration poses a threat to the security of the Russian Far East, Chinese scholars object to using the term "migrants" (*yimin*) to refer to the Chinese working in the region and instead refer to these workers as overseas workers (*waipai laowu*).

Chinese labor export (*laowu shuchu*) originated as a component of the PRC's development assistance for Third World countries such as Bangladesh and Tanzania.[40] With the onset of economic reform in the 1980s, companies that obtained licenses to work on project overseas were given the right to hire Chinese project workers. There were 211 such firms by 1992.[41] Specialized labor supply firms began to develop in the 1990s and there were 48 by 2001. Some of these firms are subordinate to the Ministry of Economics and Trade while others are affiliated with provincial level labor ministries, but most are in the non-state sector. Many companies integrate labor export with other business activities, such as construction.[42] By 2001, more than 475,000 Chinese workers had participated in labor export programs since such opportunities began.[43] Most of these workers (approximately 400,000) were involved in projects operated by provincial level authorities or non-state companies. China's southern provinces provided the largest number of workers for overseas projects (Fujian accounted for 17% and Jiangsu 15.9%), compared to 17.6% for all three Northeastern provinces together (32,073 workers from Liaoning, 8% of total personnel sent overseas; 30,255 from Jilin, 7.5% of total; and 8,262 from Heilongjiang, or 2.1% of total).[44] Workers from Heilongjiang account for 65% of the Chinese contract laborers in the Russian Far East, with Jilin accounting for 10-25% and the rest coming from the Liaoning, Shandong, and Jiangxi provinces.[45]

Chinese policy-makers view labor exchanges as mutually beneficial, but fundamentally different approaches to the use of foreign workers have hindered labor cooperation. Although Japan, South Korea, and Russia all face varying degrees of worker shortages, they tend to have more closed immigration policies, which limit opportunities for China's surplus workforce.[46] For example, as a part of Sino-Russian discussions about Russia's entry into the WTO, China has urged Russian leaders to open the Russian market completely to Chinese labor and service providers as a part of Russia's accession, a move that has been met with opposition in Moscow.[47]

Moscow now allocates certain numbers of slots for foreign workers to each region. For example, in 2004 Primorskii Krai is entitled to bring in 15,000 foreign workers, though its labor needs are much greater. Despite being one of the first Chinese provinces to start sending workers to Russia, beginning in 1988, currently Heilongjiang province sends just 3,000-5,000 workers. These are mostly farmers and workers in construction and forestry who are sent to participate in projects in Amur Oblast, Khabarovsk Krai, and Birobidjan, though smaller numbers also go to Chita Oblast and Krasnoyarsk Krai.[48]

Chinese officials recognize that despite the need for foreign labor in the Russian Far East, these regions often prefer to bring in labor from North Korea, Vietnam, and the Commonwealth of Independent States (CIS) states.[49]

Chinese labor exports to Russia are relatively small and constitute less than 3% of China's total labor exports.[50] For example, Heilongjiang and Inner Mongolia saw their labor exports fall by an average of 10% from 1992 to 2001.[51] Since 2001, the number of Chinese contract workers being sent to Russia has declined because of a rise in the cost of obtaining required permits. Moreover, in an effort to promote regional cooperation, some Chinese companies are compromising with Russian firms seeking to use Russian labor and technology.[52]

Why do Russians speak of a Chinese migration threat since the numbers of Chinese participating in legal Chinese exchanges is small and these workers return home at the end of their contracts? There are two related problems here: 1) the quasi-legal visa status of Chinese, who circumvent Russian visa rules for overseas workers by traveling on tourist visas; and 2) the inadequate enforcement on both sides of the border of legal procedures for tourists.

Despite Russian and Chinese pledges to expand trade and economic ties between their two countries, business travel remains onerous and costly. After a brief interlude of visa-free travel, visas have been required for business travel since January 1, 1994 in response to the chaos of the "hot" period in Sino-Russian border trade in the early 1990s. Business visas for Chinese citizens wishing to travel to Russia cost 700 yuan ($84.50) for regular two-week processing and 1,200 yuan ($145) for a rush job. The only Russian consulate in Northeast China is in Shenyang in the Liaoning province. A personal interview is sometimes required, which adds to the cost and inconvenience of the application process. Consequently, it is much simpler and cheaper for a business person to join a tour group to Russia for 600-700 yuan and avoid all the bureaucracy involved in obtaining a business visa.[53] Even Chinese workers with contracts for particular projects end up joining tour groups to return to Russia if they have trouble extending their work visas in order to complete their projects.[54]

As a result, cross-border tourism has been expanding rapidly, which is a testimony to the growth of cross-border trade, since few of the participants are actually engaging in tourism. According to figures from the Heilongjiang provincial government, in 2002 there were 630,000 instances of border crossings by tourists traveling between the Heilongjiang province and Russia (largely to the Russian Far East), a 21% increase over 2001, while 2003 figures show a decline to 568,626 such crossings.[55] Chinese tourists from the Heilongjiang province accounted for 160,000 of the 630,000 crossings in 2002, or 25.3% of the total.[56] The Russian government is well aware that business travelers from China circumvent the business visa rules by joining tour groups and, in response, has tightened restrictions on tourism between Russia and China. Tour group participants are only allowed to stay a maximum of 30 days and are restricted to cities specified in advance on their tour agenda. Tour group leaders hold on to the passports of all group members and must present a list of all participants at entry and departure. If any tourist fails to return with the rest of the group, then Russian customs fines the tour organizer 5,000 rubles and the company risks losing its right to engage in border tourism.[57] As with Chinese tour groups to Southeast Asia, organizers who are concerned about tourists failing to return to China may charge a "deposit" of 15,000 yuan ($1,811), to be repaid upon return to China.[58]

Chinese officials attribute problems with tourists overstaying their visas on lax Russian enforcement of visa rules and corruption among the Russian police.[59]

Enforcement of stricter rules on tour groups varies wildly. Although Chinese tour groups face fines if they fail to return with all of their registered tourists, in practice the penalties incurred depend on the relationship between the tour group and Russian and Chinese authorities.[60] According to many Chinese business travelers, instead of requiring that the Chinese who overstay leave Russia immediately, local officials demand regular "payments," thereby creating a mutually beneficial criminal situation, allowing Chinese to remain beyond their allowed time limit while providing a source of regular illegal income for Russian officials. Chinese visitors who travel to Russia legally also complain of being harassed by Russian authorities, taken to the police station to show their documents, and charged "fees" as high as 500 rubles to be left alone, even if they hold valid passports and visas.[61]

Do Chinese who travel to the Russian Far East to work plan to settle there, as many Russians fear? The author's July 2004 survey shows a pattern of migratory labor–a majority of respondents (76%) stayed less than one year at a time and traveled back and forth to Russia over a five-year period (refer to Table 8.6).

1-3 Months	14.8%
4-6 Months	31.6%
7 Months-1 Year	29.6%
1-5 Years	15.6%
More Than Five Years	7.6%
No Answer	0.8%

Table 8.6: How Long Did You Stay in the Russian Far East?

While previous surveys of the Chinese working in Russia showed a population interested in putting down roots,[62] the author's July 2004 survey of Chinese in the Heilongjiang province shows a transient population, temporarily residing in Russia for work purposes, but retaining family and cultural ties to China. A majority of respondents remained tied to their families in China, as most respondents were married (79.2%) and, of those, only 3.6% lived in the Russian Far East with both spouse and children. A majority of respondents lived in temporary quarters in the Russian Far East–56.8% in dormitories and 14% in hotels–though some rented apartments (22%) or stayed with friends or relatives (4.4%), and a few (1.6%) owned housing. More than half (50.8%) reported little interaction with Russians and 69.2% admitted to limited Russian language ability.

Respondents sought work in Russia for a variety of economic reasons and many returned home for economic reasons as well (32.4% complained of too much competition from other Chinese in their industry; 23.2% completed their contract or project), although 14% cited visa problems as the primary factor in their return. Although a majority of respondents described their experience in Russia as satisfactory or positive, there was much less consensus about the desirability of a permanent move to the Russian Far East, as Table 8.7 shows.

Definitely	16.0%
A short term stay is sufficient	14.8%
Maybe	36.8%
Absolutely not	21.6%
Don't know	8.4%
No answer	2.4%

Table 8.7: If You Had the Opportunity, Would You Choose to Work in the Russian Far East Permanently?

These results reflect the many difficulties that Chinese workers experience during their stay in the Russian Far East, especially crime and corruption (refer to Table 8.8).

1. Problems with boss or colleague	5.6%
2. Difficulties with Russian officials	14.0%
3. Problems in relations with local Russians	4.8%
4. High cost of living	14.0%
5. Missed home/family	7.2%
6. Visa problems	23.6%
7. Corruption	26.0%
8. Victim of crime (robbery, attack, etc.)	34.0%
No answer	0.4%

Table 8.8: What was the most significant problem you encountered?[63]

Conclusion

Inadequate economic security in the Chinese Northeast creates a combination of push-and-pull factors that provide powerful economic incentives for Chinese residents of the Chinese Northeast to seek temporary employment in the Russian Far East, despite hardships. Residents in the Russian Far East, however, interpret the steps that Chinese traders take to enhance their economic security as a threat, creating a "security dilemma" with potentially adverse implications for Sino-Russian bilateral and regional relations.[64]

Although Chinese provincial level authorities and non-state labor export companies are largely responsible for sending Chinese workers to the Russian Far East, officials in Beijing have welcomed labor cooperation as a natural component of economic globalization and regional economic cooperation with the Russian Far East. However, the Chinese government's tendency to discount Russian security concerns has only served to increase distrust between the two countries, a factor that continues to stymie regional economic cooperation between the Chinese Northeast and the Russian Far East.

Chinese Migration to Russia: Road to Conflict or Harmony?

Chapter 9

Chinese Migration to Russia: Road to Conflict or Harmony?

Vladimir Portyakov

Introduction

Soon after the Russian Federation became an independent state in the wake of the collapse of the Soviet Union in late 1991, it found itself exposed to an influx of Chinese–a problem it had rarely been confronted with before. Later developments confirmed apprehensions that inbound migration could turn into a lasting nuisance instead of a temporary inconvenience. For more than a decade, the "new Chinese migration" to Russia has been a sore spot in the eyes of both national and local authorities, a major media issue, and a subject of debate for political scientists.

The issue of Chinese migration is regularly raised at Russian-Chinese talks at any level, including bilateral summits. It was discussed at several hearings in the State Duma (Parliament), the most memorable of which were held on April 15, 1994 and November 13, 2003 with regards to development prospects for the Russian Far East. Experts at the Moscow Center of the Carnegie Endowment for International Peace examined it at their *ad hoc* workshops devoted to migration in post-Soviet Russia and Russian-Chinese relations (between 1995 and 1999), and the issue was also brought up within the framework of the Moscow Migration Research Program (2001-2003) sponsored by the International Organization for Migration (IOM). One of the first international conferences on "new Chinese migration" to the Russian Far East and Siberia was convened by the School of International Affairs of the Georgia Institute of Technology in Atlanta, U.S.A., in December 1994. Underscoring the popularity of this theme in the Russian media is the fact that more than 12,000 documents and publications on

Chinese migration to Russia can be found today on the Russian language website www.rambler.ru alone.

Four Dimensions

The Chinese presence in Russia is undoubtedly a major social and political issue for the Russian society. Chinese migration to Russia, which shares a common 4,300 kilometers long border with China, has many dimensions. At least four of them—*demographic, economic, ethno-psychological, and geopolitical*—merit special attention. Chinese migration to Russia may be viewed today as a key factor both in Russian-Chinese relations in general as well as in a regional context; in direct relationship to development prospects in Siberia and the Russian Far East; from the perspective of the deteriorating demographic situation in Russia, and in the context of overall foreign immigration to Russia. This diversity of a Chinese migration phenomenon in Russia accounts for a relatively broad spectrum of views among government officials and experts about its favorable and adverse effects for Russia today, and even more so in the long run.

The geographical proximity of Russia and China and the history of their controversial relations make a significant proportion of the Russian population very sensitive, and at times apprehensive of their rapidly developing Asian neighbor. Caught in the middle of transition from the past to future, the Russian society's feelings are further hardened by syndromes and phobias of various kinds. Understandably, Russians' consciousness is burdened with plain fantasies and political over dramatization of Chinese migration, obstructing, in a way, the sober assessment of the problem and frustrating government efforts to come up with a viable policy.

How it All Began

For some fifteen years, after the last group of Chinese undergraduate and post-graduate students left the Soviet Union for home due to the "Cultural Revolution" in 1966, Russia did not see many Chinese crossing over to its side of the border. When, however, exchanges of trainees resumed in 1983 and Soviet-Chinese trade and economic ties were reactivated, followed up by the opening of previously closed Far Eastern areas to foreigners conducting short visits, a few Chinese did come over, but the number was nowhere near significant. After all, the Soviet-Chinese relations were not fully normalized until 1989 and more importantly, the government had undivided monopoly over foreign trade quite a discouraging factor for the would-be merchants and peddlers.

The situation turned around completely with the collapse of the Soviet Union. Russia's government policy to forge market reforms, liberalize foreign trade, and facilitate travel for Russian nationals and foreigners created a breeding ground that rapidly swelled the influx of Chinese. Economic common sense on both sides of the border was, however, the main factor behind the influx.

With domestic production in a deep slump and a slack in interregional industrial ties in Russia, its outlying regions and their businesses were compelled to look for closer relations with their foreign counterparts just to survive. Flourishing barter, an instinctive response to wholesale shortages and the plunging ruble, made China an almost ideal choice to supply consumer manufactures and food items (both quite scarce in Russia in the early 1990s) in exchange for minerals, chemical fertilizers, trucks, and much else, as the demand for such was very low on the domestic market. Shortages on the Russian side of the border came exactly at a time, in spring 1992 through mid-1993, when China was amidst a real economic boom set off by Deng Xiaoping's appeal to boost economic growth in the country. Aside from pushing up the demand for capital goods, the boom was also fueled by foreign trade privileges for the country's border regions. Barter benefited both sides immensely with swarms of petty traders and self-made adventurers joining in the scramble for easy profit, availing themselves of visa-free cross-border trade controls that were in force in 1992 and 1993. This period of Russia's recent history went down as the years of "shuttle" trade when outlines were sketched for the new Chinese migration to Russia that actually got underway in 1992 and 1993. That migration brand had economic and mostly commercial motivations. An overwhelming majority of Chinese, including those who carried papers of tourists or students, came to Russia to conduct trade. Russian authorities took a lenient view of the Chinese looking for jobs in their country. Their attitudes were reflected in a five-year bilateral agreement of August 19, 1992 that regulated Chinese employment in Russia. By all appearances, it strengthened the belief fostered in China since the Soviet days that Russia should use a large Chinese labor force for years ahead in order to guarantee the development of its Asian regions. Chinese journal *Dongbeiya Luntan* ("Northeast Asian Forum") published in Changchun estimated labor shortages in Siberia and Russia's Far Eastern areas at 50 to 80 million (No. 1, 1993, p. 55) against the total of 33 million people living to the east of the Ural Mountains in the early 1990s.

The actual number of job-seeking migrants from China was, however, significantly smaller. According to official statistics that were first compiled in 1994, there were 20,301 Chinese migrants in Russia in that year [1] and the experts claim that their number was approximately the same back in 1992 and 1993. As the migrants started arriving, their geographic preferences went for southern Far East and East Siberia (including the Primorie and Khabarovsk territories and the Amur, Irkutsk and Chita regions), as well as Moscow city and the surrounding region.

Phobias and Fears

The Russian society was poorly prepared psychologically for the influx of Chinese migrants. Indeed, apprehensions of a "creeping Chinese expansion" were voiced and, much to the discredit of the Chinese, fueled by the impression of high criminality of the migrants and their irresistible desire to stay, rightly or wrongly, in Russia forever. The Chinese migrants' evident reluctance to integrate into Russian society looked suspicious, too, even if it was largely caused by language problems (few migrants could speak Russian) and low ethnic tolerance among a great majority of common Russians.

Rumors of mounting numbers of Chinese in Russia, with some papers citing millions of migrants, prompted the country's authorities to tighten controls over guest workers in general and Chinese migrants in particular. On December 16, 1993, the Russian President issued a decree on foreign labor recruitment and employment in Russia, according to which the Federal Migration Service was authorized to issue permits for labor to be invited from other countries. On December 29, 1993, Russia and China signed an intergovernmental agreement that went into effect within a month's time for travel visas to be issued to their respective citizens without time limits attached. The agreement required an overwhelming majority of ordinary citizens in both countries to obtain visas, which actually was a departure from the old practice of visa-free travel either way, with the exception of tourist groups.

The years 1994 to 1999 saw a waning of interest among the Chinese in coming to work or conducting trade in Russia, and a decline in the number of Chinese migrants to Russia. In the author's view, this migration reversal is explained by economic causes. As Russian consumer markets were glutted, the niche for Chinese manufactures contracted. General demand for them also dropped, with the exception of the poorest segments of the Russian population under the competitive pressure from Turkish products in the country's western areas and South Korean textiles, as well as footwear in its Far Eastern areas. Besides, Russia's unsteady economic situation, which exploded into a dramatic debt default in August 1998, alarmed the Chinese small businesses and they started to withdraw from the Russian market. China's market, too, cooled toward Russian goods, such as trucks and rolled steel, or was limited by the authorities, who, for example, banned imports of nitrogen fertilizers.

Another factor was that, even though several Russian regions were experiencing a demand for Chinese builders and vegetable farmers, labor could hardly be recruited in China in any large numbers in a situation when unemployment was high and the economic situation was deteriorating in Russia. To illustrate, in the Primorie Territory the number of registered Chinese workers dropped from 8,349 in 1995 to 6,360 in 1999.

A discouraging factor was also the regular passport and visa checks of all foreigners, which included the Chinese, who lived in Russia. As a rule, checks resulted in penalties, such as fines or, in extreme cases, deportation from Russia. Again, in the Primorie Territory 6,640 Chinese nationals were deported and another 12,389 fined in 1995 and 2,500 and 8,000, respectively, in 1999. As some 80% of deportations involved Chinese tourists who came to Russia on visa-free tours and over-stayed, immigration service officers focused their attention on making sure that tourists went back home at the end of their tours. As a result, the number of Chinese visa-free tourists going back to China on-time from the Primorie Territory rose from 68% in 1995 to over 99% in 1997-1999 [2]

Overall, the Chinese migration problem lessened for Russia in the late 1990s. The migratory flow stabilized and thinned out significantly in several regions, such as Moscow, where fewer Chinese could be seen in the streets. Moreover, some experts believe that the Russian population gradually accepted the Chinese, whose presence was no longer felt as painfully as it had been years before.[3]

Chinese as Part of a Broader Picture

Chinese migration to Russia has acquired a number of previously unknown characteristics in the years since the resignation of President Yeltsin at the turn of 2000. First, Chinese immigration is now viewed, more than it was in the past, as an element, and not a significant one, of the general influx of foreign immigrants into Russia. According to V. Zorin, Chairman of the Government Migration Policy Commission, a total of eleven million foreigners came to Russia between 1989 and 2003, and out of them only five million left, which placed Russia third in world migration rankings after the U.S. and Germany. According to A. Chekalin, Russia's Deputy Interior Minister, who cited figures for late 2003, some 400,000 foreigners lived in Russia legally, another 3.5 million worked illegally, and another 1.5 million could not be classified under any definite category. [4] It was only natural for the Russian government to pay more attention to migratory flow regulation. The law, "Legal Status of Foreign Nationals in the Russian Federation," enacted on July 25, 2002, introduced migration cards for foreigners entering Russia, after filling out which foreigners were to be issued temporary permits for periods up to three years under annual job quotas to be approved by the national government for the country as a whole and for regions, subject to payment of federal duties at a rate of 4,000 rubles per worker. In 2003, the quota established for foreign entrants was established at 530,000, and, as reported by the Federal Migration Service, the quota for 2004 was 205,633, which includes 10,450 for the country's Far Eastern areas. [5]

Significant changes have occurred in the quality and professional orientations of Chinese migrants to Russia. Now more students (real, rather than "pseudo," as the case was in the early 1990s), Chinese medicine practitioners, and catering professionals are arriving. After a strategy was launched in China to stimulate national business to expand beyond the country's borders, there are also more business people, managers, and skilled labor in general. More Chinese are now seen in some Russian regions, including Moscow, than they were in the late 1990s.

Strategic Interaction and Bilateral Regulation

Russia and China continued to improve their good-neighbor relations. Their policy of "equitable trust-based partnership and strategic interaction" was mirrored fully in the Treaty of Good-Neighborliness, Friendship, and Cooperation between the Russian Federation and the People's Republic of China signed on July 16, 2001. Under Article 20 of the Treaty, the two countries committed themselves to "control illegal migration, including illegal movement of people across their territories." The legal framework for labor migration was reinforced significantly by the three-year intergovernmental agreement of November 3, 2000, "Temporary Employment of Citizens of the Russian Federation in the People's Republic of China and PRC Citizens in the Russian Federation," which came into force on February 5, 2001 and is automatically renewable every year. The agreement reaffirmed the good prospects both countries have for cooperation in the sphere of labor employment and their "mutual interest" in regulating labor movement from one country to the other.

It was important for Russia to have a provision built into the agreement that "the host country shall be guided, in deciding on the number of workers of the other Party to be recruited, by the demand for foreign labor in the national labor market." The agreement sets the duration of employment at one year, subject to extension for a maximum of one year upon the employer's motivated request. The parties declared their intention to set up a working group to address issues related to the implementation of this agreement.

Alarmists Persist

It would seem now that the obvious across-the-board improvement of bilateral relations between Russia and China and improvement in the legal regulation of labor migration, more specifically from China to Russia, were to dispel the air of apprehension and suspicion around Chinese migrants in Russia. That was not the case, however, and just the opposite, as a new spate of alarmist publications about a "potential threat" of Chinese demographic expansion in Russia's Asian part appeared in Russian print and electronic media in 2003. It was most likely triggered by the following developments. The first was that the 2002 Census in Russia left no doubt about the fact that the central and regional authorities had been unable to reverse the depopulation process in the Russian Far East, as the population of this vast region of 3.6 million square kilometers fell from 8 million in 1990 to 6.7 million in 2002. Across the border in China, 110 million people live in just three northeastern provinces. Some people in Russia voice concerns that this difference in demographic potentials would, sooner or later, tilt toward a greater balance. High economic growth rates and the national goal of quadrupling the country's GDP by 2020 have contributed to the image of China projected across the world as a huge steamroller capable of flattening all and everything on its way. Geopolitical dread of China has been augmented by common human fear of contact with the Chinese because of the severe acute respiratory syndrome (SARS) epidemic. Not least, these concerns were intensified by the behavior of the Chinese delegation at the negotiations on Russian accession to the World Trade Organization (WTO), who made an unimpeded access for the Chinese to the Russian labor market a condition for supporting Russia's bid to join the WTO. Meanwhile, Beijing continued to procrastinate about efficient interstate migration controls. Three years after the signing of an intergovernmental agreement on labor migration, the working group to be set up under the agreement had not yet been established. There is an increasing need for the working group as China has stepped up its already active exploitation of foreign labor markets. According to China's statistics, the number of Chinese citizens working in other countries had grown from 352,000 in 1998 to 488,000 in early 2002. [6]

There is only a single, and yet very revealing, proof of a certain official encouragement of labor migration in China, at least in the last few years. According to the Beijing-based *VIP Persons* journal, Luo Gan, a member of the Standing Committee of the 16th CPC Central Committee's Political Bureau, stressed many times that "practical policy measures are to be used to encourage and support the travel and settling of [China's] citizens abroad, of course, avoiding open propaganda of the emigration encouragement policy." With Luo Gan's backing, China's Ministry of Public Security authorized, by way of experiment, foreign passports to be issued to Shanghai residents on request, beginning September 1, 2002. The experiment, with passport formalities simplified significantly, is to be extended to all major and medium-size cities in China starting in 2005.[7]

How Many is Many?

The number of Chinese in Russia is still disputable. According to the 1989 Census figures, it was approximately 5,000 in the territory of present-day Russia, and 11,300 in the whole of what was formerly the U.S.S.R.[8] The 2002 Census in Russia estimated the number of Chinese living in Russia as 35,000, of whom 30,000 were Chinese citizens. [9] Obviously, the latest census could only cover a segment of the Chinese residing in Russia permanently (to remind, the census count was taken voluntarily), while other categories of China's citizens living in Russia, including actual or hypothetical illegal immigrants, tourists, and seasonal workers arriving for short periods clearly failed to make these statistics. A majority of experts estimate the total number of Chinese living at any time in Russia within the range of 200,000 to 450,000. It is not improbable that official statistics are accurate, and that the Federal Migration Service, now placed under the Interior Ministry, has exact figures about the number of Chinese in Russia now after the introduction of migration cards. Oleg Mironov, Russian Human Rights Ombudsman, mentioned exactly 311,000 Chinese in his 2001 report. Also, President V. Putin's adviser on foreign policy affairs Sergei Prihodko refers to 150,000-200,000 Chinese in Russia.[10]

It is another matter that some influential forces in the country tend to ignore statistics and experts' estimates and continue to play up the figures of millions of Chinese allegedly settled in Russia, or even in its Far Eastern areas only.

Another important consideration is that not all of the Chinese living in Russia at any time can be regarded as immigrants in the true sense of the term, that is, persons residing, or attempting to reside, permanently in Russia. Many new arrivals look at their employment or commerce in Russia as a starting point for opening or expanding their businesses in China.[11] Between 10% and 15% of Chinese in Russia would want to take out permits and invest their money in Russia. [12]

Chinese migrants in Russia differ widely across cultural, educational and property lines. These differences are almost completely ignored by ordinary Russians. Opinion polls show that the favorable image of the Chinese that existed in the U.S.S.R. in the 1950s almost reversed itself after two decades of interstate confrontation, and particularly after the "shock" of large-scale people-to-people contacts between Russian and Chinese citizens in the early half of the 1990s. It is noteworthy that Russian citizens living in the country's Far Eastern areas find the Chinese hardworking (83% of the respondents) and enterprising (34%), but, at the same time, consider them cunning (40%), aggressive (20%), and extremely tight-fisted–in fact, only 1% of the respondents called them "generous," while the figure for Russians was 65%. [13]

It is to be noted, however, that adverse feelings displayed towards "others" in today's Russia are by no means limited to the Chinese alone, as they also extend to an overwhelming majority of arrivals from across the borders, including ethnic Russians from other former Soviet republics (a factor that basically hinders practical implementation of all resettlement programs). Besides, adverse feelings toward the Chinese typically take abstract forms and do not involve discrimination in everyday circumstances. Moreover, Russia is steadily keen on elements of the Chinese culture, from *wushu* wrestling, *fengshui*, and Chinese characters on interior decorations to quotations from Confucius and Laozi that are quite popular in Russian society, all of which softens the largely unfavorable impression produced by the real Chinese—traders and laborers.

As for constant accusations of "criminality" and frequent aspersions the Russian media are hurling at Chinese migrants, the offenses committed by the Chinese (quite often with complicity of the Russians) can be largely explained by high levels of criminality in the country and many Russian citizens' low incomes, rather than by "Chinese specifics."

In general, it should be argued that despite all personal frictions and cultural differences, the Russians and the Chinese can live side-by-side quite happily. For now, Chinese expatriates, like other foreign construction workers or traders, remain a favorite target for illegal extortions by government officials of every rank and by racketeers—their own and Russian. This discourages Chinese migrants from having firm roots in Russia or breaking ties with their compatriot communities, which are naturally quite strong.

Official Policy

The Russian authorities' official attitude toward Chinese migrants can be described in the following terms. Guided by its interests in strengthening Russian-Chinese relations, the Kremlin has opted to keep a low profile on Chinese migrants and refrain from fanning tempers that flare up now and then in the Russian media over the issue. During private meetings with their Chinese counterparts, Russian officials however regularly voice, even if in subdued tones, their concern over the issue and their readiness to seek a mutually acceptable settlement. That is actually the underlying purpose of the proposed working group on migration.

The Russian authorities clearly realize that the country's growing trade and economic relations with China and the implementation of the Program for Multilateral Trade and Economic Cooperation among member countries of the Shanghai Cooperation Organization in the years up to 2020, adopted in September 2003, will cause the number of Chinese in Russia to rise, whether they like it or not. It is important to find acceptable legal formats to regulate migration and to correlate, on a regular basis, a possible increase in the number of Chinese in Russia with the demographic situation in the country and its various regions, and to measure current economic gains against long-term economic effects.

Judging by its policies, Moscow is well aware of the importance of a stable population in its Far Eastern areas and the significance of its economic development for the destiny of the Russian state. In this context, a definite clue can be found in the speech Russian President Putin made during his visit to Blagoveshchensk in summer 2000, "Unless we make real efforts to develop our Far Eastern areas soon, the ethnic Russian population will, within a few decades, have Japanese, Chinese or Korean as their native language." [14] It is to be hoped that a correct vision of the situation in legal terms will be followed by prompt steps to correct it fundamentally.

Schools of Thought

The following basic approaches can be identified in the analysis of Chinese migration by Russian scholars as a subject of their research:

1. *Sinological Approach* - As a rule, Russian Sinologists address the Chinese migration problem in the general context of Russian-Chinese interstate relations, placing much reliance on Chinese sources which they attempt to use in an unbiased and balanced analysis of the situation.

The monograph "Russia's China Reality" by V.G. Gelbras (Moscow University's Institute of Asian and African Studies) is based on the results of polls taken among groups of Chinese in Moscow and

Russia's Far Eastern areas. The author holds that Chinese migrants must be given "humane living conditions without encouraging formation of territorial enclaves with ethnic Chinese majorities in Russia." [15]

A.G. Larin (Institute for Far Eastern Studies of the Russian Academy of Sciences in Moscow), in his monograph "Chinese in Russia Yesterday and Today," gives most of his attention to "old Chinese migration" in imperial Russia, in Russia in the period of the revolutions and the civil war, and in the Soviet Union. A special note must be made, though, of the author's view of the Chinese migration problem in modern Russia as a phenomenon bound to grow in significance "with each passing year." [16]

S.N. Goncharov (Russian Foreign Ministry) offers a profound analysis of the situation of the Chinese in Moscow in his article "The Chinese in Russia: What Are They?" based on his study of materials published by Chinese expatriates in Moscow on their web sites.

V.V. Karlusov and A.P. Kudin put Chinese migration in Russia in the general context of globalization under way in China's economy, and V.Y. Portiakov views it from the perspective of Russian-Chinese trade and economic relations and integration of Russia's Far Eastern areas into the world economy.

2. *Regional Approach* - A research endeavor in the sphere of Chinese migration (A.S. Vashchuk, A.N. Bogaevskaya, E.L. Motrich, and G.B. Dudchenko), to an extent where it bears on any one Russian region (mostly on the country's Far Eastern areas), reveals its authors' good knowledge of local realities and heavy reliance on regional statistics. A special credit must be given to monographs by V.I. Diatlov (Irkutsk University), "Present-Day Merchant Minorities: A Factor of Stability or a Source of Conflicts? (Chinese and Caucasus Migrants in Irkutsk)" and by V.L. Larin (Vladivostok, Institute of the History, Archaeology, and Ethnography of Peoples in the Far East, Far Eastern Branch of the Russian Academy of Sciences), "China and the Russian Far East in the Early Half of the 1990s: Regional Crosscurrents." Both studies, like the authors' previous works, venture far beyond the formal regional boundaries and touch on a series of major issues of national policy on Chinese migration. As V.I. Diatlov writes, the goal of that

policy is "to bring about such a situation when as many and such Chinese come here (for long or short periods) as Russia, and not China or the Chinese, wants." [17] In V.L. Larin's opinion, who makes it a point of going through the standard ritual of chastising Moscow, or the federal center, for lack of an articulate policy on either its Far Eastern areas or China, Chinese migration is for certain politicians a "way to distract the population from the true causes of the economic crisis in the country's Far Eastern regions." [18]

3. *Demographic Approach* - A number of demographers, for example, Zh.A. Zayonchkovskaya (Economic Forecast Institute of the Russian Academy of Sciences), consider Chinese migration to Russia as a natural way to compensate, even if in part only, for increasing depopulation in the country (according to UN forecasts, Russia's population is expected to drop from 145 million today to 138 million in 2025, the most optimistic outlook of all now available). In Zh.A. Zayonchkovskaya's view, the number of Chinese in Russia could reach seven to ten million by the mid-21st century, to make them, if these forecasts come true, the second largest ethnic group after Russians in the country. Her strongest argument in favor of this option as a response to Russia's declining population is that unless the Chinese are brought in, the vast expanses of Siberia and the Russian Far East will never be fully settled. [19] Without going into detail, it must be said that far from finding broad-based public support, this option is runs into vigorous criticisms.

4. *Geopolitical Approach* - Certain political scientists in Russia regard Chinese migration, particularly in the long run, as a direct threat to national interests and even to Russia's territorial integrity, and as a factor likely to alter the world balance of power in China's favor. Materials appearing on Russian web sites have forceful titles such as "Will Russia Hold on to Its Far Eastern Territories?" (Lifshitz) or "Russia in 2010-2020: Less Siberia?" (Ivashchenko) In truth, these apprehensions are heightened by the balance of the two countries' economic potentials rapidly shifting in China's favor and the frequent references Chinese scholars make to this day, in a great majority of materials published in China on the history of Russian-Chinese

relations, to the one and a half million square kilometers China allegedly lost to Russia.

As a powerful "pro-globalization" lobby has emerged in Russia, some Russian political scientists are making public their positive views of a possible growth of Chinese migration. To the author's mind, these views mirror the interest the big private businesses, which includes its transnational branches, have in the construction of large infrastructure projects, above all oil and gas pipelines, in Russia's Asian part, the realization of which could require Chinese labor.

Brief Summary

To sum up briefly, the "new Chinese migration" in Russia is a complex and many-sided phenomenon that could have various repercussions for the recipient country and, for this reason, spawn diverging judgments. From the author's point of view, this phenomenon may be a source for both harmony and conflict in Russian-Chinese bilateral relations and, to some extent, for harmony and conflict in international relations in Northeast Asia as a whole. The constructive cooperation between Russia and China on migration and economic issues, a stronger social platform for their bilateral relations, as well as robust economic development of the Russian Far East and Northeast China could minimize "the conflict side" and enforce the harmonizing effect of Chinese migration into Russia. All real and imaginary fears and suspicions of Russian citizens regarding the "Chinese presence in Russia" can be dissolved by the show of genuine concern for the transformation of Siberia and the Far East into a really livable place.

Related Sources and Bibliography

1. Agreement Between the Government of the Russian Federation and the Government of the People's Republic of China on Temporary Employment of Citizens of the Russian Federation in the People's Republic of China and of Citizens of the People's Republic of China in the Russian Federation (effective February 5, 2001).

2. Alexeev, Mikhail (U.S.A.), "Chinese Migration and Challenges to Sovereignty in the Russian Far East: Preventive Monitoring with Opinion Surveys and Event Data Analysis," in Russia, China and Japan in Northeast Asia: Regional Cooperation in the 21st Century, Vladivostok, 2000, pp. 34-42.

3. Bogaevskaya, A.N., "Chinese Migration to Russia's Far East." http://www.crime.vl.ru/docs/books/book_4.htm.

4. Collection of Russian-Chinese Treaties. 1949-1999, Terra-Sport, Moscow, 1999.

5. Conference on Chinese Immigration in the Russian Far East (Compendium of Papers), 12-13 December, 1994, Georgia Institute of Technology, Atlanta, Georgia, USA.

6. Dudchenko, G.B., "Sectoral and Territorial Structure of Chinese Labor Migration in Russia Today," in The Russian Primorie and the People's Republic of China at the Turn of the Third Millennium: Present Day and Prospects of Cooperation, Vladivostok, 1999, pp. 44-47.

7. Goncharov, S., "Chinese in Russia: What Are They?" Far Eastern Affairs, Moscow, No. 4, 2003, pp. 13-31.

8. "Irregular Migration Through Russia's Eastern and Western Borders: The Primorie Territory and the Kaliningrad Region," in International Organization for Migration (IOM) Open Forum, Moscow Migration Research Program, Information Series, Issue 4, July 2002.

9. Ivashchenko, Oleg, "Russia in 2010-2020: Less Siberia?" Center for Strategic Studies of the Volga Federal District. http://www.antropotok.archipelag.ru/text/a116.htm (2002).

10. Karlusov, V.V., and Kudin, A.P., "China and Russia: Globalization and Migration," in Globalization of China's Economy, Moscow, 2003, pp. 339-353.

11. Larin, V.L., China and Russia's Far East in the Early Half of the 1990s: Regional Cooperation Problems, Dalnauka, Vladivostok, 1998.

12. Legal Status of Foreign Citizens in the Russian Federation, Federal Law No. 115-FZ, July 25, 2002.

13. Lifshitz, R.L., "Will Russia Hold on to Its Far Eastern Territories?," Report at a Conference in Khabarovsk, February 12-13, 2003. http://www.festrategy.ru/article.php?id=19.

14. Motrich, E.L., "Demographic Potential and Chinese Presence in Russia's Far East," Far Eastern Affairs, Moscow, No. 6, 2001, pp. 55-63.

15. Motrich, E.L., "Foreign Labor in the Khabarovsk Territory," in Russia, China and Japan in Northeast Asia: Regional Cooperation in the 21st Century, Vladivostok, 2000, pp. 60-67.

16. Nomokonov, V.A., "Transnational Organized Crime in Russia's Far East," Bulletin of the Far Eastern Branch of the Russian Academy of Sciences, Vladivostok, No. 2, 2002, pp. 103-110.

17. Portyakov, V., "Are Chinese Coming? Migration in Russia's Far East," International Affairs, Moscow, No. 2, 1996, pp. 79-86.

18. Portyakov, Vladimir, "Migration in Russia's Far East," in Migration to the Far East and Russia's Policy, Moscow Carnegie Center, Moscow, 1996, pp. 37-57.

19. Portyakov, Vladimir, Integration of Russia's Far East in the

World Economy, Politekonom, Moscow, No. 3-4, 1997, pp. 149-160.

20. Portyakov, Vladimir, "Russian-Chinese Trade and Chinese Migration into Russia," in Vladimir Portyakov, The People's Republic of China: Economic Policy of the 1990s, Institute for Far Eastern Studies, Moscow, 1999, pp. 174-182.

21. Vashchuk, A.S., et al., Ethno-Migrational Processes in Primorie in the 20th Century, Vladivostok, 2002.

22. Vitkovskaya, Galina, and Panarin, Sergei, eds., Migration and Security in Russia, Interdialect, Moscow, 2000.

23. Vitkovskaya, G., and Zayonchkovskaya, Z., "A New Stolypin Policy in Russia's Far East: Aspirations and Realities," http://www.eraa.ru/EraaRus/vostok.htm,1999.

Part Four
The Diaspora in Russia's Security Strategy

Managing the Ethno-Strategic Security Implications of Russia's Demographic Crisis

Chapter 10

Managing the Ethno-Strategic Security Implications of Russia's Demographic Crisis

Graeme P. Herd

Introduction: Demographic Decline & Conflict

Although some studies have focussed on the impact of demographic variables on state power and the relationship between population change and conflict,[1] little attention has been paid to the link between demographic decline and migration patterns within the Russian Federation. With the publication of the official preliminary results of Russia's first national population census in post-Soviet history that took place from October 9th through October 16th, 2002, the question of how to manage the foreign and security policy implications of such decline can be addressed.

The Russian October 2002 Census results have confirmed trends already anticipated by many demographers. According to the U.S. Census Bureau, Russia's population is set to fall annually by 400,000 and therefore by ten million by 2025.[2] The UNDP calculates the annual decline at 840,000 or a total decline of twenty one million by 2025.[3] The Russian population dropped by 4,371,200 between 1992 and 2002 – "the natural decline of the population was 7,399,800, a decline of 5% from the 1989 to the 2002 census: this figure consisted of 20,540,000 births and 27,939,800 deaths."[4] The Russian population is declining fast, by an estimated 700,000 to 750,000 people each year. While birth rates have been consistently falling for more than two decades, a number of longer-term factors, not least poor health conditions, have brought about an increase in the death rate.[5] As a result, in 2000 the number of deaths exceeded the number of births – for every ten babies born as many as seventeen Russians die.[6] If these tendencies were not inverted or offset by mass immigration, by 2050 the Russian population would have fallen by fifty million, taking it below 100 million.[7][7]

Given the scale of the population decline, it is hardly surprising that Russian political elites have begun to frame the issue in terms of its rising strategic importance for national security, which has prompted observers to predict in apocalyptic terms an "extraordinary demographic crisis" and a "demographic catastrophe." Nationalists in the State Duma have lamented the "fact" that "the Russian nation is in a state of collapse, with unpredicted consequences for its survival and historical life."[8] Concern has also been voiced within the presidential administration. Risks of depopulation have been rated so high that the latest concept of national security, adopted in January 2000, devotes a paragraph to the demographic situation in the country.[9] Indeed, President Putin in his first address to the Federal Assembly of the Russian Federation noted that demographic decline was first amongst 16 "acute national problems":

> With each passing year, we citizens of Russia are becoming fewer and fewer in number. For several years now, the country's population has been decreasing by an average of 750,000 annually. If one believes the long-term forecasts, [...] 15 years from now Russia could have 22 million fewer citizens. If this trend continues, Russia's survival as a nation, as a people, will be in jeopardy. We are really threatened with the prospect of wasting away as a nation. The demographic situation today is one of the alarming problems.[10]

Migration to Russia of ethnic Russians and Russian-speaking populations from outside the Russian Federation fails to compensate for the natural decrease in the population. The general characteristics of population decline, such as changes in internal migration patterns with the depopulation of the Far North and Far East, the internal migration flow from rural to urban settings, differential birth and death rates between different religious and ethnic communities (not least between Slavic regions and "ethnic homelands"),[11] the aging nature of the population and changing sex balance and the devastation caused by HIV/AIDS are well understood with the demography community and amongst political geographers. The 2002 Census reveals that the Russian population has declined from 81.3% to 79.8% of the population of Russia, the lowest since the first Soviet census of 1926.[12] As Russia is an extremely large and diverse country, one can expect that there will be a regional aspect to almost every socio-economic, political and military issue. However, little research has assessed the implications of changes in demographic variables, such as population size, growth, distribution and composition, and how these changes influence the emergence of real or perceived threats to a state's stability and national security, not least its exposure to ethno-strategic vulnerabilities through minority separatism.

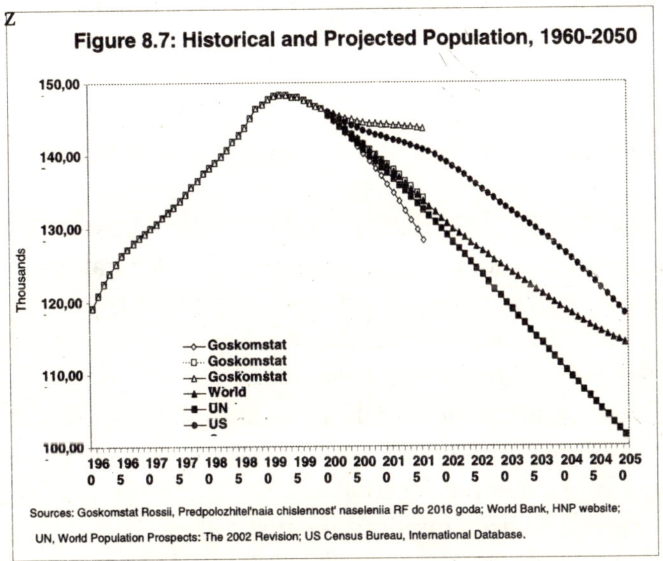

Figure 10.1: Historical and Projected Population, 1960-2050

Identifying Ethno-Strategic Implications of Demographic Decline

It should be acknowledged from the outset that there are degrees of "separatism" apparent within the Federation, not all of which lead inexorably to secessionism, and not all of which weaken the integrity of the Federation. Analysts have noted political, legal, economic and fiscal separatism, military fragmentation, and provincial particularism that accompanied the decentralization of state power during the Yeltsin presidencies (1991-2000).[13] However, ethnonationalist minority separatism projects proved unsuccessful, with the partial exception of Chechnya between 1996 and 1999. On the basis of the Chechen experience, it was generally accepted that for minority separatist movements to successfully secede from the Federation and emerge as independent sovereign entities, certain preconditions had to be met: the ethnic group must form a majority upon the territory which they live, the territory ideally had a history of independent statehood, shared a border with neighbouring states and had a charismatic leader able to mobilise the population around a separatist ideology that rested upon a set of shared grievances and the expected benefits of independence.

Political Security Implications: Minority Separatism Aspects

The demographic decline raises a series of issues concerning the political security and stability of the Russian federal system. These are related not only to potential changes in voter preference, the political weight of constituent parts and the viability and sustainability of the current federal architecture, but also to the rise of gender politics and the potential politicisation of Islam within Russia. The economic security implications include the increasing difficulty in capacity building, a labour reserve shortfall, the economic costs of HIV/AIDS and the societal security implications that follow.

Can one be more conclusive about demographic-induced changes to the political geography of the Federation? Vladimir Kontorovich has noted that "the political implications of uneven population distribution are not well understood."[14] On the basis of the results of pan-Federation presidential and parliamentary elections, an electoral geography is emerging with certain features. Voting turnout and orientation is partially influenced by the age composition of the regions' populations. A left-leaning red belt of regions stretching from southwest to the southern portions of the country with high aging populations (pensioners with high voter turn out discipline) voted for the Communist Party in the 2000 presidential elections and to a lesser extent in 2004.[15] Also, over 50% of the registered voters that comprise the total electorate reside in twenty of the most populous regions, which is a radical change to the political geography and hence the political security implications of demographic change for the Russian Federation are not as important as one might at first suppose. Whilst not radically impacting the political geography of the Federation, the demographic decline does however increase the politico-military security importance of sparsely populated border regions to the centre. Indeed, the role and significance of the state border increases in significance as global stocks of raw hydrocarbons, drinking water and agricultural land diminish and the world's population grows.[16]

Throughout the Yeltsin and Putin presidencies the Russian state has propagated a civic, not ethnic, national identity project, in an effort to build *Rossiyanin* (all the citizens of Russia) not *Russkiy* ("ethnic Russians"). In fact, it is the conservatives (communists, agrarians, and LDPR) who have played the ethno-national card, rather than the executive-backed "parties of power." Nevertheless, it is possible that demographic decline and the gradual consolidation of an ethnic Russian population in Russia's European core and the decrease of the proportion of ethnic Russians in non-Russian ethnic republics, especially those where titular nationalities are predominantly Islamic, could increase pressure to re-centralize state power and allow "the politics of Putinism" to become more associated with Russian ethno-centrism.

The advent of the second Chechen campaign, the perceived threat of "Islamic terrorism," and the reduction of the sovereignty of Russia's ethnic republics have all provided an environment within which the re-centralization of state power has greater legitimacy. Moreover, the adoption of a set of specific policies, namely the creation of the Federal District structure, the association of State and the Orthodox Church and Putin's calls for a national idea based on the "traditional values" of the Russians - patriotism and social solidarity (*sobornost*) – has established a clear link between Putinism and Russian ethno-centrism.[17] If this phenomenon emerges, then the variable geometry of demographic decline (migration from ethnic republics on the periphery to the European core and differential birth and death rates) will exacerbate such initiatives.

This risk is particularly relevant in view of Russia's Muslim minority status, an extremely controversial topic of debate in today's Russia, with the very definition of Muslim hard to determine: what constitutes someone of Islamic faith? Despite the ambiguities associated with these calculations, it is generally accepted that in the late Soviet period Muslims constituted 40% of the total population of the USSR and were projected to cross the 50% threshold by 2005. A more accurate figure for the number of Russian Muslims will be revealed by the 2002 Census, but it is currently estimated that their number ranges between 20 to 30 million, approximately 15-20% of the total population of the Russian Federation.[18] One analyst, Dmitry Glinski, has argued that the state imposition of Orthodoxy and political uniformity from above, combined with an increasing assertiveness in Islamic society from below, will exacerbate the current political asymmetry between the size of Russia's Muslim minority and its representation in the national elite.[19] This in turn could encourage "radicalism and the use of undemocratic means in political struggle on the part of Russia's Muslims." In the current context of a war against Chechnya and Russia's support for the global war on terror (GWOT), a return to pre-Soviet Russo-ethnocentrism would have international repercussions.[20]

Economic Security Implications: Minority Separatism Aspects

Russia adopted an economic security concept in 1996, but it was outdated by 2002, failing to take into account the impact of the demographic changes upon the Russian economy. Although the economic security implications of uneven population distribution and net population decline are not yet well understood, President Putin has noted that the core factors that affect the Russian economy – the demographic situation, illegal migration, border and customs issues and threats to the energy and transport systems - had rapidly changed in the new century.[21] Analysts have already highlighted the current impact of the demographic decline on "capacity deepening" amongst the labour force (building on existing skills in order to increase productivity) and the reduction in savings and rates of investment reinforces the decline in economic growth.[22] Despite the fact that the population decline is predicted and to an extent can be factored into long-term economic planning, it is extremely difficult to calculate the impact of an apparent reduction in savings, rates of investment and economic growth on the economic security of Russia because the nature of the decline – who dies and when – is unpredictable and non-linear and therefore imposes variable economic costs.[23]

Russia faces the problem of widespread elderly poverty. With male life expectancy at 58, the Russian state is relieved from paying a consistent percentage of its pension bill. Nonetheless, because of a chronic lack of resources, the social safety net is still unable to fulfil its obligations. To address the crisis of the pension system, Prime Minister Mikhail Kasyanov announced plans to launch a 50-year pension reform, which would take into account the country's current and expected demographic and economic situation.[24] As Kasyanov put it, the major shortcoming of the Russian pension system is that it was "designed for an age structure of a population of a nation that no longer exists, where population pressures would not have been great, but whose pension mandates cannot now be easily changed."[25]

As the First Deputy Economic Development and Trade Minister Ivan Materov, noted, the development of the demographic situation is "an important component of the forecast" of Russia's socio-economic development in the period between 2002 and 2004. Despite the fact that the average annual population of Russia is expected to decrease by 1.5m in the period between 2002 and 2004 (142.2m), it is unlikely that the anticipated rates of economic growth will support an adequate increase in the employment rates.[26] The workforce supply will probably continue to exceed the demand and the dependency ratio – the ratio of persons not of working age ("dependants") to those of working age – will actually decrease from 42% to 36% of the population. This creates a small window of opportunity for the Russian government to reform the pensions system as the young born in the 1980s baby boom will only join the job market in the next few years, swelling the workforce by 1.0 million.[27]

However, in the longer-term, the dependency ratio will swing in the other direction by 2006-2010, resulting in the diversion of greater state finance towards the elderly and less upon the economy or military. According to Anatoly Sudoplatov: "These demographic trends block any attempts to raise the standard of living in Russia, because the government has to allocate such large sums of money to look after the ageing and sick population."[28] In other words:

> Russia may face particularly acute problems in supporting its elderly when the large number of persons born in the 1950s leaves the workforce and is replaced by a much smaller number of persons born in the 1990s. Such problems may be overcome by increasing capital, and thereby productivity per worker, but contraction of the Russian economy may prevent this option.[29]

The demographic crisis also impacts the economic health of the state through the growing HIV epidemic, which develops into full-blown AIDS 8-10 years after the infection is contracted. Most HIV-infected people are in the 15 to 30 age group and may die without having healthy children. Aware that AIDS is a strong demographic and geopolitical factor, the government has allocated R165m for the federal anti-AIDS programme in 2002. The programme includes treatment, prevention, examination and even social aid for those infected with HIV. According to the estimates of a noted AIDS expert, Professor Pokrovskiy, the treatment of one patient costs 10,000 dollars a year. Budget funds will be enough to treat only 500 to 600 people, while there are fears that the government will be unable to foot the 75m dollar bill required to fulfil the HIV and AIDS prevention programme.[30]

As well as facing a shortfall in the labour reserves, Russia faces an economic security dilemma in some parts of the Federation. Sergey Mironov, the head of Russia's Federation Council highlights the critical importance of the Asia-Pacific region to Russian economic growth and modernization, stating that this region accounts for 55% of the world's GDP and 60% of the global market.[31] If moderate economic growth is recorded in the Russian Far East, for example, then it is calculated that this will increase the mobility of the population and allow the current deferred migrants to leave for European Russia. It is economic stagnation that keeps the emigration at current levels and only a massive economic resurgence would return incentives, subsidises and benefits to workers in these peripheral regions, thus increasing immigration.

Societal Security Implications: Migration and Minority Separatism Aspects

As opportunities for repatriation decline, immigration from the countries of the "far abroad" becomes increasingly important as a source of population growth. However, the fact that "foreign" immigration is a relatively new phenomenon for Russia makes it difficult for ordinary citizens and the state authorities to adjust to it.

By 2050, the proportion of immigrants in the labour reserves will rise at least to 20%, while some sociologists have forecasted that 7-10m Chinese will live in the Russian Federation. Zhanna Zayonchkovskaya, head of the population migration laboratory at the Russian Science Academy's Institute of Economic Forecasting, for example, has predicted that by 2050, the Chinese in Russia may become the second largest ethnic group after ethnic Russians. Chinese will constitute an inalienable component of the Russian work force, capable of reviving the national sector of services, construction, municipal transport, and agriculture.[32] However, on the basis of the current Chinese population in the Russian Far East (RFE), these assessments appear exaggerated. The most realistic assessment is that no more than about 300,000 Chinese migrants can be found in the RFE on any given day, and around 90 or so percent of them are most likely to be transient, temporary cross-border migrants.[33] The issue of Chinese migration can easily be politicized, and in the context of the de-Europeanization of the RFE as "ethnic Russians" migrate westwards, it is highly likely that the economic role of Chinese migrants will increasingly be framed within political and societal security contexts by the centre.

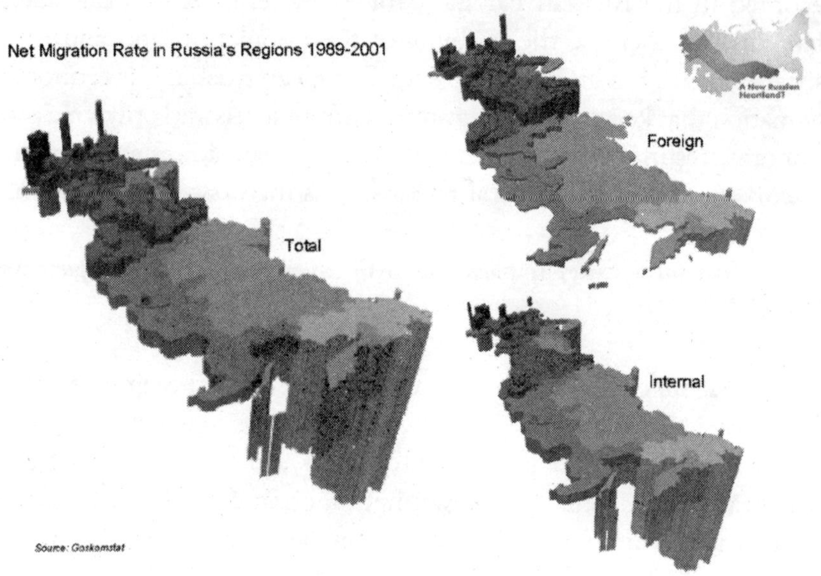

Figure 10.2: Net Migration Rate in Russia's Regions 1989-2001

A special task force was established that helped elaborate a Concept of Demographic Development in the Russian Federation in the period up to 2015, and was finally approved in 2001. The Concept focuses primarily on improving the birth rate, giving families an incentive to have children and improve the general health of the population.[34] However, some demographic experts, such as Anatolii Vishnevskii, appear to consider it unlikely that the demographic decline can be offset by a natural increase in birth rate in the immediate future. In their view, an increase in immigration remains the only possibility to guarantee the "preservation or increase of [Russia's] demographic potential in terms of its natural growth." Replacement migration is calculated in the region as at least 500,000 immigrants every year. It is estimated that if these levels are maintained, the size of the population could return to its 1990s level by the first decade of the 21st century and could keep increasing steadily.[35]

The debate over migration and the type of measures adopted to regularize migration flows reveal a deep uneasiness among the Russian public and elite opinion. As the very existence of Russia, its culture and identity are considered at risk as a result of the demographic decline, the stimulation of immigration has proved to be a sensitive and controversial policy, one that some have argued could disperse rather than consolidate Russian national heritage. Responding to divergent remits and responsibilities, different Ministries have proposed policies that appear conflicting and self-defeating. As a *Noviye Izvestiya* noted:

> [...] The minister [of Internal Affairs] has some strange ideas about how to save [the demographic situation of the country]; by this logic, Russia should be fenced off with an iron curtain from all those people outside who are willing to go to any lengths to obtain Russian citizenship. In other words, better we should die out slowly and quietly among our own than augment our ranks with foreigners. Our skinheads, Nazis and other fascist-minded citizens can relax: the Internal Affair Ministry itself is taking up their slogan 'Russia for Russians.'[36]

In the late 1990s, the focus of migration shifted from the repatriation of the Russian Diaspora in the Commonwealth of Independent States (CIS) to the arrival of economic migrants and refugees from both CIS countries and countries of the so-called "far abroad". Between the 1989 Census and the October 2002 Census, Russia absorbed a net influx of migrants – a total net addition of 5.5m was recorded.[37] Throughout the 1990s, the inflow of migrants played a crucial role in balancing out the demographic decline in Russia, but with the stabilization of economic and political conditions in many CIS and Baltic states, the number of migrants has fallen. In the period of 1995 to 1999, migration compensated for only 45% of the population decrease, and in 2000 only 25%.[38] Estimates of the Ministry of National and Migration Policies claim that to keep the country's population at 140 million, between 700,000 and 1,000,000 immigrants need to be attracted annually, while in 2001 only 380,000 people moved to

Russia.[39] The diaspora population has fallen from 25.2 million in 1989 to 18.2 million according to the first round of censuses in post-Soviet space, reflecting partly a real decline and also a decline in those that identify themselves as "Russian".[40]

In the migration debate, public attention has been focused on the categories of newcomers that would be considered "acceptable." While many seem to agree that Russia should set in place more advantageous conditions to attract "compatriots" living in the CIS countries, the very definition of compatriots is highly contested: compatriot status carries with it the right to Russian citizenship and financial support.[41] There are four categories of migrants whose presence in Russia is looked at with anxiety. A number of Chinese, Vietnamese and Korean immigrants were invited to work in Russia during the 1980s and stayed in the country even after their contracts expired. Afghan, Somali and Ethiopian refugees reached Russia after the country signed the 1951 UN Convention on Refugees and its supplementary 1967 protocol in 1992. Forced migrants and internally displaced persons from the conflict-torn Caucasus have also become more visible in the streets and the markets of the big cities. Finally, over the last decade, Russia has become an increasingly attractive destination for "transit migrants" on their way to Western countries. While the number of illegal immigrants is visibly high, Russian statistics, ranging from 700,000 to 15,000,000, seem to be unable to provide reliable data of the phenomenon.[42]

A rising number of well-documented racist attacks to individuals of Caucasian and Central Asian origin and an increasing emphasis placed by the authorities upon the illegal aspects of immigration are testimonial of the growing discomfort around the issue of migration.[43] Experts note the emergence of forms of "migrantophobia" that paradoxically appears to be strongest among members of the public seldom in contact with immigrants. Increased societal tension and the development of cultural stereotypes by local and national authorities eager to gather the political rewards of chauvinism are equally responsible for an inconsistent policy line increasingly geared towards a discriminatory understanding of immigration.

Demography and Minority Separatism: Policy Recommendations

Russia population is falling and this demographic decline has induced interlinked instabilities in the political, economic and societal spheres, which the state has begun to address. *Population migration* has increased minority separatism in that the majority ethnic Russian Europeanised population is physically becoming more separated from the Eurasian minority periphery population, and in this instance "separation" can be measured in terms of ethnicity, age and wealth. This internal migration and population decline has foreign and security policy aspects, not least the management within bilateral relations of competition between Russia, Ukraine and Kazakhstan for the desirable but diminishing diasporan population, and the emphasis that population decline and citizenship places upon the management of intractable separatist projects on Russia's borders. It also refocuses attention on the continued sustainability of an EU and China strategic partnership in the face *of* "brain drain" and Schengen border tightening as well as the perceived threat of Chinese colonization of the Russian Far East.

Demographic decline and the security challenges it poses has promoted responses from the centre in terms of policy initiatives designed to manage the current decline and control the re-distribution of the population within the Federation. This includes the elaboration of a migration policy, a demographic concept and policy, and a reformulation of a citizenship policy. Because these policies are in part contradictory, their implementation will increasingly reveal the relative effectiveness (strengths, weaknesses, limitations) of federal power under Putin and Putin's priorities during his first- and second- term presidencies (2000-2008).

As the threats to the country's security posed by the demographic crisis are so extensive and profound, one would have expected a more vigorous governmental intervention to combat the population decline, by both providing support to a natural population growth (aiming at increasing fertility or curtailing mortality) or by encouraging immigration. Although both policies have been adopted, on current evidence, Russia's demographic decline has elicited more

rhetorical and contradictory than practical and coherent responses from the state. It appears that Russia's reformulated citizenship law places restrictions on the inflow of migrants to the Russian labour force deemed necessary to stimulate economic growth. Rather than these brakes and filters reflecting a understanding that economic growth cannot occur at the expense of a breakdown of political stability or a societal identify which might result in a rise in ethnic or religious tensions within the Federation, the state has adopted a restrictive migration policy that the Russian Prime Minister himself has admitted runs counter to Russia's national interests. At present, the state lacks the political will to deploy
adequate economic resources towards managing the population decline and regional elites, and powerful bureaucratic interests appear to be hijacking migration and demographic policies to further their own power bases and institutional interests.

Over the second term of the Putin presidency a coherent population policy will have to emerge. This policy must untangle the dilemmas associated with promoting economic growth whilst maintaining political stability and societal security. President Putin ought to continue to formulate demographic policy in terms of national security concerns and strategic threats to Russia, in order to forge a consensus at elite, federal, and expert levels on the necessity of funding natural population growth and less restrictive immigration. This consensus should allow the elite to overcome public alarm and the special interests of regional elites that favour opposing immigration and bureaucracies, which want to own the process rather than implement the policies. The short-term erosion of Putin's popularity and the political instability that such a project entails are easily offset by the longer-term gains made through the sustainability of the Federation and the reduction of ethno-strategic vulnerability as well as the resultant diminution of minority separatism tendencies.

Diasporas in Russia's Security Strategy

Chapter 11

Diasporas in Russia's Security Strategy[1]

Igor Zevelev

Introduction

From a Great Power strategy perspective, diasporas in neighboring states may be viewed from two major perspectives. First, diasporas may be considered an instrument of international influence and power politics. Second, they may be perceived as an important factor in identity construction and nation-building. Both perspectives suggest that under certain circumstances, a Great Power with significant diasporas in neighboring states may easily undermine regional and even global security. This may happen if a Great Power destabilizes the neighbor-states by claiming the loyalty of part of their populations and assertively influencing their politics and policies. Another even more threatening scenario is a Great Power's nation-building on an ethnic basis and an attempt to redraw the borders in the region.

Russia claims to be a Great Power and it has a twenty million-plus diaspora of ethnic Russians in neighboring states. The term "diaspora" has become popular in Russia since the mid-1990s.[2] It has been often used together with or instead of such terms as "Russians and Russian-speakers" or "compatriots," which appeared in political and theoretical discourse earlier in 1991-1994. There was the re-conceptualization of large groups of the population in neighboring states as the Russian Diaspora reflected the attempt to emphasize the connection of these people to Russia proper, a collective memory and myth about common homeland, a traumatic experience and a troubled relationship with host societies.

It took several years before diaspora issues made their way to the official security discourse in Russia. The National Security Concept of the Russian Federation of 1997, the first comprehensive official document of this kind in post-Soviet Russia, was silent about Russian citizens or compatriots in neighboring states.[3] Russia's National Security Concept adopted by presidential decree on January 10, 2000 stated that the foreign policy of the Russian Federation should be designed, among other purposes, "to protect the lawful rights and interests of Russian citizens abroad, through the use of political, economic and other measures."[4] The Military Doctrine of the Russian Federation, approved by a presidential decree dated April 21, 2000, went further and named discrimination and suppression of the rights, freedoms and legitimate interests of citizens of the Russian Federation in foreign countries among the main external threats.[5] The Foreign Policy Concept of July 2000 named not only the fate of Russian citizens, but also "compatriots" in the list of policy concerns.[6] The document specified that "the Russian Federation will seek the adequate ensuring of the rights and freedoms of compatriots in the states where they live permanently, maintain and develop all-round ties with them and their organizations."[7] The July 2000 documents are still in force, but in 2004 it was announced that work on a new Security Concept had started. The new document is expected to be finished in 2005 and it remains to be seen how it addresses issues related to Russian Diasporas. However, President Putin and other officials addressed the issue in major statements in 2000-2004 and this provides a good basis to analyze official attitudes.

All Russian official documents and policies, as well as the Russian discourse, suggest that Russian Diasporas in neighboring states are viewed first of all as people whom the Russian state has an obligation to protect. It is clear that policies of "protection" may constitute an instrument of influence in the post-Soviet space. For example, Putin justified Russian involvement in the Ukrainian elections and political crisis that evolved in the country in late 2004 by evoking the fact that many ethnic Russians live in Ukraine. He told Ukrainian President Kuchma:

> We are far from indifferent to what is happening in your country. Ethnic Russians make up 17 percent of Ukraine's population according to the official census results. I think that in reality the figure is much higher.

> Russian is spoken throughout Ukraine, both in the western and eastern regions. It is no exaggeration to say that every other Ukrainian family, if not more, has family and personal ties to Russia. We therefore take very seriously everything that is happening in Ukraine and have been following the events with great concern.[8]

Theoretical literature contains the concept of "securitization," meaning the transfer of some issues into the realm of national security, after which they begin to be viewed as challenges and threats.[9] Is there enough evidence to claim that Russia "securitized" the issues of the diasporas and made their protection one of the major goals of its security and foreign strategies? Assertive Russian policies towards its neighboring states, especially under President Putin, have become a matter of concern to many observers and policy-makers in the West. However, this article will claim that Russia has clearly chosen a civic identity for its nation-building project, and its actual use of the diasporas for power politics in the post-Soviet space has been minimal thus far. Is it Russia's political choice or are there "objective" cultural and historical factors that leave few options to policy-makers in Moscow but to "protect" their compatriots, mainly rhetorically? To answer these questions it is necessary to examine Russian strategy in the post-Soviet space, internal nation-state building, the nature of Russian Diasporas in neighboring states, and specific Russian policies aimed at the diasporas.

Russian Strategy in the Former Soviet Republics

The Russian vision of the former Soviet republics is the product of the inherent belief that former Soviet states comprise Russia's natural zone of influence because Russia is a legitimate regional leader in this common historic and cultural space. There are several notable factors intimately linked to the Russian collective identity that have influenced this mainstream political elite's perception of Eurasia.

First, the Russian Empire and its successor, the Soviet Union, were contiguous land-based empires, similar to those of the Hapsburgs or the Ottomans,[10] with no natural boundaries between the center and the periphery. It was geography that played an important role in the formation of Russian identity, a fundamental characteristic of which was the combination of ethnic and imperial components.[11]

The second factor that played an important role in the formation of Russian geopolitical perceptions was the overlap of cultural, linguistic, and historical distinctions between Russia, Belarus, and Ukraine, which led to a confused boundary between Russians and other Eastern Slavs.[12]

The third factor is the concept of the "Soviet people" and the reality that supported it. People from mixed marriages, those living outside their "homelands," and Russians from large urban (and more cosmopolitan) centers were the most responsive to this concept. Russians accepted it more readily than other ethnic groups, because to be "Soviet" implicitly meant being a Russian-speaker and acknowledging the "civilizing" mission of the Russian culture and its extraterritorial nature throughout the entire Soviet Union.

However, not only abstract historic notions drove concrete Russian policies in the post-Soviet space. They did play a background role, but pragmatic considerations and understandings of real-world constraints were present as well. The ideas of integration of the post-Soviet space that are present in the programs of practically all political parties and major security and foreign policy documents reflect attempts of the Russian political elite to reconcile the post-Soviet realities with the nostalgia for a mighty state that existed for centuries within the broad domain of Eurasia. Economic ties and common security institutions are seen as major instruments in achieving integration.

Rhetorically, protection of the Russian Diasporas' interest has been one of the major goals of Russian policy. President Putin reiterated this in summer 2004: "The prime task still remains to protect the rights and interests of our co-citizens and our fellow-countrymen in CIS and the Baltic countries."[13] In reality, Russian Diasporas have been seen rather as an instrument, not the ultimate goal for Russian policies toward the former Soviet republics. Moreover, this instrument has not been widely used in relations with most of the countries in the region, with the notable exception of Latvia and Estonia. The European Union (EU) membership of these two states since 2004 further limited Russian options. From now on, Moscow has to address Brussels, not Riga or Tallinn, if it wants to draw the international community's attention to the rights of non-citizens, most of whom are Russians and other Russian speakers, in Latvia and Estonia.

Preparation of the Joint Statement on EU Enlargement and EU-Russian Relations in spring 2004 gave Russia an opportunity to raise the issue of Russian Diasporas in the two Baltic states in the European context. After weeks of bitter wrangling, Russia achieved very little. Even the naming of specific countries or groups of states that suffer from minority issues was declined by the EU. The final version of the statement, signed on April 27, 2004, contained only a very vague provision: "The EU and the Russian Federation welcome EU membership as a firm guarantee for the protection of persons belonging to minorities. Both sides underline commitment to the protection of human rights and the protection of persons belonging to minorities."[14] This provision gave Russia a right to raise the issues of Russian minorities in the Baltic states in future meetings with the EU, but the goal of their integration into Latvian and Estonian societies as Russian diplomats wanted to phrase it, was not mentioned.

In spite of a ritual reference to co-citizens and fellow countrymen, the main instruments of Russian policies in Commonwealth of Independent States (CIS) and the Baltic countries are found in the economic and security fields. In addition to this, Russia tried to exercise its influence by meddling in the electoral process, with the Ukrainian presidential elections in 2004 being the most striking example. In order to understand the reasons for the very timid use of the diasporas card in relations with its neighbors, it is necessary to have a closer look at internal nation-building in Russia.

Nation-Building

The problems of the interrelationship between nation-building, diasporas, and security in Russia might be analyzed by studying Russian identity transformation and its impact on the system of international relations and security arrangements in Eurasia. A new Russia has begun to define its identity from the ground up; very little from its past can be applied to the present. Intellectual history has not provided contemporary thinkers and politicians with adequate tools for assessing how Russia's age-old quandary concerning national identity fits in the new geopolitical situation. Nevertheless, three major options for the future development of a new Russian identity may be identified: neo-imperial, ethnic, and civic.

Throughout the past three centuries, the Russian culture was formed within an imperial framework. "Universalism" (*vselenskost'*) became the key feature of Russian "high culture." On the one hand, it helped it to gain worldwide recognition. Far from being "provincial" or "narrow-minded," it easily absorbed the achievements of other, particularly European, cultures and made outstanding contributions to humankind. On the other hand, attempts to include everyone, culturally and otherwise, into a limitless, universal Russia were in constant conflict with the particular aspirations of neighboring peoples who largely did not want to become "universal." They saw Russification behind such universalism and perceived it as a threat to their very existence. These historical and cultural messianic traditions stand in sharp contrast to the new geopolitical situation in which Russia finds itself today.

Most of the current literature on foreign policy and security issues in Eurasia is devoted to threats emanating from Russian attempts to restore the Soviet Union or dominate the post-Soviet space. This concentration on the neo-imperialist option has overshadowed serious perils to international security associated with the likely rise of Russian ethnonationalism, as well as the difficulties of building a new civic identity in Russia.

No longer hidden under an imperial veil, ethnic identity has become more salient to Russians after the collapse of the Soviet Union. Although ethnonationalism in Russia is not politically well-organized, it might emerge ascendant, especially if the goal of nation-state building is introduced into contemporary political discourse, since the term "nation" has had a strong ethnic, not civic, connotation in Soviet and post-Soviet academia, public opinion, and politics. As has happened many times in the history of Europe, a well-articulated common culture may come to be defined as the ideal political boundary, leading to ardent claims that all Russians must be reunited under one political roof. As Anthony Smith notes, "aggrandizing their homelands through the mobilization of ethnic sentiment among kinsmen outside the 'homeland' was the mark of many a European irredentism in the last century and later . . . and it has often led to sharp conflicts and even full-scale wars which threaten the stability of regional inter-state systems and attract great power involvement."[15]

The redefinition of Russia in more concrete ethnic terms, in line with those of all Soviet successor states, may become one of the most dangerous undertakings in its history, primarily due to the inevitable redrawing of Eurasia's borders which would accompany the implementation of an ethnonationalist project. The essence of the ethnonationalist program is to restore geographical congruence between the state and the nation by building the Russian state within the area of settlement of the Russian people and other Eastern Slavs. Politically, this means the reunification of Russia, Belarus, eastern and southern Ukraine, and northern and eastern Kazakhstan.

If the experience of other countries is any guide, nation-building on the rubble of an empire is usually the endeavor of ethno-nationalists. Kemalist Turkey started its experiment with a nation-state by subjecting its Armenian, Greek, and Kurdish minorities to genocide and expulsion.[16] Austrians welcomed the Anschluss following twenty years of living in a small post-imperial state. Serbia and Croatia became aggressively nationalistic and began to redraw the post-Yugoslavian political map through the use of brutal force. All former Soviet republics have adopted ethno-political myths and identified the state as a homeland of "indigenous" people. Intellectually, all these policies have relied on the romantic historicist tradition, claiming that humanity could be divided neatly into nations, stipulating that culturally—or ethnically—defined nations possessed sacred rights, and consequently allowing these nations' leaders to downplay individual human rights and due respect for minorities.[17] The policy of ethnonationalism is especially dangerous when it is supported by powerful outside forces that prefer to see an anti-imperial struggle cast in rosy hues, while ignoring the darker side. The real trouble in Eurasia will begin if Russia adopts a similar doctrine of nation-building, if Russians "go ethnic." The rhetoric of "historic justice" adopted by many ethnonationalists in Eurasia might result in a backlash if Russia does the same, as the notion of "historic justice" is always subjective and one-sided.

The development of civic identity also de-legitimizes Russia's current boundaries by questioning the collapse of the Soviet Union and its results. Why was it impossible to build a de-ethnicized, democratized, state within the old borders? The "politically correct" answer is that this option would not have met ethno-national aspirations of the non-Russians; they did not want to live in the old empire and thus created their own states. Russians, on the other hand, have again found themselves in a multiethnic milieu within new borders, and twenty five million of them were left outside. The "national question" for Russians was not resolved by the collapse of the Soviet Union. On the contrary, it was created. Within its current borders, Russia is "more a bleeding hulk of empire: what happened to be left over when the other republics broke away."[18]

The development of a civic identity hardly matches the other options in the sense of a rapid mobilization potential; in fact, it may result in a rather weak state for an extended period of time. In order to build a true civic identity, it is necessary to have or develop a common idea, history, heritage, traditions, legitimate boundaries accepted by all citizens, and strong and effective state institutions. Many of Putin's policies can be properly understood in this context only. Regular elections, political institutions, and common economic and social problems and policies might gradually serve as the glue for this new political nation and further separate it from the other Soviet successor states. However, internal divisions, first between ethno-territorial units and the center, remain strong. Separatist Chechnya is an extreme example of the difficulties in building a common civic identity in Russia.

Russia is not alone in confronting immense difficulties in building a civic identity. As Walker Connor observed, "scholars associated with theories of 'nation-building' have tended either to ignore the question of ethnic diversity or to treat the matter of ethnic identity superficially as merely one of a number of minor impediments to effective state-integration."[19] States in many parts of the world have been unsuccessful nation-builders, and many governments have failed to induce their subjects to shift their primary loyalties from informal subdivisions (ethnic, religious groups) to formal, legalistic state structures.[20] Commenting on the perils of nation-building "from above" with little input from society, Karen Barkey and Mark von Hagen emphasized: "the consequences of this pattern of nation-building are to be seen today in relatively fragile, mutable, and wavering definitions of nationhood, in the absence of a sense of unity in a common project, and in the vulnerability of the societies to find appeal in particularly militant variants of communist or nationalist ideologies."[21]

Many in Eurasia and the West view the vague boundaries of the Russian people as an unnerving and threatening phenomenon that could very well lead to imperial restoration. A Russian nation-state, on the contrary, is seen as a well-tested, familiar, and peaceful alternative. The approach of nation-state builders overlooks many of the grave threats to international security that may evolve from an attempt to mechanically line up Russia with its (mostly ethnonationalist) neighbors, none of which have diasporas comparable in size and potential political significance to the Russian one. Inarticulate Russian nationhood is one of the key factors that explains why the Soviet Union's demise occurred so peacefully, especially when compared to the debacle of another communist federation—Yugoslavia, where most Serbs encountered no ambiguity over their nation or national identity. A Russia without clear-cut frontiers may be the only peaceful solution to the "Russian question" after the break-up of the Soviet empire. Inconsistent and messy relations between Moscow and ethnic republics within the Russian Federation, and moderate, though hardly effective, policies toward Russians in the "near abroad" might be a better solution for security in Eurasia than attempts to shape a clear-cut approach toward nation-state building and the inevitable redrawing of borders. However, it should be noted that the Russian government often pursues such an ambiguous policy not because of its wisdom, but because of its weakness.

The issue of Russian ethnic diasporas can play a crucial role in building a new Russian nation. Political choices made by the Russian government seem to prove that "the Russian government's responsibility to this diaspora was the issue that could not be wished away. Yet addressing it entailed highlighting the contradiction between Russia as a consolidating nation-state and Russia as the heir to an empire."[22] In other words, debates on Russian nationhood in modern Russia have gone beyond state boundaries. Establishing special relations with "compatriots" might be viewed as an attempt to extend Russia's political space, but Russia lacks the resources and political will to become truly assertive in this field. However, the perception of the post-Soviet space as something not yet totally separated from Russia remains strong.

Russian Diasporas

It seems logical to assume that the plight of the Russians in the "near abroad" might strengthen ethnonationalist sentiments in Russia. However, the present problem of Russians in the "near abroad" seems to be politically important, but less intense in the Russian Federation than anyone would have predicted in 1990-1991. There have been no vigorous efforts to reunite Russia proper with the diasporas, though many in Russia perceive Russians as a divided nation. Why is this the case? Will moderation hold on? In order to answer these questions, one must look at the key features of the Russian communities. Are there distinct boundaries that separate Russians from non-Russians in "the near abroad?" What make Russian communities different from titular groups and the "core" Russians in the Russian Federation, as well as from each other? In other words, some conditions of the cohesiveness of ethnic Russians must be tested.

There are two basic features that all Russians living in what is now called the "near abroad" undoubtedly share, namely the feeling of connection with the Russian culture and the existence of an external homeland. However, culture and a remote homeland are rather abstract categories, often detached from daily life. Significant intellectual and political efforts must be made by the elite in the homeland and by the leaders of the diasporas themselves in order to have these abstract categories conceptualized and internalized by millions of common people. Meanwhile, the differences between the Russian Diasporas are numerous and their concrete situations—such as the degree of integration into the host country, economic well-being, and political rights—vary considerably. Moreover, for any analytical purpose it is practically impossible to separate Russians from other Russian-speaking populations in the "near abroad." It can be argued that the important reasons for Russia's moderation in its relations with the co-ethnics in the "near abroad" are the significant differences among the Russian communities and the blurred ethnic boundaries between them and non-Russians. It would be more appropriate to refer to them as different Russian *Diasporas* in some cases—only potential diasporas, rather than as a divided Russian nation or a single Russian Diaspora.

There are three major forms of Russian cultural influence in the newly independent states. First is the presence of ethnic Russians. Second is Russification of part of the titular population, occurring in the Soviet period, which was particularly mass-based in Belarus, Ukraine, and Moldova. In some other cases, it was mainly socially selective Russification of the titular urban elites. This was true for Kazakhstan and Kyrgyzstan. Third, there is Russification of many non-titular, non-Russian groups. Together with ethnic Russians, they serve as a barrier to nationalization (nation-building on ethnic basis) in the newly independent states. This is an important factor in Ukraine, Moldova, Kazakhstan, Kyrgyzstan, and the three Baltic states.

There are significant groups in all former Soviet republics that culturally represent fragments of a collapsed Soviet Union. Ethnicity has played a less important role for their identity as these groups contain both ethnic Russians and non-Russians. The titulars, even if they are Russian-speakers, seem to differ from the others in their feelings on the situation. They became more comfortable with new political realities and changes in linguistic policies after their respective republics acquired independence. The rest of the Russian-speaking population is little differentiated between ethnic Russians and non-titular non-Russians in many of the republics. There are significant differences between the newly independent states and the linguistic, cultural, and political situations that Russians and Russian-speakers found themselves in after the collapse of the Soviet Union.

Russian ethno-national consciousness may become stronger in the Russian communities outside Russia than in Russia itself. This is typical for the periphery of most nations, where there is more intensified interaction with the neighboring peoples in building a stronger common identity. However, without Russia's support, these communities can hardly unite under a single political roof on the basis of their common culture. It is safe to assume that the "near abroad" policy of the Russian Federation is the key potential factor for raising the Russian Diasporas to international significance. These communities are poorly organized and have almost no links with each other.

Russian Policies toward the Russian Diasporas

Interaction between Russia and the Russian Diasporas is a transnational relationship between state and non-state actors. This relationship has been incorporated into the Russian foreign policy agenda and reflects an attempt of the Russian state to address the "Russian question" as it was shaped by the collapse of the Soviet Union. It has not been the driving force of Russian foreign policy toward newly independent states, though it has the potential to become one and reshape the Eurasian geopolitical landscape if Russia took a more nationalistic path.

The impact of the diasporas on a new Russian collective identity is different from what is known about the experience of classic diasporic peoples: for example, Jews, Greeks, Armenians, and Chinese. The intellectual and political influence of Russians from the "near abroad" on their "historic homeland" has been minimal thus far, unlike the effect of Jewish, Greek, or Armenian Diasporas on their respective homelands. However, those "other Russians" play an important role as subjects of Russian theoretical, political, and foreign policy deliberations and actions. The reference group for those who debate, conceptualize, and shape a new Russian identity by political means has been extended beyond the state borders of the Russian Federation. This is a new phenomenon for Russia. Throughout the last several centuries, the state reached well beyond the territory where Russian culture, language, religion, and traditions held sway. After the collapse of the Soviet Union, however, the official Russian political body no longer covered the entirety of this domain, while it continued to include entities that can hardly be said to belong to Russia culturally. Chechnya is the most striking example. The issue of minorities exists in many countries. While having this problem as well, Russia is also confronted by the question of its diasporas. In this way, there is a double challenge to nation-building in Russia–internal and external. Russia must address the issues of both the minorities inside and ethnic Russians outside state boundaries.

Across the political spectrum, there is a consensus that Russia does have some responsibility to those people who identify themselves as Russians or Russian-speakers and who live in the successor states. There is a sense of obligation shared by many citizens of the Russian Federation in this matter. There is broad agreement among both the Russian elite and the common people that they must not abandon the diasporas. It is politically impossible for even the most liberal Russian politician not to express some concern for the fate of those Russians. That is why the programs of all the important political parties, from communist to liberal, contain provisions on this issue. All successive Yeltsin governments, as well As Putin's administration, expressed, at least rhetorically, their commitment to protect "compatriots" in the "near abroad."

The Russian government has felt the tension between the concept of a Russian state within the allegedly arbitrarily-drawn borders of the former Russian Soviet Socialist Federative Republic (RSFSR), on the one hand, and the actual domain of Russian culture, language, and national consciousness, on the other hand. The idea of dual citizenship that took shape in the Russian establishment by the mid-90s was originally perceived as something of a panacea for all the problems associated with this discrepancy between the boundaries of the newly emerging state and those of the newly emerging nation. Seizing upon this idea, the Russian government decided to grant Russian citizenship to all Russians, as well as to people of other nationalities who had some sort of historic tie with the territory of

Russia. This was to be a supplement to a local citizenship granted by another independent state.

In the opinion of officials in the Russian government, the advantages of dual citizenship for Russians in the "near abroad" seemed to be threefold. First, such a policy looked much more "civilized" (a favorite term of the Russian political elite in early 90s) than would the establishment of some sort of "special relationship" with co-ethnics abroad. It stressed the civic, not ethnic, nature of Russian polity and policy, and thus held the promise of protecting the Russian nation without exacerbating ethnic conflict.

The second perceived advantage of dual citizenship policy was that it could help to curb an uncontrolled flow of migrants to Russia by providing them with some sort of security and peace of mind in their host state. At the same time, it could also help to prevent irredentism.

The third advantage of dual citizenship was more self-aggrandizing than geared toward conflict-avoidance. The policy could serve as a conve-nient source of leverage and influence on neighboring states and as an instrument for implementing Russian policy of domination and hegemonism. The protection by a powerful state of its citizens abroad has become normal practice in modern international relations. This policy has been often used by the United States in Latin America and by France in Africa. If Russia could have millions of its citizens in neighboring states, no one would be able to challenge its absolute and unrestrained domination in Eurasia.

However, de jure introduction of dual citizenship in Eurasia, once elevated as a strategic task of Russian foreign policy, started disappearing from the political and negotiation agenda by 1995 as an issue in bilateral or multilateral relations. Despite energetic efforts by the Russian government, a very important instrument of the Russian policy of hegemony and domi-nance has not been created within the framework of international law. When Moscow encountered determined resistance from the governments of the neighboring states on this issue, it simply backed off. However, the poorly controlled process of multiplying citizenships is taking place in Eurasia, and Russian officials effectively encouraged it.

It would be premature to argue that the spread of de facto dual citizenship will lead to Russia obtaining unquestionable leverage in relations with neighboring states. The newly independent states do not acknowledge dual citizenship and regard individuals with two passports simply as their citizens. There is a significant difference between the fact of possessing two passports by an individual and acknowledgment of the dual citizenship of this individual.[23] It creates a legal deadlock for any Russian attempts to protect these dual citizens or intervene on their behalf from the perspective of international law as codified by the Hague Convention of 1930.[24] For Russia, it is much easier to justify protection of those Russian citizens who reside in a successor state and do not have local citizenship. However, the proliferation of de facto dual citizenship creates some additional prerequisites for Russian preponderance vis-à-vis Eurasian states.

In 1996-2004, the Russian idea to introduce de jure dual citizenship in Eurasia existed in a dormant form, only to be revived during the presidential campaign in Ukraine in late 2004. President Vladimir Putin paid two high-profile visits to Ukraine during the campaign and brought home the message:

> The Ukrainian leadership - the President and Prime Minister Viktor Yanukovich - and also Ukrainian citizens, during the live television broadcast, repeatedly raised the issue of dual Russian-Ukrainian citizenship. ...I think that, given the special relation between our two countries that developed over hundreds of years when our peoples lived within a unified state, given the close ethnic, religious, cultural and even linguistic ties that our peoples share, the huge number of family ties and mixed marriages, given the economic demands and the close cooperation that has emerged between many of our companies over recent years and decades, given all the benefits in the broadest sense that our two countries stand to gain, I think that we should react to this signal from Ukraine and come back to this question once again.[25]

This may suggest that under favorable circumstances, Russia is prepared to revisit its allegedly abandoned decade-old strategy of introducing dual citizenship in Eurasia. Meanwhile, in accordance with international norms, Russia constitutionally acknowledges that dual citizenship could exist only in the context of a special treaty relationship with a particular state. In the absence of such a treaty, Russia, like many other states of the world, treats an individual de facto possessing a citizenship additional to the Russian one only as a Russian citizen, but at the same time it does not object to or deem this possession criminal. The Russian law on citizenship, including the latest amendments of 2003, is very friendly to those former Soviet citizens who reside in other successor states and wish to move to Russia and become Russian citizens. Though facing strong opposition from virtually all its neighboring states, Russia effectively extended the same rights to those who preferred to stay in their host state.

In most cases, proliferation of Russian citizenship in the post-Soviet states does not constitute an immediate security problem. However, in the non-recognized separatist regions of Pridnestrovye, South Ossetia, and Abkhazia, this became a factor that to a significant extent shapes the security environment in Moldova and Georgia. Estimates of the Russian citizens' share in the total populations of these territories vary, but most probably it is about 20 percent in Pridnestrovye, 60-70 percent in Abkhazia, and up to 90 percent in South Ossetia. In the last two cases, the absolute majority of Russian citizens are not ethnic Russians.

In sum, there are three categories of people who may be viewed as Russian Diasporas in the post-Soviet space. First, there are ethnic Russians. Second, there are "compatriots" who may feel affinity to Russia irrespective of their ethnicity. Third, there are a growing number of Russian citizens in the neighboring states. These three entities partly concur and partly diverge.

Russia's future attempts to help the Russians in the near abroad could range from neo-imperialistic ambitions to efforts to ensure their human rights. Russia may respond to the problems confronted by its diasporas in the former Soviet states in a variety of ways—some of them quite constructive. The tendency today is to automatically assume that any talk about the Russians in the successor states is potentially aggressive, but this is not necessarily the case.

On the imperialistic side—much feared by international observers as well as by leaders of the successor states—it is possible Russia could use the Russian populations to help re-establish its domination, perhaps turning the successor states into protectorates or semi-independent entities in a buffer zone around Russia. In countries where the diasporas are adjacent to Russia, Russia could stir up the populations to form breakaway regions that would reunite with Russia. Politicization of the diasporas and efforts to redraw state borders along ethnic lines are among the potential threats to security in the region.

It is also possible that Russia will pursue a constructive and humanistic course. Such a course might include helping Russians in the diasporas maintain their distinct culture, for example, by helping to develop educational institutions, cultural centers, and periodicals. Or it might include efforts to protect Russians' human rights by acting within the framework of existing international institutions designed for the protection of both individual human rights and the rights of minorities, such as the Council of Europe and the Organization for Security and Cooperation in Europe (OSCE).

The Russian government emphasizes that Russia would concentrate on helping compatriots living abroad in solving their cultural, educational, and social problems. For example, the importance of providing textbooks to Russian-language schools, educating teachers, and supporting Russian-language newspapers within the existing laws of respective countries is often pointed to. The necessity of working within the Council of Europe and OSCE frameworks in the field of protecting the human rights of Russian-speakers is routinely underlined.

How will Vladimir Putin's policy toward the compatriots abroad look in the near future? Should one expect any significant transformations in this field in comparison with the period of 1991-2004? It is safe to argue that policy towards the Russian Diasporas will be a function of broader national security and foreign policy strategies of the Russian Federation. President Putin has vowed to rebuild the Russian state and restore Russia's standing in the world. He declared that he would lead Russia to regain its strength, its sense of national pride and purpose. Analysis of Putin's policies, as well as his statements and interviews suggest that he is first of all a strong state-builder.

How may of Putin's strategic goals and perception of the tasks of state and nation-building in Russia influence more concrete policies toward the diasporas? It may be plausible to suggest that diaspora issues will remain instruments rather than goals of Russian policy in the "near abroad." In this sense, there will be no radical departure from the previous course. The questions of Russian compatriots in the "near abroad" are addressed by the president primarily in the context of the interstate relations with the newly independent states, which are driven by security considerations and "economic pragmatism." This means that issues regarding diasporas will be concerned primarily with human rights and cultural as well as educational issues.

It may be argued that a violent crisis directly involving Russian Diasporas may dramatically change Russia's pragmatic, cautious, and benign policy. Judging by Putin's handling of the second Chechen war, his response may be immediate, decisive and forceful. However, the scenario of Russian military intervention to protect Russians in the "near abroad" is very unlikely. The prospects for violence against Russians in the post-Soviet space are practically zero. The leaders of all newly independent states are well aware of possible consequences of a crisis involving Russian Diasporas and would certainly try to prevent any use of force against them.

The Russian Diasporas are seen as convenient instruments to support Russian claims to be a leader in Eurasian common historic and cultural space. However, this instrument has consistently been compromised for the sake of other policies considered to be of higher priority. The most important of them is building good neighborly relations with the former Soviet republics and playing the role of a legitimate regional leader that is not feared, but loved.

Concluding Remarks

Robert Dahl argued that power was not the resource-based property of one actor, but a relationship between at least two actors when A causes B to do something that B otherwise would not have done. In other words, power is not based on what a country has, but what it can get other countries to do.[26] Joseph Nye further developed this "relational power" approach and said that power was the ability to affect the outcomes one wants, and if necessary, to change the behavior of others to make this happen. [27] From this perspective, the diasporas have not played a significant role in enhancing Russia's power in the post-Soviet space. The main reasons for this are the civic definition of nation in Russia, the blurred boundaries between ethnic Russians and other Russian-speakers in former Soviet republics, and moderate and ineffective Russian policies towards its diasporas. Russian leaders gave higher priority to state-to-state relations in the post-Soviet space. As a result of both moderation and ineffec-tiveness, there is a great discrepancy between the assertive rhetoric of Russia's leaders and the actual policy of Russia in its relations with Russian Diasporas.

Diaspora is first of all a political phenomenon and its members must be ready to do well to their historic homeland.[28] After the collapse of the Soviet Union, Russia got an opportunity to create a functioning active Russian Diaspora in the neighboring states out of those people who were ethnic Russians or non-Russians feeling affinity with the Russian Federation. The Russian state, with the help of its official rhetoric and laws, did take some steps in this direction, but the results have not been impressive thus far because they were not always supported by concrete and consistent policies. The members of the (potential in many cases) Russian Diasporas in the neighboring states are not politically, socially, or civically organized, and they expect the Russian Federation to do good by them, not necessarily vice versa.

Russian speakers in the Baltic states probably have the best prospect to become a classic diaspora. They have vibrant intellectual discourse on their own problems and relation to Russia, and they are getting politically and civically organized. All this is lacking in Central Asia and South Caucasus, but many Russian-speakers there feel alienation from their host societies and thus can make their own way to form a kind of diaspora that looks mainly for support granted to them by their alleged historic homeland. In Belarus, there are no significant differences between ethnic Russians and Byelorussians.

Paradoxically it may seem, the whole population of Belarus or nobody at all will develop a Russian Diaspora mentality in the coming years.

The most important issues and those most difficult to conceptualize are related to the fates of the Russian Diasporas in Ukraine and Kazakhstan. Ethnic Russians comprise at least 17 and 30 percent of the population of these countries, respectively. This is about thirteen million people and two-thirds of all ethnic Russians in the neighboring states. Almost half of the citizens of Ukraine and Kazakhstan prefer to speak Russian. It is hardly plausible to think about these groups as "minorities." As legitimate founders of the Ukrainian and Kazakhstan states, they feel like titulars and consider themselves to be "indigenous" groups. This is where the "Russian question" is crucial to security, political stability, success of the nationalization process, and construction of nation-states. Both Ukraine, where ethnic Russians are intermingled with ethnic Ukrainians, and Kazakhstan, where the community of about four million Russians lives compactly in the area adjacent to the Russian border, are extremely important countries for the Russian security strategy, self-perceptions of all Russians, the redefinition of "Russianness," and stability of Eurasia.

In 1991–2004, nation-building in both Ukraine and Kazakhstan took mostly a civic form, though it was accompanied by governments' efforts to promote the traditions and language of the titular groups, often at the expense of Russian culture. It may be argued the situation in Ukraine may change after the political crisis in late 2004. There were efforts during this calamity to mobilize the multi-ethnic Russian-speaking population in the eastern and southern parts of the country. If the new government of Ukraine adopts cultural and foreign policies that look anti-Russian, the Russian-speaking population in some regions may gradually acquire a Russian Diaspora mentality, as has already happened in the Crimea. In this case, Russia will obtain an important instrument of influence.

In summary, Russian policies towards its actual and potential diasporas in neighboring states have been driven by humanitarian concerns and the intent to enhance its "soft power." These policies have been balanced and constrained by other foreign policy and security goals in the post-Soviet space, an inarticulate sense of ethnicity and nationhood among Russians, and a lack of political mobilization, with few exceptions, among the members of the diasporas.

The Ethnic Russian Diaspora in Moscow's Central Asia Strategy

Chapter 12

The Ethnic Russian Diaspora in Moscow's Central Asia Strategy

Charles E. Ziegler*

Introduction

Diasporas can have a significant impact on the domestic and foreign policies of states. The American Jewish community, for example, constitutes a powerful voice within the United States in support of Israel, and shapes American policy toward the Middle East. The Armenian community has for years influenced U.S. policy toward Turkey and the Caucasus, while Florida's Cubans have pressured Washington to maintain a hard line against Castro's regime. Ethnic Chinese living in the United States, Canada, Australia and Taiwan have invested heavily in the People's Republic of China (PRC), contributing substantially to the mainland's phenomenal economic growth. When the Soviet Union collapsed, some twenty-five million ethnic Russians were living in the fourteen non-Russian republics, with several million more scattered around the globe.

This chapter focuses on Russians in Central Asia and attempts to assess the importance of this segment of the population for Russian foreign policy and regional stability. The Russian Diaspora issue has resurfaced periodically in Russian politics, and one can assume it should play a more important role as Russian nationalism waxes and Russian foreign policy becomes more assertive. Since taking office, Vladimir Putin has made policy toward the Commonwealth of Independent States (CIS) a top priority. Moscow is pursuing greater influence in the southern border regions, which pose the greatest security challenge to Russia, and the Russian Diaspora is frequently cited as a potential instrument of Russian statecraft.

* I would like to thank Igor Danchenko, Vitaly Kozyrev, Ruslan Kazkenov, Valentina Kurganskaya, and Jim Thurman for their kind assistance in assembling materials for this project.

Has Vladimir Putin's administration adopted a substantially different approach to Russian compatriots abroad than that of Boris Yeltsin? What has been Russia's ethnic strategy in the critical security region of Central Asia? How does the ethnic factor fit into Russia's overall strategy toward Central Asia? This paper will assess the situation of Russians, and the role of the Russian Diaspora in Russian and Central Asian foreign policies. The first task will be to outline the demographic and political situation of ethnic Russians in Central Asia following the dissolution of the Soviet Union.

Russians in Central Asia

Russians moved into Central Asia in various waves over the past four hundred years. The first settlers were Cossacks who settled in the region around the Ural and Irtysh Rivers in the 16th to 18th centuries. In the latter half of the 19th century Cossacks, peasants, and former officers and soldiers from the Turkish wars settled in Central Asia, largely in the towns. Another wave of Russians followed the Revolution, civil war, and accompanying famine of 1921. More Russians, Ukrainians and Belarusians were displaced by collectivization, industrialization, and the terror of the 1930s, and by the Second World War. Stalin's forced deportations included Russians and other Slavs, along with Koreans, Chechens, Ingush, Crimean Tatars, and others who were relocated to Central Asia. The last major influx occurred in the late 1950s during Nikita Khrushchev's Virgin Lands project; the bulk of these agricultural workers settled in Kazakhstan.

In the Stalin and Khrushchev periods, the share of Russian population in Central Asia increased, in part due to the influx of Russians and other nationalities, but also from repressions carried out against the native peoples. For example, collectivization is estimated to have caused the deaths of close to 40 percent of the Kazakh population, with the bulk coming in the famine of 1932-33. Kazakhs has become a minority within their own republic, according to the 1959 census. In that year, Russians accounted for 43 percent of Kazakhstan's population, and 30 percent of Kyrgyzstan's. However, by the 1960s and 1970s the trend was slightly reversed, due to high Central

Asian birth rates and some Slavic out-migration. Table 12.1 outlines the growth and decline of Russians as a percentage of local populations in the Soviet period, based on census data.

	1926	1939	1959	1970	1979	1989
Kazakhstan	20	40	43	42	41	38
Uzbekistan	5	12	14	13	11	8
Kyrgyzstan	12	21	30	29	26	22
Tajikistan	0.7	9	13	12	10	8
Turkmenistan	8	19	17	15	13	10

Source: S. I. Kuznetsova, Russkie v Tsentral'noi Azii (Moscow: Izdatel'stvo "Gumanitarii," 2002), p. 9.

Table 12.1: Russian Share of Population in Central Asian Republics, 1926 to 1989, in Percent

During the Soviet era, Russians and other Slavs in Central Asia were concentrated in the cities, and they were heavily overrepresented in the skilled labor force. Russians also constituted a large proportion of the population in the capitals: in 1989, 37 percent of Bishkek's population was Russian, 39 percent of Ashgabad's, 42 percent of Dushanbe's, and 49 percent of Tashkent's. Kazakhstan and Kyrgyzstan had the largest proportion of rural Russians, but even in these countries the Russian population was largely urban. Throughout Central Asia, Russians dominated in the intelligentsia, political and economic sectors, as well as the military.

Central Asia is often described as a colonial appendage of Russia, and yet Soviet rule did bring benefits, particularly in the areas of literacy and education. On many indicators Central Asians surpassed their brethren in neighboring states. However, Russia displaced the indigenous languages in government and education, while Russian cultural symbols and heroes supplanted those of the Central Asian peoples. Soviet developmental priorities skewed the economies of the republics. Uzbekistan became dependent on a single crop—cotton—while irrigation practices in the Amu Darya and Syr Darya basins created an environmental disaster with the shrinking of the great Aral Sea. In Kazakhstan, the Semipalatinsk nuclear testing range and Baikonur cosmodrome poisoned huge regions of the steppe. The relationship was colonial, and despite Soviet censorship, was recognized as such and was resented in varying degrees among the indigenous populations.

Russians in Central Asia, 1992 to the Present

In the uncertain and unstable milieu of Central Asia immediately after the disintegration of the USSR, Russian ethnics felt especially vulnerable. Russian national organizations had emerged in the later stages of perestroika, in response to growing national awareness within the republics. In Central Asia, the Russian groups included Lad (Kazakhstan), the National Association of Russian Culture (Uzbekistan), Slavonic Diaspora and Slavonic Foundation (Kyrgyzstan), and the Russian Society (Tajikistan).[1] Perceptions of discrimination increased as the Central Asian states began to adopt national constitutions, and promote the indigenous languages and cultures. In addition, with the exception of Turkmenistan, the new governments resisted pressure from Moscow to grant dual citizenship.

Perhaps the most tenuous situation for ethnic Russians existed in Tajikistan, which descended into a bloody civil war that lasted from 1992 to 1997. Moscow supported the existing government and employed the 201st Motorized Rifle Brigade, which is still deployed in the country. S.I. Kuznetsova estimates that 161,000—nearly half of Tajikistan's Russian population—emigrated during the civil war (see Table 2), and by 2003 the U.S. State Department estimated the country's ethnic Russian population at 3.5 percent, down from 8 percent in 1989. Although the situation was less drastic for Russians in the rest of Central Asia, large numbers left Uzbekistan, Kyrgyzstan and Turkmenistan in the first years of independence.

Table 12.2 presents data on the number of ethnic Russians departing Central Asia for the Russian Federation in the 1990s. Kazakhstan accounts for just over half of the Russian emigrants during this period. Migration peaked during the mid-1990s when language laws and indigenization policies were beginning to take effect, and shortly after the Central Asian states had adopted their own currencies. By this point, the likelihood of the newly independent states reintegrating with Russia had begun to recede, and ethnic Russians were faced with the classical choice of exit, voice or loyalty.[2]

	1990	1991	1992	1993	1994	1995	1996	1997	1998	1990-1998
Kazakhstan	55	30	82	104	234	114	98	151	131	1006
Uzbekistan	66	36	65	51	94	64	23	20	23	407
Kyrgyzstan	21	18	41	66	43	13	7	5	3	211
Tajikistan	40	18	47	41	26	22	15	10	7	215
Turkmenistan	5	5	11	7	13	12	14	10	6	82
Total	187	107	247	269	410	255	157	196	160	1921

Source: S. I. Kuznetsova, Russkie v Tsentral'noi Azii (Moscow: Izdatel'stvo "Gumanitarii," 2002), p. 10.

Table 12.2: Net Migration of Russians to Russia ('000)

In Kazakhstan, President Nursultan Nazarbaev pursued a delicate balancing act. Although completely russified and, like his fellow Central Asian rulers, a part of the Soviet power structure for many years, Nazarbaev quickly joined the bandwagon of cultural and national revival. At the same time, he was careful to reassure Kazakhstan's large Russian community, and Moscow, that the new state would be multinational and would cooperate closely with Russia through the Commonwealth of Independent States and other organizations.

Kazakhstan leaders were sensitive to the possibility that Russian nationalists in Kazakhstan and Russians might lobby for the return of heavily Russian areas of the north to the Russian Federation. Nazarbaev's decision to move the capital to Astana was clearly an attempt to consolidate Kazakh political control over the northern regions. To make the move more palatable to the country's Russian minority (and to Moscow), the government emphasized the danger of earthquakes in Almaty. However, this is hardly a convincing reason to move the center of government from a cosmopolitan metropolis of 1.2 million to a town of 300,000 in the frozen steppe, and spend at least $400 million in the process.

Obviously, the Kazakh leadership was convinced that Russians in northern Kazakhstan constituted a sort of fifth column that might press for the region's reincorporation into Russia. Russian nationalists, most prominently Aleksandr Solzhenitsyn and Vladimir Zhirinovsky, had claimed that these territories were historically Russian. The issue of Russian irredentism became more acute after Zhirinovsky's nationalistic Liberal Democratic Party made a strong showing in the December 1993 parliamentary elections.

The hopes of Russian nationalists and the fears of Central Asians may be exaggerated. There is considerable evidence that Russians in Central Asia (and in the former Soviet republics more broadly) do not seek a return to the motherland. For example, surveys conducted by the Center for Study of the Russian Minority in the Near Abroad in Kazakhstan in 1994 indicated that only 36 percent of Russians favored the northern regions remaining part of Kazakhstan. One-quarter wanted to integrate with Russia, and 14 percent indicated a preference for administrative autonomy.[3]

It is important not to view Russians in Central Asia as homogeneous. Just as they differ in terms of how long they have lived in Central Asia, whether or not they were born there, and what were the circumstances that brought them there (voluntary or involuntary), so too their attitudes may vary considerably. For example, it would be misleading to assume that all ethnic Russians in Central Asia identify closely with their Russian homeland. Nor should one assume that all Russian in northern Kazakhstan favor reunification with the Russian Federation. Identities, particularly those in the post-Soviet space, tend to be complex and difficult to categorize.

Survey research conducted in the late 1990s by a team of American, Russian and Ukrainian scholars found little support for the assumption that Russians living in the near abroad feel a strong identification with Russia. The researchers found that 58.7 percent of Russians living in Kazakhstan identified that country, or part of it, as their "homeland," while only 22.4 percent identified Russia or a location in Russia as their homeland. Likewise, in Kyrgyzstan 60.8 percent of Russians living there named Kyrgyzstan or some part of it as their homeland, with 20.7 percent citing Russia as their homeland.[4]

The same study found that Russians living in Kazakhstan and Kyrgyzstan overwhelmingly considered themselves national minorities (59.3 and 67.0 percent respectively), while only a small proportion of those living in Ukraine and Belarus (18.8 and 9.2 percent) viewed themselves in this way. The implication is that a non-Slavic cultural environment heightens awareness of an ethnic difference among Russian minorities, but they may nonetheless identify more closely with their country of residence than with mother Russia. Interestingly, Russians who were not born in the republics but who identified with the republics (Kazakhstan, Kyrgyzstan and Belarus) as their homeland expressed higher levels of pride in their adopted country than did Russians who were born in the republic and identified with it as their homeland.

An ongoing study conducted in Kazakhstan by V.D. Kurganskaya and V. Iu. Dunaev has found that a majority of ethnic Kazakhs and nearly three-fourths of Russians polled prefer the formation of an inclusive state that would not grant privileges to any ethnic groups. Just over one-third of Kazakh respondents indicated they would prefer a multi-national state that would single out Kazakhs for special privileges (see Table 12.3).

	Kazakhs	Russians	Others
Formation of a state for all ethnic groups without any sort of privileges	53.4%	73.5%	76.1%
Formation of a multinational state with defined Privileges for Kazakhs	36.2%	13.3%	12.5%
Formation of a mono-national Kazakh state	5.2%	3.1%	3.1%
Assimilation of representatives of all nationalities and formation of a unified nation	3.4%	10.2%	6.3%

Source: V.D. Kurganskaya and V. Iu. Dunaev, Kazakhstanskaya model' mezhetnicheskoi integratsii (Almaty: Tsentr gumanitarnykh issledovanii, 2003), p. 78.

Table 12.3: What Sort of Policy Should Kazakhstan Follow in Relations Among Nationalities During the Process of State Formation?

Pal Kolsto, a leading expert on Russian Diasporas, makes the important point that Russian national organizations in the former Soviet republics have been small, weak and for the most part lack coordination. Constant infighting and schisms among and within the groups have caused them to lose authority and respect among the diaspora communities. They have not been able to effectively mobilize the local Russians, nor have they had any significant impact on Russian foreign policy toward the region.[5]

There have been relatively few instances of overt Russian opposition in Central Asia. Clearly, the authoritarian nature of the regimes discourages most forms of political protest. Few are brave enough to openly confront Saparmurat Niyazov's Stalinist personality cult in Turkmenistan, or Islam Karimov's repressive dictatorship. In addition, some of the states have constitutional bans against ethnically-based political parties. Nonetheless, Uzbekistan, one of the most repressive Central Asian states, has a relatively vigorous religious opposition movement, which has taken violent and non-violent forms. If Russian grievances were strong, one would expect to see more examples of national opposition than those cited below.

Kazakhstan and Kyrgyzstan are the most tolerant regimes in Central Asia. Russian nationalists have been allowed to form political movements in Kazakhstan, most notably Lad (Harmony) and organizations linked to Dmitrii Rogozin's Congress of Russian Communities (KRO).[6] Russia's Ministry of Foreign Affairs website lists a total of twelve compatriot organizations registered in Kazakhstan, and seventeen in Kyrgyzstan.[7] The Republican Slavic Movement Lad, founded in 1992, had 15 regional branches (*filiali*) in Kazakhstan in 2002, publishes a newspaper, and lobbies for Slavic causes. Its stated goal is to preserve the ethnically distinct culture and language of Slavs, develop and strengthen democracy, and defend the political, social and cultural interests of the Slavic population in Kazakhstan.[8]

Despite the relatively relaxed political environment in Kazakhstan, Russian national movements there have experienced difficulties. Kazakh law prohibits organizing political parties on an ethnic or religious basis. While the Constitution states that the Russian language may be officially used on an equal basis with Kazakh in organizations and local government, in practice the government discriminates in favor of ethnic Kazakhs in employment.[9] Early on, the Russian government made strenuous efforts to persuade Nazarbaev to adopt a law on dual citizenship, but the wily Kazakh leader rejected the proposal. Russia and Kazakhstan did sign an agreement in 1995 that made it easier to acquire citizenship and clarify the legal status and property rights of Russians living in Kazakhstan.[10]

In Kyrgyzstan, President Askar Akayev followed a strategy similar to that of Nazarbaev. As a weak and poor country, Kyrgyzstan is vulnerable to powerful neighbors like Russia, and so must tailor its policies accordingly. Kyrgyzstan's economy is also heavily dependent on Russians and Russian speakers. In 2000, Kyrgyzstan designated Russian as an unofficial language, in an attempt to dissuade skilled workers from leaving, and Akayev has promised to protect ethnic Russians, who comprise about 15 percent of the population, from discrimination. Still, in early 2004 the parliament passed a bill that mandated government officials to learn Kyrgyz, and Akayev signed the bill into law in April.[11] Among those who voiced concern about the measure was the leader of the Slavonic Fund of Kyrgyzstan and Moscow's ambassador to Bishkek, Evgenii Shmagin.[12]

At the same time that Kyrgyzstan is gradually moving to strengthen its cultural identity, Akayev continuously reassures Moscow of his country's support for Russian language and culture, and attention to Russia's foreign policy goals. On a September 2004 visit to Moscow, Akayev described relations with Russia as occupying a "special role" in Kyrgyzstan's foreign policy, which he described as multi-vectored diplomacy (*mul'tivektornoi diplomatii*, the same term used by Nazarbaev to describe Kazakhstan's foreign policy). The Kyrgyz president assured a group of listeners at the Ministry of Foreign Affairs Diplomatic Academy that "Russians (Rossiane) should not be troubled over the fate of their compatriots in Kyrgyzstan."[13]

There has been only one prominent case of potentially violent Russian opposition to Central Asian rule. In 1999, the Kazakh government announced the arrest of twenty two Russians (twelve of whom were Russian Federation citizens) in the town of Ust Kamenogorsk in Northeastern Kazakhstan on charges of planning to overthrow the oblast leadership and establish a Russian Altai republic. Despite the intervention of a Russian delegation of parliamentarians that included Duma Speaker Gennadi Seleznev and CIS Affairs Committee chairman Boris Pastukhov, the plotters were sentenced to lengthy prison terms.[14] Nationalists in Russia criticized the trials' outcome, but it appeared to have no discernable effect on official Russian policy.

Moscow's Policy Toward the Russian Question in Central Asia

In the first year of Boris Yeltsin's administration, Russia focused on Europe and the United States and neglected the near abroad. By 1993, however, the nationalist backlash against the Yeltsin-Kozyrev Western orientation shifted attention more toward the "near abroad," with the goal of restoring Russian influence in the border regions and protecting Russian nationals abroad.

Several laws and decrees on Russians abroad were enacted in the 1990s. In 1994, Yeltsin's government adopted "Basic Directions of State Policy of the Russian Federation in Relation to Compatriots Living Abroad," and the Duma formed a Committee on CIS Affairs and Compatriots Abroad. The following year saw the founding congress of representatives of Russian societies, centers and organizations from countries of the near abroad.[15] In 1998, the Russian parliament adopted a "State Policy of the Russian Federation toward Compatriots Abroad." The emphasis in these documents was on addressing political discrimination against Russian compatriots, and what assistance Russia could provide.[16]

For the most part, however, the Yeltsin administration did not devote attention or resources to the issue of Russian compatriots abroad, nor did it seek to make them a factor in Russian foreign policy. Moscow's goals for stability in Central Asia coincided with those of regional leaders. A serious Russian national opposition movement, say in Kazakhstan, could have further destabilized the southern arc. Given all the problems in this part of the world—the Taliban's extremist regime in Afghanistan, Tajikistan's civil war, Chechnya and the various Caucasus conflicts, as well as the rapid penetration of the oil-rich

Caspian region by Western oil companies–Moscow did not need the additional distraction of having to choose between diaspora movements and its Central Asian partners.

Vladimir Putin appears determined to reassert Russia's presence in Central Asia. Putin's policies call for increased centralization and authoritarianism domestically, while restoring Russia's status as a great power internationally. A pragmatist, Putin recognized that a nationalistic defense of Russians abroad could be one means of enhancing Russian influence in the near abroad (Central Asia and the Baltics, Ukraine and Belarus). Putin has taken a greater interest in the welfare of the Russian Diaspora in Central Asia than did Yeltsin. Putin was the first Russian leader to meet with representatives of Kazakhstan's Russians during his visit to Astana in October 2000. Putin has also worked assiduously to integrate certain CIS states–Kazakhstan, Ukraine, Belarus–into a Moscow-dominated confederation.

Putin's strategy seems to have paid off. Kazakhstan's president has skillfully shaped his country's foreign policy to coincide with Russian foreign policy interests. Nazarbaev has been one of the strongest proponents of a renewed union of post-Soviet states, specifically through the proposed common economic infrastructure of Russia, Kazakhstan, Ukraine and Belarus. Kazakhstan has also been a prominent backer of the Shanghai Cooperation Organization, which brings together Russia, China, Kazakhstan, Uzbekistan, Kyrgystan and Tajikistan in an effort to stabilize Central Asia and stem terrorism, separatism, and drug trafficking.

Promoting these organizations serves several purposes, namely reassuring Moscow that Kazakhstan is attuned to its national interests and its position as a great power in the region, demonstrating to official Russia and Russian nationalists that the Kazakh leadership (if not the people) continue to identify with the Slavic community, and assuring ethnic Russians in Kazakhstan that the country's future is tied to that of its Slavic neighbors. Kazakhstan's large Russian population is one reason Nazarbaev has pursued a pragmatic foreign policy, as he has stated that the multi-ethnic character of Kazakhstan and its geopolitical situation has made political rather than military means dominant in ensuring the country's national security.[17]

Nazarbaev has also followed a "multi-vectored" foreign policy of good relations with the country's immediate neighbors (such as Turkey and China), and with other more distant powers (the United States, Germany, and South Korea). Nazarbaev's pragmatism gives him the advantage of having a unique relationship with Russia among Central Asian states, while keeping the door open to other countries and appearing statesmanlike. Many Kazakh intellectuals, however, are concerned that Nazarbaev is too close to Russia, and is playing into Putin's hands.

Courting ethnic Russians and encouraging them to return to the motherland was at one point early in Putin's tenure seen as a means of dealing with Russia's demographic decline. Speaking in Novosibirsk in November 2000, Putin encouraged workers from the former Soviet Union (FSU) to migrate to Russia, particularly Siberia and the Russian Far East, which were losing population, rather than Moscow or the Black Sea coast, where there were housing shortages. Yet, not surprisingly, it seems this strategy had limited appeal to Russians living abroad, most of whom realized that conditions in Magadan were far harsher than those in Almaty.[18]

The Russian ethnic factor is also apparent in the attempt to develop a broader Siberian regional entity. Cossack organizations in the Eastern Kazakh oblast have been active in trying to establish a Siberian Cossack Union that would link northeast Kazakhstan's Russian communities with Russian Siberia. Kazakhstan has three major Cossack organizations–the Semirechye Cossacks in the south and central regions, the Ural Union of Cossacks in the west–and the Union of Cossacks of the Gorki line in the northern and eastern regions. These groups have close ties to the Cossack organizations in Russian Siberia, and constitute a strong separatist movement. They have not been successful, though, in garnering official support from Moscow for their goals.[19]

Promoting the interests of Russians abroad is also a means of garnering political support among a political elite and a population that is increasingly nationalistic, although there is far more rhetoric than action. The Turkmen gas deal of 2003 is one example. As part of Putin's and Gazprom's plan to tie Central Asia more tightly into the Russian energy grid, Putin and Turkmen President Niyazov in April 2003 concluded a 25-year agreement that provided natural gas on terms highly favorable to Russia. Niyazov abruptly declared that he would abrogate Turkmenistan's dual citizenship law within two months, which would force the 100,000 ethnic Russians who held Russian and Turkmen passports to decide whether to stay in the repressive dictatorship or leave for an uncertain future in Russia.

Many Russians, both within Turkmenistan and in Russia, saw the gas deal as a sellout by President Putin.[20] From April 2003 through February 2004, about 1500 Russians per month left Turkmenistan, according to Russia's Deputy Foreign Minister, Alexei Fedotov. The Turkmen government assured Moscow that welfare of local Russians would be protected, but the situation for ethnic Russians was already worsening before the gas agreement. Numerous Russian-language schools have been closed down, and while twenty two newspapers are published in Turkmen, as of 2003 there was only one Russian paper. The Turkmen government has cut off deliveries of all Russian language newspapers into the country–they are far more critical than anything the Turkmenbashi is willing to tolerate–although the population can still receive restricted satellite TV broadcasts from Russia.[21]

Duma member and KRO head Dmitrii Rogozin criticized Turkmenistan a month after the deal for drug trafficking, supporting terrorist groups, and abusing the human rights of ethnic Russians. Since human rights have not been a priority in the Putin administration, and given the strong control over the parliament exercised by the President, it is likely that Rogozin's remarks were a coordinated effort to convince the Russian public that the government was concerned about the plight of their compatriots prior to the December 2003 Duma elections and the March 2004 presidential contest.[22]

Additional evidence that Moscow's concern for Russian compatriots in Turkmenistan is tactical can be gleaned from the February 2004 visit to Ashgabad by Valentina Matviyenko, governor of St. Petersburg and a close associate of Putin's. Matviyenko fawned over Niyazov's accomplishments and described his *Rukhnama* (a spiritual handbook) as a serious philosophical work. Governor Matviyenko signed an agreement covering cooperation in the fishing, mining and gas industries, but she ignored the ethnic question entirely.[23]

Publicly, there is substantial government support of the Russian Diaspora. The Russian Federation government in November 2002 allocated a budget line for support of Russian compatriots abroad. The budget line included money for: celebrating holidays and significant cultural days, marking the Great Fatherland War, purchasing Russian language books for schools, purchasing art and reference literature for libraries and social organizations, teacher training, supporting Russian culture (theaters), health of children and WW2 veterans, staging Olympiads in Russian language and literature, and for children's centers.[24] A total of 210 million rubles was allocated to support compatriots abroad in 2003, with 252 million rubles allocated for 2004.[25]

Russian nationalism and the ethnic factor were evident in the December 2003 Duma elections and the March 2004 presidential contest. Of the four parties that surmounted the 5 percent barrier to make it into the Duma, three–United Russia (Edinaya Rossiya), Motherland (Rodina) and Zhirinovsky's Liberal Democratic Party–advocated nationalistic positions, in particular the rights of Russian nationals abroad. The two democratic parties–the Union of Right Forces and Yabloko–failed to make the cutoff. The leaders of the new Duma's factions–Dmitrii Rogozin, Sergei Glazyev, and Vladimir Zhirinovsky–have been among the strongest proponents of Russian rights in the former republics. Yet it remains to be seen whether nationalists holding key positions in the parliament can translate their electoral victory into political clout.

The outcome of the 2003 parliamentary elections may be an indication that Russia's voting public is increasingly disillusioned with the more democratic political forces and more nationalistic. The rise of nationalism seems to be linked to frustration arising from Russia's lack of influence on world politics, including in the unstable southern arc. Moreover, Russian nationalism may be fueled by terrorist actions in the Islamic areas of Central Asia and the Caucasus. Since 2000, the Duma has been converted largely into an appendage of presidential policy-making by Putin. The President's authoritarian tendencies and his hard-line approach to terrorism and instability on Russia's borders resonate with Russians, most of whom seem willing to accept less democracy if it means greater security.

Conclusion

Russian security is now focused on the threat of terrorism and Islamic extremism in the unstable southern arc of Central Asia and the Caucasus. The same threats have brought American troops and bases to Central Asia, in Uzbekistan and Kyrgyzstan. American troops may provide short-term stability, which is in Russia's interest, but a longer-term term presence would undermine Russia's position in this volatile and energy-rich region.

Russia has four sources of leverage in Central Asia, and President Putin has proved quite skillful in using them to reassert Russia's influence. The first is the military, which has been employed primarily in Tajikistan and Kyrgyzstan. Granted, Russia's armed forces are weak and beset with problems, but in the context of even weaker Central Asian states and militaries, the Russian army can be effective. A second source of leverage is energy and economics. Russia has lost much economic influence over the past decade, but recent moves to tie Central Asia into a regional energy infrastructure have been met with success. Third, Russian participation in regional organizations like the Shanghai Cooperation Organization, and the emerging concept of a unified economic space among Russia, Kazakhstan, Ukraine and Belarus demonstrate a pragmatic willingness to work with neighboring states, turning Russia's weakness into a form of diplomatic strength.[26]

Less effective but still important is the ethnic influence, namely the presence of millions of Russian expatriates in Kazakhstan, Kyrgyzstan, Tajikistan, Turkmenistan, and Uzbekistan, and their ties to mother Russia.[27] The actual impact on Russian politics, however, has been more apparent in the domestic sphere than in foreign policy, with the Kremlin adopting largely symbolic policies. Two peak periods of support for the Russian Diaspora can be identified. There was a brief flurry of activity in the mid-1990s, as the Yeltsin administration responded to nationalist pressures within Russia by adopting a few decrees and passing some laws. Likewise, Putin actively promoted the cause of Russians abroad in 2000-01, allocating limited funds to promote Russian culture and language. However, Putin has devoted more attention to using the other three sources of leverage to promote Russia's foreign policy goals in Central Asia.

Russian nationalism could reinvigorate the role of Russia's Diaspora in foreign policy. The strong showing of nationalist parties in last year's parliamentary elections and the surge of patriotism in the wake of recent terrorist attacks may lead to greater pressures to "defend" Russians abroad. A triggering event would be more likely to occur in Kazakhstan than in any other Central Asian country. However, the leaders of both Kazakhstan and Russia are in firm control of their governments and both, realizing the potential for instability and bloodshed, have rejected using the ethnic card in foreign relations.

Notes: Chapter 2

[1] Czech Prime Minister Milos Zeman ignited an international furor in February 2002 when he reportedly told an Austrian magazine that the Sudeten Germans had been "Hitler's fifth column" and that they were, in effect, fortunate to have been expelled from Czechoslovakia in 1945 rather than to have been executed for treason. Nearly three million ethnic Germans were expelled from Czechoslovakia and substantial numbers of them (the figures are highly controversial) perished in internment camps or on the long march to Germany or Austria. P. Wallace, "Putting the Past to Rest: The Sudeten Question Is Still Causing Trouble in Central Europe," *Time Europe* online edition, 18 March 2002. Zeman had created a row some years earlier when, as speaker of the Czech parliament, he reportedly commented that "the deportation of the Sudeten Germans was the logical consequence of World War II and of the activities of the German population in the former Czechoslovakia." *Time International* online edition, v. 148, no. 6 (5 August 1996). Not all Czechs agree with Zeman. In 1990, the Nobel prize-winning Czech President Vaclav Havel called the expulsion of ethnic Germans "deeply immoral."

[2] Hugh Thomas, *The Spanish Civil War* (New York: Harper & Row, 1961), p. 317. Not all Czechs agree with Zeman. In 1990, the Nobel prize-winning Czech President Vaclav Havel called the expulsion of ethnic Germans "deeply immoral."

[3] The term's notoriety was given a boost by Ernest Hemingway, who wrote a play in 1937 called "The Fifth Column," performed in New York in 1940, about a pro-Loyalist war correspondent. *The Fifth Column, and Four Stories of the Spanish Civil War* (New York: Scribner, 1969). Film actor Humphrey Bogart also contributed to the term's notoriety as the star in the 1942 movie *All Through the Night*, a spy thriller about "Axis fifth columnists" infiltrating the United States.

[4] There were, of course, non-German collaborators with Hitler Germany. This study focuses exclusively on those whose ethnic ancestry was German. The most comprehensive postwar account of the German fifth column phenomenon is Louis De Jong, *The German Fifth Column in the Second World War* (London: Routledge & Kegan Paul, 1956).

[5] A bibliography on Nazi fifth columns prepared at the Library of Congress in 1943 and consisting only of books and major articles in American periodicals contained 290 entries. De Jong, *The German Fifth Column*, p. 136.

[6] De Jong, *The German Fifth Column*, p. 136.

[7] Quoted in De Jong, *The German Fifth Column*, p. 105.

[8] De Jong, *The German Fifth Column*, p. 109.

[9] The argument that there was considerable wisdom in U.S. plans to defend the Western Hemisphere against the threat of Nazi attack, including fifth column attack, is ably set forth in Alton Frye, *Nazi Germany and the American Hemisphere 1933-1941* (New Haven: Yale University Press, 1967).

[10] For propaganda purposes, the Nazis were fond of claiming a world total of 100 million Germans. Their somewhat exaggerated reckoning included some three million German-Swiss, whose attachments to Germany were dubious in spite of language, and eight million German-Americans, the great bulk of whom were quite irrecoverably lost to American culture. For country-by-country estimates, see Hans-Adolf Jacobsen, *Nationalsozialistische Aussenpolitik 1933-1938* (Frankfurt/Main: Alfred Metzner Verlag, 1968), pp. 160-61; for the Nazi tabulation, p. 698.

[11] Estimates of their total number varied considerably. According to a 1937 Nazi reckoning, there were roughly 500,000 *Reichsdeutschen* abroad, excluding the rather large number in North America. Inclusion of the North American contingent would have raised the figure by at least one million.

Jacobsen, *Nationalsozialistische Aussenpolitik*, p. 129n. See also De Jong, *The German Fifth Column*, p. 243.

[12] *Volksdeutschen* were further subdivided into *Grenzdeutschen* (inhabitants of ethnically compact areas on Germany's borders), *Binnendeutschen* (in contrast to the *Grenzdeutschen*, these were ethnic Germans supposedly living *willingly* on the edge of the German frontier, as in Switzerland); *Inseldeutschen* (those residing in enclaves of densely German settlements away from Germany's borders, as in the Soviet Union); *Streudeutschen* (those living in scattered settlements); and *Ueberseedeutschen* (the overseas Germans, as in the Western Hemisphere). Z. A. B. Zeman, *Nazi Propaganda*, 2nd edition (New York: Oxford University Press, 1973), p. 73.

[13] Ralph F. Bischoff, *Nazi Conquest through German Culture* (Cambridge: Harvard University Press, 1942), pp. 78-83.

[14] Bischoff, *Nazi Conquest*, p. 80. *Volkstumsarbeit* has been defined as "an intense concern for the welfare of ethnic German groups and an attempt to foster closer ties between these groups and the Reich German population through social, economic, and cultural assistance." Ronald M. Smelser, *The Sudeten Problem 1933-1938: Volkstumspolitik and the Formulation of Nazi Foreign Policy* (Middletown: Wesleyan University Press, 1975), pp. 4-5.

[15] Ibid., p. 100.

[16] Arthur L. Smith, Jr., *The Deutschtum of Nazi Germany and the United States* (The Hague: Martinus Nijhoff, 1965), pp. 5-6; and Bischoff, *Nazi Conquest*, pp. 102-09.

[17] Jacobsen, *Nationalsozialistiche Aussenpolitik*, p. 165.

[18] The compilation is reprinted in Jacobsen, *Nationalsozialistische Aussenpolitik*, pp. 692-96.

[19] The gradual nazification of *Volkstum* organizations in Germany is treated at length in Smelser, *The Sudeten Problem*.

[20] On the Germandom organizations, very useful are the studies by Jacobsen, *Nationalsozialistische Aussenpolitik* (in German); Smelser, *The Sudeten Problem*, Bischoff, *Nazi Conquest*, pp. 73-109; Smith, *The Deutschtum of Nazi Germany*; and MacAlister Brown, "The Third Reich's Mobilization of the German Fifth Column in Eastern Europe," *Journal of Central European Affairs* 19, no. 2 (1959): 128-48.

[21] Jacobsen, *Nationalsozialistische Aussenpolitik*, pp. 690-91.

[22] German migrants to the United States, for example, were prolific organizers. Just prior to the outbreak of World War I, there were well over 6,000 clubs and organizations, exclusive of even more numerous church-related associations, catering to ethnic German interests in the United States. Frederick C. Luebke, *Bonds of Loyalty: German Americans and World War I* (DeKalb: Northern Illinois University Press, 1974), p. 43.

[23] In the United States, for example, there were almost 800 German-language newspapers and journals published in the 1890s. While this figure had been reduced to 522 by 1919, the latter figure was still "nearly as great as that of all other foreign-language publications in America combined." Luebke, *Bonds of Loyalty*, p. 45.

[24] Bischoff, *Nazi Conquest*, p. 105.

[25] Smith, *The Deutschtum of Nazi Germany*, p. 22.

[26] Smelser, *The Sudeten Problem*, p. 116.

[27] Smith, *The Deutschtum of Nazi Germany*, pp. 33-4.

[28] Jacobsen, *Nationalsozialistische Aussenpolitik*, p. 144.

[29] Ibid., p. 144.

[30] Jacobsen, *Nationalsozialistische Aussenpolitik*, p. 146. On the fourth such commemoration in 1936, over 5,000 *Reichsdeutschen* leaders from all over the world were in attendance.

[31] Ibid., p. 143.

[32] See, for instance, Carleton Beals, "Totalitarian Inroads in Latin America," *Foreign Affairs* 17 (October 1938): 80. Italian fascists often stood accused of the same misdeeds. See, for example, the widely discussed account of Marcus Duffield, "Mussolini's American Empire: The Fascist Invasion of the United States," *Harpers* 159 (November 1929): 661-72.

[33] J. W. Bruegel, *Czechoslovakia Before Munich: The German Minority Problem and British Appeasement Policy* (Cambridge: Cambridge University Press, 1973), p. 120. Bruegel seizes upon this particular transaction to make the case for Hitler's unambiguous and early sponsorship of a Sudeten German fifth column. "The suggestion," he writes, "that even a fraction of this huge amount of money [330,000 Reichsmarks] which was smuggled into Czechoslovakia could be granted to a political party not in thrall to Hitler is too absurd even to be discussed." Smelser, in contrast, concludes that the process of appropriation looked "like anything but the smooth, well oiled machinations that have come to be associated with Nazi 'synchronization'.... Through all the financial maneuvering, it is clear how little in touch the Berlin agencies—official and nonofficial—were, both with each other and with the situation in Czechoslovakia. As one observer noted, all any two-bit organization in Czechoslovakia had to do was scream 'Germandom', and the money immediately started pouring in from Berlin with no questions asked." Smelser, *The Sudeten Problem*, pp. 113-14.

[34] Smelser, *The Sudeten Problem*, p. 138.

[35] Ibid., pp. 166-89.

[36] On Trans Ocean's operations in the Western Hemisphere, see Frye, *Nazi Germany and the American Hemisphere*.

[37] Zeman, *Nazi Propaganda*, pp. 50-1.

[38] Ibid., p. 59.

[39] Ibid., pp. 57-8.

[40] Ibid., p. 60. For an analysis of the contents and techniques of Nazi radio propaganda, see Harwood L. Childs and John B. Whitton, *Propaganda By Short Wave* (Princeton: Princeton University Press, 1942).

[41] Smelser, *The Sudeten Problem*, p. 221.

[42] Smith, *The Deutschtum of Nazi Germany*, p. 27; Bischoff, *Nazi Conquest*, p. 4.

[43] In these two cases were "found indications of military Fifth Column activity on a considerable scale ..." De Jong, *The German Fifth Column*, p. 294.

[44] De Jong, *The German Fifth Column*, pp. 290-94. De Jong rated the Austrian Nazi party a political fifth column group "in the highest measure conceivable." It is omitted from this discussion of ethnic minority fifth column activity since the German-Austrians were obviously the majority group.

[45] Polish and German writers have never ceased arguing about events involving ethnic Germans in September 1939 at the outset of World War II—Poles insisting that German fifth columnists actively aided the oncoming Nazi forces, Germans insisting that the Poles slaughtered thousands of innocent ethnic Germans. For the Polish view, see, for instance, Polish Ministry of Information, *The German Fifth Column in Poland* (London: Hutchinson and Company, 1941), and Zachodnia Agencja Prasowa, *Irredentism and Provocation: A Contribution to the History of German Minority in Poland* (Warsaw: Wydawnictwo Zachodnie, 1960). For the German point of view, see Peter Aurich, *Der Deutsch-Polnische September 1939: Eine Volksgruppe Zwischen Den Fronten* (Munich: Olzog, 1970); and Edwin Erich Dwinger, *Der Tod in Polen: Die volksdeutsche Passion* (Jena: Eugen Diederichs Verlag, 1940), translated into English in 2004 as *Death in Poland: The Fate of the Ethnic Germans*, available on the Web at www.wintersonnenwende.com. See also Elizabeth Wiskemann, *Germany's Eastern Neighbors* (London: Oxford University Press, 1956), pp. 33-47; and De Jong, *The German Fifth Column*, pp. 39-53, 147-57.

[46] The best argument for the partial autonomy of Henlein's movement is by Smelser, *The Sudeten Problem*. Studies that suggest greater control from Berlin include Bruegel, *Czechoslovakia Before Munich*; Josef Korbel, *Twentieth-Century Czechoslovakia: The Meanings of its History* (New York: Columbia University Press, 1977), pp. 112-20; and Radomir Luza, *The Transfer of the Sudeten Germans: A Study of Czech-German Relations, 1933-1962* (New York: New York University Press, 1964). For a well-informed and balanced discussion by a contemporary, see Elizabeth Wiskemann, *Czechs and Germans*, 2nd edition (New York: St. Martin's Press, 1967), originally published in 1938. See also Bischoff, *Nazi Conquest*, pp. 110-31; and Robert W. Seton-Watson, "The German Minority in Czechoslovakia," *Foreign Affairs* 16 (July 1938): 651-66.

[47] Smelser, *The Sudeten Problem*, p. 243.

[48] They are summarized, in somewhat different form, in De Jong, *The German Fifth Column*, pp. 290-94.

[49] Joachim Remak, "'Friends of the New Germany': The Bund and German-American Relations," *Journal of Modern History* 29 (March 1957): 38-41. The *Bund*, according to Remak, almost certainly had links with Bohle's *Auslandsorganisation*; but these could not have profited Germany very much, since the *Bund* was decidedly a fringe group. Not even Nazi Germany ever estimated the size of its membership at more than 6,000. On Nazism among German-Americans, see Sander A. Diamond, *The Nazi Movement in the United States 1924-1941* (Ithaca: Cornell University Press, 1974); and Frye, *Nazi Germany and the American Hemisphere*. Interesting for their contemporary perspective are Martin Dies, *The Trojan Horse in America* (New York: Dodd, Mead, 1940); Bischoff, *Nazi Conquest*, pp. 132-81; and Frank C. Hanighen, "Foreign Political Movements in the United States," *Foreign Affairs* 16 (October 1937): 1-20.

[50] Hitler's decision encountered strong resistance from within Germany as from the Tyrolean Germans themselves. The area was finally annexed by Germany following the Italian armistice in September 1943. By the end of the war, roughly 70,000 Tyrolean Germans had been resettled in Germany. See Mario Toscano, *Alto Adige—South Tyrol: Italy's Frontier with the German World* (Baltimore: The Johns Hopkins University Press, 1975), pp. 1-67. Toscano notes (page 49) as proof of the enormous magnetism of Nazi German power in 1939 the results of a poll taken of the German minority in the Alto Adige shortly after the fall of Poland. Of 266,985 eligible voters, 185,085 opted for emigration to Germany.

[51] Zeman, *Nazi Propaganda*, p. 50. In the early years of the Nazi regime, Berlin seems to have been equally concerned to avoid contaminating its foreign policy with the activities even of the Sudeten Germans. Although given generous encouragement, German-Czechs were typically left to their own, usually confused and sometimes self-defeating, devices. Smelser, *The Sudeten Problem*. On the German minority in Hungary as a source of friction between the Magyars and Nazi Germany, see

Gerhard L. Weinberg, *The Foreign Policy of Hitler's Germany: Diplomatic Revolution in Europe 1933-36* (Chicago: The University of Chicago Press, 1970), pp. 110-16.

[52] Henlein's party, with 1,249,530 votes (roughly 60 per cent of the total *German* vote cast), polled more votes than either of the two leading Czechoslovakian parties. Bruegel, *Czechoslovakia Before Munich*, p. 124.

[53] In the 1935 election, some 600,000 German voters (about one-third the total of German voters) cast ballots for Czechoslovakia's *democratic* parties. Bruegel, *Czechoslovakia Before Munich*, p. 124.

[54] Luebke, *Bonds of Loyalty*, pp. 29-30.

[55] Ibid., p. 252.

[56] Italian-Americans were apparently less impervious to appeals from abroad than were Americans of German background. On this, see John P. Diggins, *Mussolini and Fascism: The View from America* (Princeton: Princeton University Press, 1972), and the partisan but useful study by Gaetano Salvemini, *Italian Fascist Activities in the United States* (New York: Center for Migration Studies, 1977). See also Duffield, *Mussolini's American Empire*; and Alan Cassels, "Fascism for Export: Italy and the United States in the Twenties", *American Historical Review* 69 (April 1964): 707-12.

[57] Frye, *Nazi Germany and the American Hemisphere*, p. 65.

[58] Ibid., pp. 67-8.

[59] George F. W. Young, *The Germans in Chile: Immigration and Colonization* (New York: Center for Migration Studies, 1974), pp. 165-70.

[60] Franz Neumann, *Behemoth: The Structure and Practice of National Socialism 1933-1944*, reprint (New York: Octagon Books, Inc., 1963), pp. 98-102.

[61] Zevedei Barbu, *Democracy and Dictatorship* (New York: Grove Press, 1956), p. 147.

[62] Smelser, *The Sudeten Problem*, p. 244.

[63] Ibid., p. 206.

[64] Adolf Hitler, *Mein Kampf* (New York: Reynal and Hitchcock, 1939).

[65] Bischoff, *Nazi Conquest*, p. 32.

[66] Neumann, *Behemoth*, pp. 160-66.

[67] "In the first flush of early and easy victories in the Baltic States," according to one account, "the Germans were so intent on exploiting the occupied Eastern territories that they ignored the political handling of the populations and were openly hostile to any manifestation of national independence. The Baltic peoples welcomed the advancing Germans as liberators from the Soviet regimes that had been imposed upon them, and they offered at once to form volunteer legions to help liberate their countries. These offers were at first rejected out of hand. Even later when, mainly under the aegis of the SS, national units from the Baltic states were finally permitted, they were organized exclusively 'for the fight against Bolshevism'. Nationalist propaganda was not permitted and officers of Baltic nationalities were mistrusted." Paul W. Blackstock, *The Strategy of Subversion* (Chicago: Quadrangle Books, 1964), p. 169.

[68] Julian Hale, *Radio Power, Propaganda and International Broadcasting* (Philadelphia: Temple

University Press, 1975), p. 3. In spite of the fact that pre-Munich Czechoslovakia, apart from its Czechs and Slovaks, contained politically significant Polish, Hungarian, Ruthenian, as well as German minorities, "Nazi propaganda," according to Hale, "was directed solely towards the German minority, in the German language." On the medium- and longwave bands employed mainly in intra-European transmission, the Nazis failed to develop a foreign-language service before the war, and even on shortwave habitually broadcast news and other spoken programmes bilingually in both German and the regional language. "On the whole," concluded another author, "broadcasting, like other expressions of National Socialist propaganda, was circumscribed by the view that the German nation was the most suitable vehicle for the Nazi revolution." Zeman, *Nazi Propaganda*, p. 62.

[69] In Germany's post-Munich campaign against Czechoslovakia, which ended in its dismemberment in March 1939, the Nazis transmitted numerous anti-Czech broadcasts from Vienna in Slovak as well as in Ukrainian, for the Ruthenian minority, apparently with poor results. Henry Delfiner, *Vienna Broadcasts to Slovakia, 1938-1939, A Case Study in Subversion* (New York: Columbia University Press, 1974). Nazi propaganda was apparently more successful among some of the Turkic-Muslim minorities of the Soviet Caucasus and Caspian Sea regions. See Blackstock, *The Strategy of Subversion*, pp. 173-76.

[70] Hale, *Radio Power*, pp. 3-4. The initials RRG refer to the *Reichsrundfunkgesellschaft* (German Broadcasting Society), an agency subordinate to Goebbels' Ministry of Propaganda.

[71] Barbu, *Democracy and Dictatorship*, p. 139.

[72] Delfiner, *Vienna Broadcasts to Slovakia*, p. 14.

[73] In remarks made near the end of his life, Hitler stated that he was "deeply distressed at the thought of those millions of Germans, men of good faith, who emigrated to the United States and who are now the backbone of the country. For these men, mark you, are not merely good Germans, lost to their fatherland; rather, they have become enemies, more implacably hostile than any others.... Transplant a German to Kiev, and he remains a perfect German. But transplant him to Miami, and you make a degenerate out of him—in other words, an American." Hitler's comment is taken from *The Testament of Adolf Hitler*, quoted in Frye, *Nazi Germany and the American Hemisphere*, p. 191.

[74] See, for example, Gerhard L. Weinberg, "Hitler's Image of the United States," *American Historical Review* 69 (July 1964): 1006-21.

[75] Kenneth R. Conklin, "Hawai'i's Fifth Column: Anti-Americanism in the Hawaiian Sovereignty Movement," 2004, online at: www.angelfire.com/hi2/hawaiiansovereignty/antiamerican.html.

[76] Steven Ferry, "Fifth Cavalry or Fifth Column? Examining Psychiatry's Role in Our Lives," 20 August 2004, online at: www.dissidentvoice.org.

[77] Stephen R. C. Hicks, "Deconstructing the Fifth Column Left," online at: www.6thcolumnagainstjihad.com.

[78] Bruce Kogut and Gordon Walker, *Restructuring or Disintegration of the German Corporate Network: Globalization as a Fifth Column*, William Davidson Institute Working Paper Number 591 (Ann Arbor: University of Michigan Business School, June 2003).

[79] Sergey Stefanov, "Fifth Column of Information Terrorists in Moscow," *Pravda* online edition, 1 November 2002, online at: http://english.pravda.ru/main/2002/11/01/38981.html.

[80] "The American Fifth Column," 1 August 2004, online at: www.parida.com/5columna.htm.

[81] Frank J. Gaffney, Jr., "Muslim Fifth Column?" *Jewish World Review* online, 23 September 2003.

[82] "Editorial: Facing China's Fifth Column," *Taipei Times* online, 1 December 2002.

[83] Lin Chieh-yu, "Tourists May Be 'Fifth Column', Official Says," *Taipei Times* online, 23 July 2004.

[84] Grover Norquist, "The New Fifth Column," *The American Enterprise* online, June 2003.

[85] Susan Katz Keating, "The Wahhabi Fifth Column," United States Committee for a Free Lebanon (January 2003), online at: www.freelebanon.org/articles/a345.htm.

[86] One of the earliest attempts at serious scholarly inquiry into the international dimension of ethnic conflict was that of Astri Suhrke and Lela G. Noble (eds), *Ethnic Conflict and International Relations* (New York: Praeger, 1977). More recent such studies include: Manus I. Midlarsky (ed.), *The Internationalization of Communal Stife* (London: Routledge, 1992); Michael E. Brown, *Ethnic Conflict and International Security* (Princeton: Princeton University Press, 1993); Ted Robert Gurr and Barbara Harff, *Ethnic Conflict in World Politics* (Boulder: Westview, 1994), especially pp. 117-46 ; and David A. Lake and Donald Rothchild (eds), *The International Spread of Ethnic Conflict: Fear, Diffusion, and Escalation* (Princeton: Princeton University Press, 1998).

[87] One fairly early study that drew essentially negative conclusions about the fifth column potential of Southeast Asia's overseas Chinese communities was Stephen FitzGerald, *China and the Overseas Chinese: A Study of Peking's Changing Policy, 1949-1970* (Cambridge: Cambridge University Press, 1972). The opposite conclusion had been drawn earlier by Robert S. Elegant, *The Dragon's Seed: Peking and the Overseas Chinese* (New York: St. Martin's Press, 1959). See also Charles P. FitzGerald, *The Third China: The Chinese Communities in Southeast Asia* (Vancouver: University of British Columbia Press, 1965).

[88] Over the past three or four decades, there has been a vast outpouring of literature signaling the rapid rise in importance and proliferation in numbers of so-called "transnational," "non-state," or "non-governmental" actors. For a sampling, see Joseph S. Nye, Jr. and Robert O. Keohane (eds), *Transnational Relations and World Politics* (Cambridge: Harvard University Press, 1971); Judy S. Bertelson (ed.), *Nonstate Nations in International Politics* (New York: Praeger, 1977); Thomas Risse-Kappen (ed.), *Bringing Transnational Relations Back In: Non-State Actors, Domestic Structures and International Institutions* (Cambridge: Cambridge University Press, 1995); Jackie G. Smith (ed.), *Globalization and Resistance: Transnational Dimensions of Social Movements* (New York: Rowman and Littlefield Publishers, 2002); William Wallace, *Non-State Actors in World Politics* (New York: Palgrave Macmillan, 2002); and Jackie G. Smith, Charles Chatfield, and Ron Pagnucco (eds), *Transnational Social Movements and Global Politics: Solidarity Beyond the State* (Syracuse: Syracuse University Press, 1997).

[89] Statistics are from typed handouts supplied to the author by RFE-RL and VOA offices in Washington, DC.

[90] The VOA was broadcasting at that time in 36 languages, augmented by RFE-RL, which was broadcasting (with some linguistic duplication) in 22.

[91] Reported by Lawrence Wright, "The Terror Web," *The New Yorker* online, 2 August 2004.

[92] Marc Sageman, *Understanding Terror Networks* (Philadelphia: University of Pennsylvania Press, 2004), pp. 160-61.

[93] Wright, "The Terror Web." Another writer respectful of the Internet's potential uses in the hands of terrorists is Audrey Kurth Cronin, "Behind the Curve: Globalization and International Terrorism," *International Security* 27, no. 3 (Winter 2002/03): 46-51.

[94] Walker Connor, "The Politics of Ethnonationalism," *Journal of International Affairs* 27, no. 1 (1973): 15. "To say that there has been a vast increase in informal penetration activities during the past half-century," in the words of an early student of these phenomena, "is only another way of saying that the assault on men's loyalties is quantitatively far greater than it once was. Since the capacity of men to withstand this kind of attack has probably not changed significantly, the increased pressure on their allegiance must necessarily result in a greater incidence of disloyal behavior." Andrew M. Scott, *The Revolution in Statecraft: Informal Penetration* (New York: Random House, 1965), p. 115.

[95] FitzGerald, *China and the Overseas Chinese*, p. 186.

[96] No contemporary work stimulated more debate over this issue than that of Samuel P. Huntington, *The Clash of Civilizations and the Remaking of World Order* (New York: Simon & Schuster, 1996). Most of Huntington's critics found particular fault in his alleged neglect of divisive *intra*-civilizational nationalisms.

[97] For example, while declaring Palestinian Arabs "an inseparable part of the Arab Nation" (Article 3), the Covenant asserts the "permanent and genuine" character of the Palestinian personality (Article 5) and the right of Palestinians to determine their own destiny in accord with their "own wishes and free will and choice" (Article 4). For a partisan but still useful analysis of the Covenant, see Yehoshafat Harkabi, *Palestinians and Israel* (New York: John Wiley & Sons, 1974), pp. 49-69.

[98] For a superb discussion of the factors involved in resolving the conflict in the South Tyrol, see Peter J. Katzenstein, "Ethnic Political Conflict in South Tyrol," in *Ethnic Conflict in the Western World*, Milton J. Esman (ed.) (Ithaca: Cornell University Press, 1977), pp. 287-323. Somalia's territorial claims against its East African neighbors are equally revealing of the diminished virtue popularly seen in irredentism. The Somali campaign to recover what Somalis insist are their ethnic Somali brethren from Ethiopia, Kenya and Djibouti was for many years the only prolonged and militant ethnic unification movement on the African continent. It made Somalia, at least until civil war in the 1990s left it in political ruin, a pariah state among Africans, and it was responsible in large part for making the African Horn the continent's record-holder for boundary disputes. The Somalis themselves, interestingly, have been careful to disclaim any expansionist designs. They claimed, for example, that the capture of the Ogaden desert from Ethiopia in 1977 was accomplished entirely by the Somali minority *within* Ethiopia—revealingly bearing the name of the Western Somalia Liberation Front. *Christian Science Monitor*, 26 July 1977. For background, see Christopher Clapham, "Ethiopia and Somalia," in *Conflicts in Africa*, Adelphi Papers no. 93 (London: International Institute for Strategic Studies, December 1972), pp. 1-23.

[99] In October 1977, President Jimmy Carter signed both this Covenant and the Covenant on Economic, Social and Cultural Rights. The U.S. Senate has never ratified either Covenant.

[100] Woodrow Wilson's Secretary of State Robert Lansing long ago entered in his diary a prophetic warning about the principle of self-determination, a phrase, he said, "simply loaded with dynamite" that would "certainly come home to roost and cause much vexation." Quoted in Alan J. Ward, *Ireland and Anglo-American Relations 1899-1921* (London: Weidenfeld and Nicolson, 1969), pp. 170-71.

[101] On this subject, see Francis MacDonnell, *Insidious Foes: The Axis Fifth Column and the American Home Front* (Guilford: Lyons Press, 2004).

[102] The Latin American angle of this issue is the focus of Max Paul Friedman, *Nazis and Good Neighbors: The United States Campaign Against the Germans of Latin America in World War II* (New York: Cambridge University Press, 2003).

[103] Already noted in this context was the postwar forced exodus from Czechoslovakia of about three million Sudeten Germans. In this category also certainly falls the unwarranted detention of over 120,000 Japanese-Americans during World War II.

[104] In his memoirs, Hitler's Foreign Minister von Ribbentrop made the disingenuous, yet revealing, admission that in his early years in that post "the activities of the National Socialist Organization of Germans Abroad caused me acute embarrassment, in South America, for instance. There, as elsewhere, such things as processions, uniforms, and rallies created the impression that National Socialism was to be exported. Indeed, however wrongly, the Organization was described as a 'Fifth Column', and furnished President Roosevelt with the grotesque propaganda argument that Germany was trying to establish a foothold in South America, which it would use as a base for action against the U.S.A.... I often pointed out that while the Organization's aim of keeping Germans abroad together was certainly right, the manner in which this was done entailed disproportionate disadvantages." Quoted in Zeman, *Nazi Propaganda*, pp. 77-8.

[105] On the Tibetans, see Barry Sautman, "China's Strategic Vulnerability to Minority Separatism in Tibet," *Asian Affairs* 32, no. 2 (Summer 2005): 87-118. On the Muslim Uigurs, see Yitzhak Shichor, "Blow Up: Internal and External Challenges of Uyghur Separatism and Islamic Radicalism to Chinese Rule in Xinjiang," *Asian Affairs* 32, no. 2 (Summer 2005): 119-35.

Notes: Chapter 3

[1]Axel, B. K. 1996. "Notes on Space, Cartography, and Gender," in Singh, P. and Barrier, N. g. (eds) *The Transmission of Sikh Heritage in the Diaspora*. Delhi: Manohar: 173.

[2] *Report of the High Level Committee on Indian Diaspora*, Government of India: V http://indiandiaspora.nic.in/diasporapdf/part1-for.pdf (Last accessed on, 2006-10-26).

[3] Dijkink, G. 1996. *National Identity & Geopolitical Visions: Maps of Pride and Pain*, London & New York: Routledge: 147.

[4] Castles, S. and Miller, M. J. 1998 (second edition), *The Age of Migration: International Population Movements in the Modern World*, Houndmills: Macmillan.

[5]Dijkink, G. 1996. *National Identity & Geopolitical Visions: Maps of Pride and Pain*, London & New York: Routledge: 11.

[6] Tesfahuney, M. 1998. "Mobility, Racism and Geopolitics," *Political Geography* 17(5):499.

[7] Ibid.

[8] Dwyer, C. 1999. "Migrations and Diaspora," in Cloke, P, Crang, P. and Goodwin, M. (eds.) *Introducing Human Geographies*, London: Arnold: 288.

[9] Foucault, M. 1980. *Power/Knowledge: Selected Interviews and Other Writings*. New York: Penguin.

[10] Harvey, D. 2001. *Spaces of Capital: Towards a Critical Geography*, New York: Routledge: 231-32.

[11] Soja, E. W. 1989. *Post-Modern Geographies: The Reassertion of Space in Critical Social Theory*, New York: Verso.

[12] Axel, B. K. 1996. "Notes on Space, Cartography, and Gender," in Singh, P. and Barrier, N. g. (eds) *The Transmission of Sikh Heritage in the Diaspora*. Delhi: Manohar.

[13] Ludden, D. 2002. *India and South Asia: A Short History*, Oxford: One World: 15-16.

[14] Vertovec, S. 2000. "Religion and Diaspora," paper presented at the conference on "New Landscapes of Religion in the West," School of Geography and Environment, University of Oxford, 27-29 September: 27.

[15] International Organization for Migration (IOM). 2003. World Migration: Managing Migration. Challenges and Responses for People on the Move: 4.

[16] Bhagwati, J. 2004. *In Defense of Globalization*, New Delhi: Oxford University Press: 209.

[17] Ibid.: 217-218.

[18] Bhagwati, J. 2004. *In Defense of Globalization*, New Delhi: Oxford University Press: 218.

[19] Ibid.: 215.

[20] Appadurai, A. 1996. *Modernity at Large: Cultural Dimensions of Globalization*. Minneapolis: University of Minnesota Press.

[21] Huang, Y. 2001. Why More is Actually Less: New Interpretation of China's Labour Intensive FDI http://www.wdi.umich.edu/files/Publications/WorkingPapers/wp375.pdf (Last accessed on 26.10.2006).

[22] *Report of the High Level Committee on Indian Diaspora*, Government of India http://indiandiaspora.nic.in/contents.htm (Last accessed on 26.10.2006).

[23] Ibid.: vi.

[24] Ibid.: viii.

[25] Ibid.: xi.

[26] Ibid.: vi.

[27] Ibid.: xxii.

[28] Ibid.: xviii.

[29] Ibid.: xviii.

[30] Gupta, A. 2004. *The Indian Diaspora's Political Effects in the United States*, Observer Research Foundation (ORF) Occasional Paper, September. http://www.observerindia.com/publications/OccasionalPapers/occasional.htm (Last accessed on 26.20.2006).

[31] *Report of the High Level Committee on Indian Diaspora*, Government of India: xx- xxi.

[32] Ibid.: xxiv-xxvi.

[33] Sharma, J. 2003. *Hindutva: Exploring the Idea of Hindu Nationalism. New Delhi*: Penguin/Viking: 7.

[34] Hansen, T. B. 2004. *The Saffron Wave: Democracy and Hindu Nationalism in Modern India*. In Omnibus: *Hindu Nationalism and Indian Politics* (with an introduction by P. B. Mehta), New Delhi: Oxford University Press: 76-77.

[35] Ibid.: 78-80,

[36] Ibid.: 80.

[37] Thapar R. 2004. *Somnath: The Many Voices of a History*, New Delhi: Penguin: 217-18.

[38] BJP Election Manifesto: Our National Identity http://www.bjp.org/manifes/chap2.htm (Last accessed on 26.20.2006).

[39] Robinson, R.2001. "Religion on the Net: An Analysis of the Global Reach of Hindu Fundamentalism and its Implications for India," Sociological Bulletin, 50 (2): 245.

[40] Robinson, R.2001. "Religion on the Net: An Analysis of the Global Reach of Hindu Fundamentalism and its Implications for India," Sociological Bulletin, 50 (2): 245.

[41] Rajagopal, A. 2004. "Non-resident nationalism," *Frontline*, 21(6). http://www.hinduonnet.com/fline/fl2106/stories/20040326005212700.htm (Last accessed on 26.20.2006).

[42] Kurien, P. 2001. "Religion, Ethnicity and Politics: Hindu and Muslim Indian Immigrants in the United States," *Ethnic and Racial Studies*, 24(2): 284.

[43] Kapoor, D. 2003. "Indian Diaspora as a Strategic Asset," *Economic and Political Weekly*, 1 February: 448.

[44] Harvey, D. 2001. *Spaces of Capital: Towards a Critical Geography*, New York: Routledge: 231-232

[45] Lacoste, Y. 2000. "Rivalries for Territory," *Geopolitics*, 5(2): 121.

Notes: Chapter 4

[1] Devesh Kapur, "Ideas and Economic Reforms in India: The Role of International Migration and the Indian Diaspora," *India Review*, Vol. 3, no. 4 (Ocober 2004), p. 365.

[2] Myron Weiner, "The Indian Presence in America: What Difference Will It Make?" In Sulochana Raghanvan Glazer and Nathan Glazer eds., *Conflicting Images: India and the United States* (Glenn Dale, MD.: Riverdale Publishers, 1990), pp. 241-56.

[3] *India Abroad* (1 October 2004), p. 8.

[4] Robert Jervis, *The Logic of Images in International Relations* (New York: Columbia University Press, Morningside ed., 1989).

[5] Dennis Kux, *Estranged Democracies: India and the United States, 1941-1991* (New Delhi: Sage, 1993).

[6] Harold R. Isaacs, *Scratches on Our Minds* (Armonk, N.Y.: M.E. Sharpe, 1980 edition), p. xxxiii.

[7] Glazer and Glazer eds, *Conflicting Images*, p. 4.

[8] Chester Bowles, "Spoken at a Conference on India and the United States," in Selig Harrison ed., *India and the United States*. New York: The Macmillan Company, 1961), p. 28.

[9] William Richter, "Long Term Trends and Patterns in Indian Opinion towards the United States," in Harold Gould and Sumit Ganguly eds, *The Hope and the Reality: U.S.-Indian Relations from Roosevelt to Reagan.* Boulder, Co.: Westview), pp. 199-217.

[10] Michael Brecher, *The Foreign Policy System of Israel* (New Haven: Yale University Press, 1972).

[11] See Shashi Tharoor, *Reasons of State* (Delhi: Vikas Publishing House Private Ltd., 1982), passim, for an elaboration.

[12] See Kux, *Estranged Democracies*, p. 70.

[13] See Steven Hoffmann, "Indo-US Strategic Worldviews," in Ashok Kapur, Y.K. Malik, Harold A. Gould and Arthur G. Rubinoff eds., *India and the United States in a Changing World* (New Delhi: Sage Publications, 2002), pp. 216-44.

[14] M.S. Venkataramani and B.K. Shrivastava, *Quit India: The American Response to the 1942 Struggle* (New Delhi: Vikas, 1979).

[15] A. Shanmugan, *Indian Parliament and the United States* (Annamalainagar: Annamalai University, 1989, pp. 93-113.

[16] Francine R. Frankel, *India's Political Economy, 1947-1966* (Princeton: Princeton University Press, pp. 299-300.

[17] A. Guy Hope, *America and Swaraj* (Washington, D.C.: Public Affairs Press, 1968), pp. 19-23.

[18] Gary R. Hess, *America Encounters India* (Baltimore and London: The Johns Hopkins Press, 1971).

[19] See Frenise A. Logan, "Racism and Indian-U.S. Relations, 1947-1953: Views in the Indian Press," in Michael L. Krenn ed., *Race and U.S. Foreign Policy During the Cold War* (New York and London: Garland Publishing Company, 1998), pp. 89-97.

[20] Karen Isaksen Leonard, *The South Asian Americans* (Westport, CN, 1997), chapter 2.

[21] Stephen P. Cohen, *India, Emerging Power* (Washington, D.C.: The Brookings Institution, 2001), p. 86.

[22] *United States v. Thind 261 U.S. 204 (1923).*

[23] See D.S. Saund, *Congressman from India* (New York: E.P. Dutton, 1960) for a discussion of efforts to redress these matters. Saund—the only legislator of Indian descent to serve in Congress—entered the United States in 1920 and earned a Ph.D. from the University of California at Berkeley. Elected to the House of Representatives as the first Democrat from the Imperial Valley of California in 1956, he served on the Foreign Affairs Committee. In 2004 Bobby Jindal (R-LA) became the second Indian-American elected to Congress. By contrast, Indo-Canadians—which account for one million people in a country one-tenth the size of the United States—currently have nine members of their community in the House of Commons.

[24] Binod Khadria, The *Migration of Knowledge Workers, Second-Generation Effects of India's Brain Drain* (New Delhi (Sage, 1999), pp. 60-61.

[25] For an elaboration see Selig Harrison, "Dialogue of the Deaf: Mutual Perceptions and Indo-American Relations," in Glazer and Glazer, *Conflicting Images*, p. 58.

[26] Milton Singer, *When a Great Tradition Modernizes* (New York: Praeger, 1972), p. 12.

[27] See Lloyd I. Rudolph, "Gandhi in the Mind of America," in Glazer and Glazer eds, *Conflicting Images*, pp. 143-77.

[28] W. Norman Brown, *The United States, India, Pakistan and Bangladesh* (Cambridge: MA: Harvard University Press, 1972), p. 392.

[29] Charles H. Heimsath, "The American Images of India as Factors in U.S. Foreign Policy Making," in Krenn ed., *Race and U.S. Foreign Policy During the Cold War*, p. 99.

[30] "National Target for South Asia Specialists," *A Report to the National Council for Foreign Languages and International Studies*, p. 18.

[31] *Asia and American Textbooks* (New York, 1976).

[32] United States-Indian Cultural Relations (Washington: Bureau of Educational and Cultural Affairs, 1982).

[33] See William Watts, *The United States and Asia: Changing Attitudes and Policies* (Lexington, Ma: Lexington Books, 1982).

[34] Hess, *America Encounters India*, p. 7.

[35] John W. Mellor, *India as a Rising Middle Power* (Boulder, Co.: Westview Press, 1979), p. 359.

[36] Christopher Van Hoellen, "The Tilt Policy Revisited: Nixon-Kissinger Geopolitics and South Asia," *Asian Survey*, Vol. XX, no. 4 (April 1980), p. 341.

[37] James Warner Bjorkman, "Public Law 480 and the Policies of Self-Help and Short-Tether: Indo-American Relations, 1965-68," in Lloyd I. Rudolph and Susanne Hoeber Rudolph, *The Regional Imperative, U.S. Foreign Policy towards South Asian States* (Atlantic Highlands, N.J: Humanities Press, 1980), p. 234.

[38] John P. Lewis, *India's Political Economy, Governance and Reform* (Delhi: Oxford University Press, 1995), p. 87.

[39] Norman Ornstein, "The Open Congress Meets the President," in Anthony King ed., *Both Sides of the Avenue* (Washington, D. C. American Enterprise Institute, 1983), p. 208.

[40] Pramod Vas, *Dawning on the Capitol, U. S. Congress and India* (Calcutta: Mascot, 1966), p. 1.

[41] Quoted from *Playboy*, March 1977, p. 78 by John W. Mellor and Philip Oldenburg, "India and the United States," in Mellor, ed., *India: A Rising Middle Power*, p. 4.

[42] U.S. Congress, House Committee on Foreign Affairs, Subcommittee on the Near East and South Asia, *Hearings, Political Trends in India and Bangladesh*, 93d Congress 1st session, (31 October 1973), p. 18.

[43] Baldev Raj Nayar, "Treat India Seriously," *Foreign Policy*, No. 18 (Spring 1975), pp. 173-54.

[44] Myron Weiner, "Critical Choices for India and America," in Donald C. Hellmann ed., *Southern Asia: The Politics of Poverty and Peace* (Lexington, Ma.: Lexington Books, 1976), p. 65.

[45] Lloyd I. and Susanne Hoeber Rudolph, "The Coordination of Complexity," in *The Regional Imperative*, p. 95.

[46] Report of an Independent Task Force, *A New Foreign Policy toward India and Pakistan* (New York: Council on Foreign Relations, 1997), p. 45.

[47] Hence, in the Senate, only the Subcommittee on Refugees of the Senate Judiciary Committee, chaired by Edward Kennedy (D-MA), held hearings on the Bangladesh crisis of 1971-1972.

[48] According to a senior analyst at the Congressional Research Service. Interview, Washington, D. C., 15 April 1986.

[49] See *India Today* (15 November 1993), pp. 207-09.

[50] On this point see Andrew J. Rotter, *Comrades at Odds, The United States and India, 1947-1964* (Ithaca: Cornell University Press, 2000).

[51] Robert Dahl, *Congress and Foreign Policy* (New York: Harcourt, Brace, 1950), p. 15.

[52] U.S. Department of State, Office of Intelligence Research, "India's Political and Economic Position in the East-West Conflict," *OIR Report No. 5526* (15 May 1951), p. 1.

[53] For an elaboration see "U.S. Attitudes towards India" in Arthur G. Rubinoff ed., *Canada and South Asia: Political and Strategic Relations*, (Toronto: South Asia Centre of the University of Toronto, 1992), pp. 63-73.

[54] For details see Arthur G. Rubinoff, "The Role of Congress in the Formulation of U.S. South Asia Policy," in Lloyd I. Rudolph and Susanne Hoeber Rudolph, *The Regional Imperative, U. S. Foreign Policy towards the South Asian States* (2d ed. New Delhi: Concept Publishing Company, 2005), forthcoming.

[55] The Brown Amendment divided the Indian and Pakistani communities which had cooperated on easing restrictions for foreign doctors to practice in the United States. The two communities played a role in the unsuccessful campaign of Larry Pressler (R-SD)—a critic of Pakistan's nuclear program—to win reelection in 1996. In 2002, a Pakistani-American managed the successful reelection campaign of Democratic Senator Tim Johnson in South Dakota.

[56] See Arthur G. Rubinoff, "Mixed Opportunities and Contradictory Policies: Indo-American Relations in the Clinton-Rao Years," *Pacific Affairs*, Vol. 69, no. 4 (Winter 1996-97), p. 514.

[57] *Indian Express* (25 September 1995).

[58] *The Hindu*, international edition, (16 December 1995), p. 5.

[59] Surjit Mansingh, *India's Search for Power* (New Delhi: Sage, 1984), p. 71.

[60] "Indians Go Home, but Don't Leave U.S. Behind," *New York Times* (24 July 2004), p. 1.

[61] Ibid. The author even encountered one member of the Indian parliament who made sure his wife gave birth in the United States, so that his child would be an American citizen.

[62] Aziz Haniffa, "India Sends Maximum Students to the US," *India Abroad* (28 January 2003), p. 6.

[63] See Arthur G. Rubinoff, "The Changing Nature of India's Parliament," in Reeta C. Tremblay *et al.*, eds., *Indo/Pakistani/Canadian Reflections on the 50th Anniversary of India's Independence* (Delhi: B. R. Publications, 1998), pp. 251-65.

[64] See Arthur G. Rubinoff, "Legislative Perception of Indo-American Relations," in Ashok Kapur, *et al* eds., *India and the United States in a Changing World*, pp. 412-57.

[65] Aziz Haniffa, "Young MPs Wow Capitol Hill," *India Abroad* (17 September 2004), p. 1.

[66] Kapur, "Ideas and Economic Reforms in India: The Role of International Migration and the Indian Diaspora," pp. 374-75.

[67] Ibid., p. 379.

[68] Robert M. Hathaway, "Unfinished Passage: India, Indian Americans, and the U.S. Congress," *The Washington Quarterly*, Vol. 24. no. 2 (Spring 2001), p. 26.

[69] On this point see Godfrey Hodgson, *The Gentleman from New York, Daniel Patrick Moynihan, a Biography* (Boston: Houghton Mifflin Company, 2000), p. 206.

[70] In January 2004 Joseph Crowley, the Co-Chair of the Caucus on India and Indian Americans, and Steny Hoyer (D-MD), the Democratic Whip, headed a fifteen member congressional delegation—the largest American legislative contingent ever to visit India. *India Abroad* (12 December 2003), p. 8.

[71] In this connection see Ralph Nurnberger, *Lobbing in America: A Primer for Citizen Participation* (Washington: India Abroad Center for Political Awareness, 2000). Nurnberger spent eight years as a senior lobbyist for the American Israel Public Affairs Committee before becoming a Washington associate of the India Abroad Center for Political Awareness.

[72] Robert M. Hathaway, "Washington's New Strategic Partnership," *Seminar*, Number 538 (June 2004), pp. 68-72.

[73] Sonalde Desai and Rahul Kanakia, "Profiles of a Diasporic Community," *Seminar*, Number 538 (June 2004), p. 49.

[74] George Joseph, "Indian Population Explodes in the US," *India Abroad* (1 September 2006), p. 1.

[75] It is no accident that Al Gore's emergence from seclusion after the 2000 election was at a highly paid speech in Atlanta to the Asian American Hotel Owners Association.

[76] *New York Times* (12 January 2003), p. 4.

[77] "U.S. is largest wealth market for Indians," *Yahoo! India News*, 15 May 2003, http// in.news.yahoo.com/030515/43/24aog.html.

[78] See Leonard, *The South Asian Americans*, pp. 77ff.

[79] See the joint website of Indian Embassy and India Abroad Center for Political Awareness, as well as www.usinpac.com for complete details.

[80] For a discussion of prominent Indian-Americans see "Indian Americans: A Saga of Success," *Asia Times online*, http://www.atimes.com/atimes/Front_Page/EJ23Aa03.html.

[81] Sadad Dhume, "From Bangalore to Silicon Valley and Back: how the Indian Diaspora in the United States is Changing India," in Alyssa Ayres and Philip Oldenburg eds., *India Briefing, Quickening the Pace of Change* (Armonk, NY:M. E. Sharpe, 2002), pp. 117-19.

[82] Hathaway, "Unfinished Passage," p.24.

[83] Dhume, "From Bangalore to Silicon Valley and Back," p. 116.

[84] According to *Fortune* (19 July 1999), p.85, twenty percent of Congressman Frank Pallone's donors have Indian surnames and sixty eight percent of those live outside of New Jersey.

[85] Miles A. Pomper and Sumana Chatterjee, "Congress Embraces India as Pakistan's Influence Fades," *Congressional Quarterly Weekly*, Vol. 58, no. 12 (18 March 2000), p. 57883.

[86] While reasonably cohesive on issues, there are evident fissures within the community. The Indian American Association's most recent past president attempted to organize a boycott of competing groups' reception for former Indian president K.R. Narayanan in Washington in May 2003. *India Abroad*, June 6, 2003. Similar rivalries were evident during the recent visit of Prime Minister Manmohan Singh. *India Abroad* (24 September 2004), p. 1.

[87] Given the overwhelmingly Democratic character of the Indian-American community, a concerted effort was made to recruit Republican members so that the community did not appear partisan. According to a 1996 study, forty two percent of Indian-Americans identified themselves as Democrats, and thirteen percent as Republicans. *Washington Post* (internet edition), 25 October 2003. In the 1988 presidential election, 56.3 percent of Indian-Americans voted for Michael Dukakis, the Democratic candidate for president and 23.0 percent voted for George H.W. Bush, the Republican nominee. Tanmay Kanjil, "The Indian-Americans in the United States: Participation in the U.S. Political Process," *International Studies*, Vol. 32, no. 4 (October-December, 1996), p.90. In 2000, Democrat Al Gore garnered fifty three percent of the Indo-American community's vote compared to just fourteen percent for George W. Bush, the Republican nominee. *India Abroad*, (24 September 24, 2004), p.8. In 2004, despite the unpopularity of John Kerry's position on outsourcing, he led President George W. Bush by forty two percent to eight percent, with twenty three percent undecided. Interestingly, the results were fifty-fifty in India.

[88] See Robert M. Hathaway, "Confrontation and Retreat: The U.S. Congress and the South Asian Nuclear Tests," *Arms Control Today*, Vol. 30, no. 1 (January-February 2000), pp. 7-14.

[89] Pallone was deposed by Gary Ackerman (D-NY) in October 1998, after being accused of using the organization for personal aggrandizement. See *India Abroad* (16 October 1998), p. 18 and 23 October 1998, p.12 for details. Jim McDermott (D-WA) succeeded Ackerman two years later. James Crowley (D-NY), whose district has the second largest population of Indian-Americans, replaced McDermott in 2002. Ackerman reassumed the leadership of the organization in 2004.

[90] Robert M. Hathaway, "Coming of Age: Indian-Americans and the US Congress," in Kapur *et al, India and America in a Changing World*, p. 399.

[91] Aziz Haniffa, "Friends of India Formed in US Senate," *rediff.com*, 31 March 2004.

[92] It is believed the BJP through its affiliate groups, such as the VHP, is especially active among the expatriate community in the United States.

[93] "Swaminomics: Foreign Policy Impact of Indian Americans," http://syndication.indiatimes.com/articleshow.cms?msid=20448957

[94] Mike McIntyre, "Indian-Americans Test Their Clout on Atom Pact," *New York Times* (5 June 2006), p. 1.

[95] Arthur G. Rubinoff, "Changing Perceptions of India in the U.S. Congress," *Asian Affairs*, Vol. 28, no. 1 (Spring 2001), p. 57.

[96] *India Abroad* (13 February 2004), p. 8.

Notes: Chapter 5

[1] Chandrashekhar Bhat, 'India and the Indian Diaspora: Inter-Linkages and Expectations' in Dubey (ed.) *Indian Diaspora: Global Identity* (Delhi: Kalinga Publications, 2003), 11.

[2] Hugh Tinker, *A New System of Slavery: The export of Indian labour overseas, 1830-1920* (London: Hansib Publishing Ltd, 1993).

[3] Chandrashekhar Bhat, 'India and the Indian Diaspora: Inter-Linkages and Expectations' in Dubey (ed.) *Indian Diaspora: Global Identity* (Delhi: Kalinga Publications, 2003), 11–12.

[4] <www.faculty.winthrop.edu/haynese/india/medals/VC/IndVC.html>

[5] Kim Knott, 'Hinduism in Britain' in *The South Asian Religious Diaspora in Britain, Canada and United States* (NY: State University of United States, 2000), 92.

[6] Ibid.

[7] Steven Vertovec, *The Hindu Diaspora* (London: Routledge, 2000), 124.

[8] Steven Vertovec, *The Hindu Diaspora* (London: Routledge, 2000), 138.

[9] Ibid. 128–129.

[10] Bhiku Parekh, 'Politics of Nationhood', in K.Brenda et al. (ed.), Nationalism, Ethnicity and Cultural Identity in Europe (Utrecht: Utrecht University Press, 1995), 126–127

[11] Ibid. 130.

[12] Steven Vertovec, *The Indian Diaspora* (London: Routledge, 2003), 141.

[13] Ibid. 146–147.

[14] Kim Knott, 'Hinduism in Britain' in *The South Asian Religious Diaspora in Britain, Canada and United States* (NY: State University of the United States, 2000), 92.

[15] <www.news.bbc.co.uk/1/hi/world/south_asia/669171.stm>

[16] Amrit Dhillon, 'Goodness gracious: the Brits invade Bollywood', *The Sunday Times* (26 September 2004), 29.

[17] *Gandhi* won eight Oscars in 1983 (Best Picture, Director, Actor, Screenplay, Cinematography, Film Editing, Art Direction, Costume Design) and starred Ben Kingsley, Roshan Seth, Saeed Jaffrey, Alyque Padamsee, Amrish Puri, Martin Sheen, Candice Bergen and Edward Fox.

[18] Ravindra Jain, 'A Civilization Theory of Indian Diaspora and its Global implications', in Ajay Dubey (ed.), *Indian Diaspora: Global Identity* (Delhi: Kalinga Publications, 2003), 1.

[19] Chandrashekhar Bhat, 'India and the Indian Diaspora: Inter-Linkages and Expectations' in Dubey (ed.), *Indian Diaspora: Global Identity* (Delhi: Kalinga Publications, 2003), 16.

[20] Carl Mortished, 'Indians curry favour in the West', *The Times*, Business section (30 August 2004), 33.

[21] Bhat, 'India and the Indian Diaspora', 18.

[22] Ibid.

[23] Ibid.

[24] Ibid., 19.

[25] Neelam Verjee, 'India's big push into the global market', *The Times*. Business section (30 August 2004), 34.

[26] Ibid., 34.

[27] Carl Mortished, 'Sahara, the company for all the family', *The Times*. Business section (30 August 2004), 34.

[28] Arifa Akbar, 'India looks to brain gain as new affluence draws migrants back in their thousands', *The Independent* (2 Aug. 2004), 18.

[29] Ibid.

[30] Muhammad Anwar, 'The Participation of Asians in the British Political System', in *South Asians Overseas*, edited Colin Clarke, Ceri Peach and Steven Vertovec (Cambridge: Cambridge University Press, 1990), 301.

[31] Michael White, Gift of £2m makes Mittal Labour's biggest benefactor. The Guardian. July 14, 2005.p.14.

[32] Bhat, 'India and the Indian Diaspora', 15.

[33] <www.indiandiaspora.nic.in/pressrelease.htm>

[34] Bhat, 'India and the Indian Diaspora', 19–20. <www.indiandiaspora.nic.in/mandate.htm>

[35] Chetan Bhatt and Parita Mukta, '*Hindutva* in the West: Mapping the antinomies of diaspora nationalism', *Ethnic and Racial Studies*, 23/3 (May 2000), 409.

[36] 'The Foreign Exchange of Hate. IDRF and the American funding of *Hindutva*': <http://stopfundinghate.org/sacw/appendixa.html>

[37] Jayant Lele, 'Indian Diaspora's Long Distance Nationalism', in *Fractured Identity: The Indian Diaspora in Canada* (ed.) Sushma Varma and R.Seshan (Jaipur: Rawat Publications, 2003), 80.

[38] Rowena Robinson, 'Religion on the Net: Analysis of the global Reach of Hindu Fundamentalism and its implications for India', *Sociological Bulletin*, 50/2 (2001), 239.

[39] Jayant Lele, 'Indian Diaspora's Long Distance Nationalism', 81.

[40] Ibid., 82.

[41] Rowena Robinson, 'Religion on the Net: Analysis of the global Reach of Hindu Fundamentalism and its implications for India', *Sociological Bulletin*, 50/2 (2001), 239.

[42] Maneesha Tikekar, Religion as Ethnicity: *Hindutva* in Britain' (Unpublished paper).

[43] Ibid.

[44] Chetan Bhatt and Parita Mukta, '*Hindutva* in the West', 426. The HSS is the British version of the RSS.

[45] Maneesha Tikekar, 'Religion as Ethnicity: *Hindutva* in Britain' (Unpublished paper).

[46] Ibid.

[47] Ibid.

[48] Gita Sahgal, 'Diaspora Politics in Britain: Hindu Identity in the Making', in Rahjeshwari Ghose (ed.), *In Quest of a Secular Symbol* (Indian Ocean Centre and South Asian Research Unit. Curtin University of Technology, 1996), 141.

[49] See Awaaz: South Asia Watch Ltd. In Bad Faith: British Charity and Hindu Extremism.London.2004. ISBN 0 9547174 06

[50] *The Times of India*, 20 September 2004.

[51] Ibid.

[52] <www.dawn.com/2004/09/21/top12.htm>

Notes: Chapter 6

[1] Igor Saveliev, "Globality and Diversity: Introduction," in Pal Nyiri and Igor Saveliev (eds), *Globalizing Chinese Migration: Trends in Europe and Asia* (Hampshire: Ashgate, 2002), p. 5.

[2] Pal Nyiri, "From Class Enemies to Patriots: Overseas Chinese and Emigration Policy and Discourse in the People's Republic of China," in Saveliev, "Globality and Diversity," p. 230.

[3] Nyiri, "From Class Enemies to Patriots," pp. 222-23.

[4] Ibid., pp. 230.

[5] Frank Ching, "China Maligned," *Far Eastern Economic Review* (29 July 1999).

[6] Anatoli M. Shkurkin, "Chinese in the Labor Market of the Russian Far East: Past, Present, Future," in Nyiri and Saveliev (eds), *Globalizing Chinese Migration*, p. 88.

[7] Quoted in Bertil Lintner, "Triads Tighten Grip on Russia's Far East," *Jane's Intelligence Review* (September 2003). For a complete version of the paper, see: www.csis.org/ruseura/ponars/policymemos/pm_0184.pdf.

[8] Interview with Vitaly Nomokonov, Vladivostok, 21 May 2003

[9] Bertil Lintner, "Spreading Tentacles," *Far Eastern Economic Review* (2 October 2003).

[10] Interview, Nomokonov, 21 May 2003.

[11] Ibid.

[12] Lintner, "Spreading Tentacles."

[13] Quoted in Lintner, "The Third Wave,", *Far Eastern Economic Review* (24 June 1999).

[14] Lintner, "The Third Wave."

[15] Bruce Gilley, "The Exiled Resurgent," *Far Eastern Economic Review* (8 January 1998).

[16] Julio Jeldres, "China's Growing Influence in Cambodia," in *Africana: Rivista di Studi Extraeuropei* VIII (Pisa: Italian Association of Extraeuropean Studies, 2002).

[17] According to numerous interviews with local people, including such "brokers" in Ruili. See also Bertil Lintner, "Illegal Aliens Smuggling to and through Southeast Asia's Golden Triangle," in Nyiri and Saveliev (eds), *Globalizing Chinese Migration*, pp. 108-19.

[18] See, for instance, Nyi Pu Lay, "The Python", in Anna J. Allot (ed.), *Inked Over, Ripped Out: Burmese Storytellers and the Censors* (Chiang Mai: Silkworm Books, 1994), pp. 85-101.

[19] Interview with Giff Johnson, editor of the *Marshall Islands Journal*, Majuro, the Marshall Islands, 25 May 2004.

[20] "Authorities Bust Alien Smuggling Scheme," *Saipan Tribune* (4 October 2004).

[21] Quoted in Bertil Lintner, "A New Battle or the Pacific," *Far Eastern Economic Review* (5 August 2004).

[22] See John Henderson and Benjamin Reilly, "Dragon in Paradise: China's Rising Star in Oceania," *The National Interest* (Summer 2003).

[23] Henderson and Reilly, "Dragon in Paradise," p. 98.

[24] Ibid., p. 98.

[25] Nyiri, "From Class Enemies to Patriots," p. 232.

Notes: Chapter 7

[1] Paper presented at the International Conference on Ethnic Minorities and Great Power Strategies in Asia, 12-14 October 2004, Asia Pacific Center for Security Studies, Honolulu, Hawaii.

[2] Associate Professor and Dean, Asian Center, University of the Philippines.

[3] Rizal Sukma, "Indonesia's Perceptions of China: The Domestic Bases of Persistent Ambiguity" in Herbert Yee and Ian Storey, eds. *The China Threat: Perceptions, Myths and Reality* (London: RoutledgeCurzon, 2002), 191.

[4] Abdul Razak Baginda, "Malaysian Perceptions of China: From Hostility to Cordiality" in Yee and Storey, 229.

[5] Theresa Chong Carino, *Political Leadership and the Federation of Filipino-Chinese Chambers of Commerce and Industry: Continuity and Change (1954-1994)*. Unpublished Dissertation at CSSP, 1995, 222-223.

[6] Leo Suryadinata, "China's Economic Modernization and the Ethnic Chinese in ASEAN: A Preliminary Study" in Leo Suryadinata, ed. *Southeast Asian Chinese and China: the Politico-Economic Dimension* (Singapore: Times Academic Press, 1995), 200.

[7] Ibid., 202.

[8] Ibid., 201.

[9] Taiwanese Chinese Ho Wen Lee was accused of transferring classified data from the nuclear plant he worked for; and Indonesian Chinese were charged with making illegal contributions to electoral campaign funds of U.S. President William Clinton.

[10] East Asia Analytical Unit, Department of Foreign Affairs and Trade, Australia. *Overseas Chinese Business Networks in Asia*, 1995, 7.

[11] Stephen Fitzgerald. *China and the Overseas Chinese: A Study of Peking's Changing Policy 1949-1970.* (Cambridge University Press, 1972), 186.

[12] Chinben See, "Chinese Organizations and Ethnic Identity in the Philippines" in Jennifer Cushman and Wang Gungwu, eds. Changing Identities of the Southeast Asian Chinese since World War II (Hong Kong: Hong Kong University Press, 1988), 327.

[13] Lee Kam Hing, "The Political Position of the Chinese in Post-independence Malaysia" in *The Chinese Diaspora: Selected Essays*, ed. Wang Ling-chi and Wang Gungwu (Singapore: Times Academic press 1998).

[14] Wang Gungwu, "The Southeast Asian Chinese and the Development of China", in Leo Suryadinata, ed. *Southeast Asian Chinese and China: the Politico-Economic Dimension* (Singapore: Times Academic Press, 1995), 21.

[15] Edgar Wickberg, "Chinese organizations and Ethnicity in Southeast Asia and North America since 1945: A Comparative Analysis" in Jennifer Cushman and Wang Gungwu, eds. *Changing Identities of the Southeast Asian Chinese since World War II* (Hong Kong: Hong Kong University Press, 1988), 308.

[16] Chinben See, 323.

[17] See Suryadinata, 2, 4-5, and various other sources.

[18] Chinben See, 328.

[19] Interview with Go Bon Juan, Kaisa para sa Kaunlaran. 17 September 2004.

[20] Carino, 54, citing James Blaker and similar work by Wang Gungwu.

[21]Wang Gungwu, 23-24.

[22] Wickberg, 307.

[23] Chinben See, 319.

[24] Wickberg, 307.

[25] East Asia Analytical Unit, 5.

[26] Fitzgerald, 7-8.

[27] Chinben See, 331.

[28] Yen-ching Huang. *Community and Politics: The Chinese in Colonial Singapore and Malaya* (Times Academic Press, 1995), 307.

[29] Fitzgerald, 25.

[30] Leo Suryadinata, 194.

[31] Interview with Go Bon Juan.

[32] This waning of Kuomintang influence in part had to do with the increased attraction to the booming mainland economy, as well as with the growth of pro-independence sentiments in Taiwan. Taiwan sympathizers among the Philippine Chinese are divided or indifferent on the independence issue, and the KMT itself reportedly focuses on its links with the anti-independence factions. In 1997, the KMT faction was expelled from the Federation of Filipino-Chinese Chambers of Commerce and formed their own group – the Filipino Chinese Business Club.

[33] Benito Lim, "A History of Philippine-China Relations" in Aileen San Pablo-Baviera and Lydia N. Yu-Jose, eds. *Philippine External Relations: A Centennial Vista* (Manila: Foreign Service Institute, 1998), 246.

[34] Fitzgerald, 49-50.

[35] Fitzgerald, 47.Fitzgerald made the same observation of Southeast Asian Chinese, in general.

[36] Leo Suryadinata, 203.

[37] East Asia Analytical Unit, 21.

[38] Informant, a Chinese banker.

[39] Carino, 217-218.

[40] Wickberg, 315.

[41] Chinben See, 320.

[42] Ibid., 330.

[43] Ang See, 167.

[44] East Asia Analytical Unit, 204.

Notes: Chapter 8

[1] David Held et al. *Global Transformations: Politics, Economics and Culture*, (Stanford: Stanford University press, 1999), p. 16.

[2] Held et al., pp. 18-20.

[3] James Rosenau, *Distant Proximities: Dynamics beyond Globalization*, (Princeton: Princeton University Press, 2003), p. 11.

[4] Rosenau, pp. 97-105. Rosenau defines "resistant locals" as those people who view globalization as detrimental and seek to reduce its effects on their community, though they do not live in isolation from processes of globalization.

[5] Saskia Sassen, *Globalization and Its Discontents*, (New York: The New Press, 1998), p. XXXI.

[6] U.N. Commission on Human Security, Final Report, p. 46. For example, few countries haves signed the 2002 treaty regulating the treatment of migrant workers.

[7] Stephen Castles and Mark J. Miller, *The Age of Migration: International Population Movements in the Modern World*, (New York: The Guilford Press, 1993), pp.268-270; Held et al., p. 323.

[8] Saska Sassen, *Guests and Aliens*, (New York: The Free Press, 1999), p. 104.

[9] David T. Graham, "The People Paradox: Human Movements and Human Security in a Globilizing World," in. David T. Graham and Nana K. Poku, eds., *Migration, Globalisation, and Human Security* (Routledge: London, 2000), pp. 186, 193.

[10] Amitav Acharya, "Human Security: East Versus West?" Working Paper No. 17, Institute of Defence and Strategic Studies, September 2001, pp. 3-4, 8; Kanti Bajpal, "Human Security: Concept and Measurement," Kroc Institute Occasional Paper #19: OP:1, August 2000, pp. 36-38; Roland Paris, "Human Security: Paradigm Shift or Hot Air?" *International Security*, Vol. 26, No. 2, Fall 2001, p. 100.

[11] Anatoly Vishnevsky, "Migratsiia i bezopasnost': Analiz aspektov vzaimodeistvii," [Migration and Security: Analysis of Interactive Aspects] *Migratsia i bezopasnost' v Rossii*, [Migration and Security in Russia] (Moscow: Moscow Carnegie Center, 2000), p. 36.

[12] Samuel S. Kim, "China's Path to Great Power Status in the Globalization Era," *Asian Perspective*, Vol. 27, No. 1, 2003, pp. 55-58.

[13] Thomas G. Moore, "China and Globalization," in Samuel S. Kim ed., *East Asia and Globalization*, (Lanham, Md.: Rowman & Littlefield, Publishers, Inc.2000), p. 113.

[14] Yunxiang Yan, "Managed Globalization: State Power and Cultural Transition in China," in eds. Peter L. Berger and Samuel Huntington, *Many Globalizations: Cultural Diversity in the Contemporary World*, (New York: Oxford University Press, 2002), p. 20.

[15] Moore, p. 115.

[16] Darryl Crawford, "Chinese Capitalism: Cultures, the Southeast Asian Region and Economic Globalisation," *Third World Quarterly*, Vol. 21, No. 1, pp. 78-9.

[17] Vil'ya G. Gel'bras, *Rossiya v usloviyakh global'noy Kitaiskoi Migratksii* [Russia in the conditions of global Chinese migration], (Moscow: Muravei, 2004), p. 170.

[18] Galina Vitkovskaiia, Zhanna Zayonchkovskaia, and Kathleen Newland, "Chinese Migration into Russia," in ed. Sherman Garnett, *Rapprochement or Rivalry? Russia-China Relations in a Changing Asia*, Washington, DC: Carnegie Endowment for International Peace, 2000, p. 351.

[19] "Special Report: The Other China," *The Economist*, January 10, 2004, p. 59.

[20] Cited in Dorothy J. Solinger, "Jobs and Joining: What's Effect of the WTO for China's Urban Employment," paper prepared for the conference on "The Political and Economic Reforms of Mainland China in a Changing Global Society," National Taiwan University, Taipei, Taiwan, April 25-27, 2002.

[21] "Special Report: The Other China," p.60.

[22] "Chinese Experience Gains, Pressure from WTO Membership," *Renmin Ribao*, March 8, 2002.

[23] Wang Shaoguang, Hu Angang, and Ding Yuanzhu, "Behind China's Wealth Gap," *South China Morning Post*, October 31, 2002, p. 22.

[24] David Murphy, "Nothing to Lose," *Far Eastern Economic Review*, November 7, 2002, p. 3.

[25] Human Rights Watch, *Paying the Price: Worker Unrest in Northeast China,* Vol. 14, No. 6 August 2002, pp. 15-35.

[26] Tang Qinghua, Interview with Chen Xiaoguang, Vice Governor of Jilin Province, "Northeast Plans Rejuvenation," Beijing Review, March 18, 2004, p. 29.

[27] "If the Chinese in Russia Are Driven Away, It Would Cause Inconveniences to Many Local People in Their Daily Lives," *Global Times*, November 28, 2003, in http://www.english.peopledaily.com.cn/data/russia/html.

[28] Xinhua, July 26, 2004.

[29] Text of speech by PRC President Jiang Zemin at the Institute of International Relations of Russia, September 3, 1994, in *FBIS* (PRC), September 6, 1994, p. 18.

[30] Ibid.

[31] The complete text, "Dogovor o dobrososedstve, druzhbe i sotrudnichestve mezhdu Rossiiskoi Federatsiei i Kitaiskoi Narodnoi Respubliki," [Agreement on Good Neighborliness, Friendship, and Cooperation between the Russian Federation and the People's Republic of China] was published by ITAR-TASS in *Rossiiskaia Gazeta* [Russian Newspaper] on July 17, 2001. For an English-language version, see "Text of Sino-Russian Treaty," Xinhua, July 15, 2001.

[32] Vilya G. Gelbras, *Kitaiskaya real'nost' Rossii* [Russia's Chinese Reality], Moscow: Muravei, 2001, p. 39.

[33] Sergei Prikhodko, "My ne dolzhny boyatsya Kitaya [We shouldn't be afraid of China]," *Izvestiya*, March 23, 2004.

[34] Igor' Verba, "Polzuchaia ekspansiia velikogo soseda [The Great Neighbor's Purposeful Expansion]," Source? February 17, 2001.

[35] Interviews, Beijing, October 2002 and April 2004.

[36] Interviews, Beijing and Harbin, March-April 2004.

[37] Li Zhuanxun, "ZhongE quyu jingji hezuo mianlin de wenti" [Current issues in Sino-Russian regional economic cooperation in Xue Jundu and Lu Nanquan eds., *ZhongE Jingji guanxi* [Sino-Russian Economic Relations], Beijing: CASS, 1999, pp. 237-245.

[38] Xia Huanxin, "Siboliya yu yuandong zai ZhongE guanxizhong de zhongyaoxing" [Key aspects of the role of Siberia and in the Russian Far East in Sino-Russian relations], in Xue Jundu and Lu Nanquan, eds. *Eluosi siboliya yu yuandong—guoji zhengzhi jingji guanxi de fazhan* [Russian Siberia

and Far East—the development of international political and economic relations], Beijing: Shijie Zhichi chubanshe, 2002, p. 229.

[39] Interviews, Beijing and Harbin, March-April 2004.

[40] Xiang Biao, "Emigration from China: A Sending Country Perspective," *International Migration*, Vol. 41, No. 3, p. 32.

[41] Ibid.

[42] Zhao Jinping, "Zhongguo dui Eluosi touze de fazhan qushi jiqi tedian," [The development trends and characteristics of China's investment in Russia], in Deng Peng ed. Mianshang mulai de ZhongE jingmao guanxi [Sino-Russian Economic Relations: Review and Prospects], (Beijing: Zhongguo Fazhan Chubanshe, 2003), p. 140.

[43] Yin Hao, "International Labor Migration from China: Policy and Trends," in ed. Yasuko Akase, *A Study on Trade, Investment and International Labor Migration in the APEC Member Economies*, APEC Study Center, Institute of Developing Economies, JETRO, March 2002, p. 104.

[44] Idem, p. 117.

[45] Li Zhuanxun, "Jin nian lai ZhongE pilin diqu zhengzhi jingji guanxi zoushi [Trends in current Sino-Russian border regional political and economic relations]," in Hokkaido Slavic Research Center Seminar Report, "The Sino-Russian Strategic Partnership: Current Views from the Border and Beijing," April 2003, p. 28.

[46] Wang Shengjin, "The Chinese Northeastya laodongyuan kaifa yanjiu [Research on Use of Labor Resources], Northeast Asian Research Center Report, Changchun: Jilin University, 2001, p. 23.

[47] China Eases Its Stand on Russia's Accession to the WTO," *Vedomosti*, June 10, 2002.

[48] Interview, Harbin, March 25, 2004.

[49] Interview, Harbin, March 25, 2004.

[50] Zhao Jinping "Zhongguo dui Eluosi touze...," p. 140.

[51] The two provinces sent a total of 29,789 workers to Russia in 1993, the peak year for labor exchanges, but just 6,980 by 2001. Zhao Jinping, p. 141.

[52] Interview, Beijing, April 2, 2004.

[53] Interview, Harbin, March 23, 2004.

[54] Deng Peng, "Heilongjiang shen fazhan dui E laowu hezuo de zhuyao wenti," [Key questions regarding the development of labor cooperation between Heilongjiang province and Russia], in ed. Deng Peng, *Mianshang mulai de ZhongE jingmao guanxi* [Sino-Russian Economic Relations: Review and Prospects], (Beijing: Zhongguo Fazhan Chubanshe, 2003)" p. 241.

[55] Information Office, Peoples' Government of Heilongjiang Province, *Heilongjiang Today*, Harbin: 2003, p. 44.

[56] At this writing the number of Chinese crossing from Heilongjiang to Russia 2003 has not been published.

[57] Interview, Harbin, March 26, 2004.

[58] James K. Chin, "Reducing Irregular Migration from China," *International Migration*, Vol. 41, No. 3, 2003, p. 56. Interview with Beijing tourism official, April 2, 2004.

[59] Interviews, Beijing, October 2002.

[60] Interviews, Beijing, April 2004.

[61] Interviews, Beijing and Harbin, March 2004.

[62] Vil'ya Gel'bras concludes on the basis of his 2002 survey of Chinese in Khabarovk, Vladivostok, Irkutsk, and Moscow, that a majority of Chinese have no interest in returning home and that the longer they stay in Russia, the harder it will be for them to reintegrate into Chinese society. See Gel'bras, *Rossiya v usloviyakh global'noi Kitaiskoi migratsii*, [Russia under Conditions of Global Chinese Migration] (Moscow: Muravei, 2004), p. 29, 88.

[63] The percentages do not add up to 100% because twenty respondents answered 6, 7, and 8; twenty four answered 7 and 8; one answered 2 and 8; one answered 5, 7, and 8; and one answered 3 and 8.

[64] Robert Jervis first developed the concept of the security dilemma in "Cooperation under the Security Dilemma," *World Politics*, Vol. 30, No. 2, January 1978, pp. 167-174.

Notes: Chapter 9

[1] *Rossiiskaya Gazeta*, 16 September 1995.

[2] Bogaevskaya, A.N., "Chinese Migration to Russia's Far East." http://www.crime.vl.ru/docs/books/book_4.htm.

[3] Diatlov, V.I., Modern Merchant Minorities: A Factor of Stability or a Source of Conflicts? (Chinese and Caucasus Migrants in Irkutsk), Natalis, Moscow, 2000, p.118.

[4] *Izvestia*, 29 November 2003.

[5] Ibid.

[6] *21 shiji jingji baodao*, Guangzhou, April 17, 2003.

[7] *Fengyun renwu*, Beijing, No. 318, 2003, p. 82.

[8] Gelbras, V.G., *Russia's China Reality*, Muravei, Moscow, 2001, p. 17; Larin, A.G., *Chinese in Russia Yesterday and Today: A Historical Outline*, Muravei, Moscow, 2003, p. 150.

[9] *Trud*, 5 December 2003.

[10] Prihodko, Sergei, "Moscow-Pekin: We Need Each Other," *Russia in Global Affairs*, Moscow, 2004, No.2, p.17.

[11] Gelbras, V.G., *Russia in the Context of Global Chinese Migration*, Muravei, Moscow, 2004, pp. 21-24 and 101.

[12] Goncharov, S., "Chinese in Russia: What Are They?" *Far Eastern Affairs*, Moscow, No. 4, 2003, p. 26.

[13] Larin, V.L., "Chinese Factor in Public Opinion of Russian Border Region's Inhabitants: Year 2003," *Far Eastern Affairs*, Moscow, 2004, No 4, p. 66.

[14] Larin, A.G., "Chinese in Russia Yesterday and Today: A Historical Outline," Muravei, Moscow, 2003, p.168.

[15] Gelbras, V.G., *Russia's China Reality*, Muravei, Moscow, 2001, p. 309.

[16] Larin, A.G., *Chinese in Russia Yesterday and Today: A Historical Outline*, Muravei, Moscow, 2003, p.192.

[17] Diatlov, V.I., *Modern Merchant Minorities: A Factor of Stability or a Source of Conflicts? (Chinese and Caucasus Migrants in Irkutsk)*, Natalis, Moscow, 2000, p.185.

[18] Larin, V.L., "A Periphery of the Superpowers: Russia's Far East in Russian-Chinese, Russian-American and Russian-Japanese Relations at the Turn of the Centuries," *Bulletin of the Far Eastern Branch of the Russian Academy of Sciences*, No. 1, 2002, p. 11.

[19] Zayonchkovskaya, Zh.A., "Chinese in Russia: Treat or Salvation?" http://www.eraa.ru//EraaRus/kitay4.htm(2002);Zayonchkovskaya, Zh.A., "Labor Migration to Russia," *Otechestvennie Zapiski*, Moscow, 2003, No. 3, pp. 177-188.

Notes: Chapter 10

[1] See for example, Krebs, Ronald R. and Jack S. Levy, 'Demographic Change and the Sources of International Conflict.' In Myron Weiner and Sharon Stanton Russell, eds. *Demography and National Security* (New York: Berghahn Books, 2001), pp. 62-108.

[2] Estimates and projections taken from the U.S. Census Bureau's International Data Base http://www.census.gov.ipc/www/idbagg.html.

[3] Timothy Heleniak, 'The 2002 Census in Russia: Preliminary Results', *Eurasian Geography and Economics,* Vol. 44, No. 6, 2003, pp 430 – 442.

[4] Heleniak, 'The 2002 Census', p. 433.

[5] C. Becker and D. Bloom (1998), 'The Demographic Crisis in the Former Soviet Union: Introduction', *World Development*, Vol. 26, n. 11, pp. 1913; Victor Perevedentsev (1999), 'The Demographic Situation in Post-Soviet Russia', in *Population Under Duress: The Geodemography of Post-Soviet Russia*, edited by George J. Demko, Grigory Ioffe and Zhanna Zayonchkovskaya (Westview Press), pp. 17-36.

[6] Murray Feshbach, 'A Country on the Verge', *New York Times*, May 31, 2003, A.25; Timothy Heleniak, 'Geographic Aspects of Population Aging in the Russian Federation', *Eurasian Geography and Economics*, 44, No. 5, 2003, pp. 345-367; *Rossiskaya Gazeta*, August 3, 2001, p. 5.

[7] *Novie Izvestiya*, September 30, 2000, p. 1.

[8] V. I. Ilyukhin (1999) *Natsiya-Gosudarstvo-Bezopasnost'*, (Moscow: OOO Tsentrkniga), p. 37.

[9] "The consequences of the deep social crisis are the dramatic reduction of the birth rate and life expectancy in the country, the distortion of the demographic and social structure of society, the depletion of the labour resources as the basis of the development of industries, the weakening of the family as the fundamental element of society and the fall of spiritual, moral and creative potential of the population." National Security Concept of the Russian Federation, approved by Presidential Decree no. 24, January 10, 2000, reprinted in *Rossiskaya Gazeta*, January 18, 2000.

[10] *Rossiskaya Gazeta*, July 11, 2000, pp. 1, 3.

[11] Between 1989 and 2002, "only 27 of Russia's 87 regions (excluding Chechnya and Ingushetia) registered more births than deaths. Most were located outside the central core of the country, in the ethnic homelands in the North Caucasus and the various regions of Siberia and the Far East." Heleniak, 'Geographic Aspects of Population Aging', p. 352.

[12] 'Brochure, 'Main Results of the All-Russian Population Census of 2002'. Accessed from Goskomstat web-site (http://www.gks.ru/).

[13] See: Graeme P. Herd, 'Russia: Systemic Transformation or Federal Collapse?' *Journal of Peace Research*, vol. 36, no. 3, May 1999, pp. 259-269; Graeme P. Herd, 'Russia and the Politics of Putinism', *Journal of Peace Research*, Vol. 38, no. 1, January 2001, pp 117-122; Graeme P. Herd & Anne Aldis, 'Conclusions: Russian Federal Stability and the Dynamics of the twenty-first Century' in Graeme P. Herd & Anne Aldis (eds.), *Russia and the Regions: Strength through Weakness* (London and New York: RoutledgeCurzon, 2003), pp. 267-277.

[14] Kontorovich, Vladimir 'Can Russia Resettle the Far East?' *Post-Communist Economies*, Vol. 12, No. 3, 2000, p. 380.

[15] Christopherr Marsh, Ksaren Albert and James W. Warhola, 'The Political Geography of Russia's 2004 Presidential Election', *Eurasian Geography and Economics*, 45, No. 4, 2004, pp. 262-275:

"Putin received more than 80 per cent of the vote in 16 regions, all of which were ethnic regions, including Chechnya, Dagestan, and Kabardino-Balkaria, even receiving 98.18 per cent in Ingushetia.": 267-268. Thirty one of the eighty nine constituent parts of the Federation (21 republics and 10 autonomous okrugs) have a special status as "homelands."

[16] *Nezavisimaya Gazeta*, Moscow, 30 November 2000.

[17] Simonsen, Sven Gunnar 'Putin's Leadership Style: Ethnocentric Patriotism', *Security Dialogue*, Vol. 31 (3) 2000: 377-380, see p. 378.

[18] Dmitri Glinski, 'Russia and Its Muslims: The Politics of Identity at the International-Domestic Frontier', *East European Constitutional Review*, Vol. 11, No. 2, Winter/Spring 2002, pp. 71-83. Glinski cites *Nezavisimaya Gazeta* claiming without supporting evidence that the number of "ethnic Muslims" in Russia is 13.17 million (9 percent of the population) and of this "only 0.5 million of them pray five times a day, as required," and therefore can be seen as "true Muslims." See: Mikhail Tulsky, 'Islam v neislamskom mire,' *Nezavisimaya Gazeta*, September 29, 2001.

[19] Glinski-Vassiliev, Dmitri 'Islam in Russian Society and Politics: Survival and Expansion', Programme on New Approaches to Russian Security (PONARS), *Policy Memo Series* No. 198 Davis Centre, University of Harvard: http://www.csis.org/ruseura/ponars/policymemos/pm_0198.pdf. Glinski, 'Russia and Its Muslims', pp. 71-83.

[20] Smith, Mark 'Russia and Islam', *Conflict Studies Research Centre*, Directorate General Development and Doctrine, Royal Military Academy Sandhurst, Camberley, Surrey, August 201, F73, pp. 1-12.

[21] *Interfax news agency*, Moscow, 8 July 2002.

[22] Harley Balzer, 'Human Capital and Russian Security in the 21st Century' in Andrew Kuchins, ed. *Russia After the Fall* (Washington, DC: Carnegie Endowment for International Peace, 2002), pp. 163-184; Harry Balzar, 'Demography and Democracy in Russia: Human Capital Challenges to Democratization,' *Demokratatizatsiya: The Journal of Post-Soviet Democratization*, Volume 11, Number 1, Winter 2003 – forthcoming.

[23] Bloom, David E., 'Macroeconomic Consequences of the Russian Mortality Crisis', *World Development*, Vol. 26, No. 11, November 1998, pp. 2013-2027; Buckley, Cynthia & Donahue, Denis 'Promises to Keep: Pension Provision in the Russian Federation', in Mark G. Field & Judyth L. Twigg (eds.), *Russia's Torn Safety Nets: Health and Social Welfare During the Transition*, (New York: St. Martin's Press, 2000), pp. 251-270.

[24] *Interfax news agency*, Moscow, 19 March 2001.

[25] DaVanzo, Julia & Grammich, Clifford *Dire Demographics: Population Trends in the Russian Federation* Santa Monica, Calif.: RAND, MR-1273, 2001, p 67: http://www.rand.org/publications/MR/MR1273/.

[26] *Interfax news agency*, Moscow, 19 April 2001.

[27] *ITAR-TASS news agency*, 2 July 2002.

[28] Gentleman, Amelia 'Wanted; more Russian babies to rescue a fast dying nation', *The Observer*, 31 December 2000, p. 19.

[29] DaVanzo et al., *Dire Demographics*, p 67.

[30] *Interfax news agency*, Moscow, 20 February 2002.

[31] *ITAR-TASS news agency*, Moscow, 21 August 2002.

[32] *Izvestiya*, Moscow, 23 June 2001.

[33] See, for example: Karlusov, V. and A. Kudin. 2002. 'Kitaiskoe prisutstvie na rossiiskom Dal'nem Vostoke: istoriko-ekonomicheskii analiz.' *Problemy Dal'nego Vostoka* 5: 76-87, and Alexseev, Mikhail A. 2001. 'Socioeconomic and Security Implications of Chinese Migration in the Russian Far East,' *Post-Soviet Geography and Economics* 42, no. 2 (2001): 95-114.

[34] SWB SU/4072 B/7, 15 February 2001.

[35] Vishnevskii, A. (1998) 'Demographicheskii potentsial Rossii', *Voprosy Ekonomiki*, n. 5, p. 111

[36] *Noviye Izvestiya*, April 25, 2002, pp. 1, 5.

[37] Nicholas Eberstadt, 'The Russian Federation at the Dawn of the Twenty-First Century: Trapped in a Demographic straight Jacket, N*ational Bureau of Asian Research (*NBR) Analysis, Vol. 15, No. 2, September 2004, p. 7.

[38] Spitsyn, A. (2002), 'Vliyanie Migratsii na demograficheskie protsessy i sotsial'no-ekonomicheskyyu obstanovku v strane - na primiere Oremburskoi Oblasti', *Ekonomist*, n. 3, p. 23.

[39] *Kommersant'*, July 25, 2001, p. 2.

[40] Timothy Heleniak, Migration of the Russian Diaspora After the Breakup of the Soviet Union', *Journal of International Affairs,* Vol. 57, no. 2, Spring 2004, p.114.

[41] Rybakovskii, L. L. (1996), 'Migratsionnyi potentsial russkogo naseleniya v stranakh novogo zarubez'ya', *Sotsiologicheskoe Issledovanie*, n. 11, pp. 31-42.

[42] Timothy Heleniak (2002), 'Russia Beckons but Diaspora Weary', October 1, available at http://www.migrationinformation.org.

[43] For a thorough examination of institutional as well as societal examples of racism in Russia, Moscow Helsinki Group (2002), *Nationalism, Xenophobia and Intolerance in Contemporary Russia*, available at http://www.fsumonitor.com/stories/xenophobia.pdf See also: Meredith L. Roman, 'Making Caucasians Black: Moscow Since the Fall of Communism and the Radicalization of Non-Russians', *Journal of Communist Studies and Transition Politics*, Vol. 18, No. 2, June 2002, pp.1-27.

Notes: Chapter 11

[1] Earlier versions of some sections of the chapter were previously published in Igor Zevelev, *Russia and Its New Diasporas* (Washington, DC: United States Institute of Peace Press, 2001).

[2] For a discussion of the term "diaspora," see Robin Cohen, "Diasporas and the Nation-State: From Victims to Challengers," in the *International Affairs*, Vol. 72, no.3 (1996), pp.507-20. For a discussion of the concept of Russian Diaspora, see Paul Kolstoe, *Russians in the Former Soviet Republics* (Bloomington and Indianapolis: Indiana University press, 1995), pp.1-5. The term is widely used in Russian theoretical discourse, for example, by Aleksandr Solzhenitsyn in his book *The Russian Question at the End of the Twentieth Century* (New York: Farrar, Straus, and Giroux, 1995). It is contained in the programs of many political parties. The term "diaspora" is also used in key governmental documents. Valery Tishkov, the leading Russian expert on ethnic issues, has challenged the traditional understanding of the term "diaspora." See V.A. Tishkov, "Istoricheskii fenomen diaspry (Historical phenomenon of diaspora)," in Yu.A. Polyakov and G.Ya. Tarle (eds), *Natsionalnye diaspory v Rossii i Za Rubezhom* (National diasporas in Russia and abroad) (Moscow: Institut Rossiiskoi istorii, 2001), pp. 9 – 44.

[3] *Rossiiskaya gazeta* (26 Dec. 1997).

[4] *Nezanisimoe voennoe obozrenie* (14 Jan. 2000).

[5] *Nezavisimaya gazeta* (22 Apr. 2000).

[6] There are three categories of residents of the neighboring states who qualify as "compatriots:" (1) Russian citizens residing in the "near abroad;" (2) former Soviet citizens who have not obtained new citizenships (apatriates, or stateless persons, most of whom live in Latvia and Estonia); and (3) those who obtained citizenship of the host country but wish to maintain their own culture and ties with Russia.

[7] *Rossiiskaya gazeta* (11 July 2000).

[8] http://president.kremlin.ru/eng/speeches/2004/12/02/2117_80523.shtml, last accessed December 11, 2004.

[9] See Barry Buzan, Ole Waever, and Jaap de Wilde, *Security: A New Framework of Analysis* (Boulder, CO: Lynne Riener, 1998).

[10] For a comparative analysis of the Soviet Union and the Russian, Ottoman, and Habsburg empires, see Karen Barkey and Mark von Hagen (eds), *After Empire: Multiethnic Societies and Nation-Building* (Boulder, Colo.: Westview, 1997).

[11] See discussion of this issue in Igor Zevelev, *Russia and Its New*, pp. 33-9.

[12] See Alexei Miller, *"Ukrainskii vopros" v politike vlastei i russkom obschestvennom mnenii (vtoraya polovina XIX v.)* [The "Ukrainian Question" in Official Policy and Russian Public Opinion (the Second Half of the XIX Century)] (Sankt-Peterburg: Aleteya, 2000); Igor Zevelev, *Russia and Its New Diasporas*, pp. 277-85.

[13] http://president.kremlin.ru/eng/text/speeches/2004/07/12/1323_74425.shtml, last accessed November 29, 2004.

[14] http://europa/eu.int/comm/external_relations/russia_docs/js_enlarg_270404.htm, last accessed December 8, 2004.

[15] Anthony Smith, *The Ethnic Origin of Nations* (Oxford: Basil Blackwell, 1986), p. 222.

[16] The perils of the Turkish example for Russia were highlighted by Anatol Lieven in his "Restraining NATO: Ukraine, Russia, and the West," in *The Washington Quarterly* (Autumn 1997), pp. 73–4.

[17] See more on the Romantic views of nationhood in Margaret Canovan, *Nationhood and Political Theory* (Cheltenham: Edward Elgar, 1996), pp. 6–9.

[18] Geoffrey Hosking, *Russia: People and Empire* (Cambridge, Mass.: Harvard University Press, 1997), p. 485.

[19] Walker Connor, *Ethnonationalism: the Quest for Understanding* (Princeton: Princeton University Press, 1994), p.29.

[20] Ibid., p.90.

[21] Karen Barkey and Mark von Hagen, "Conclusion," in Barkey and von Hagen (eds), *After Empire*, p. 187.

[22] George Breslauer and Catherine Dale, "Boris Yeltsin and the Invention of a Russian Nation-State," in the *Post-*

Soviet Affairs, Vol. XIII, no. 4 (October-December 1997), p. 332.

[23] See I.P. Blishchenko, A. Kh Abashidze, Ye.V. Martynenko, "Problemy gosudarstvennoy politiki Rossiiskoy Federatsii v otnoshenii sootechesvennikov (Problems of the state policy toward the compatriots)," *Gosudarstvo i pravo*, no.2 (1994), p. 8.

[24] Ibid., p. 9.

[25] http://www.kremlin.ru/eng/speeches/2004/10/30/1024_78792.shtml, last accessed December 12, 2004.

[26] Robert Dahl, "The Concept of Power," *Behavioral Science*, no. 2 (1957), pp. 201-15.

[27] Joseph Nye, *The Paradox of American Power* (New York: Oxford University Press, 2002), pp. 8-12.

[28] See Valery Tishkov, "Istoricheskii fenomen diaspory," pp. 21, 33.

Notes: Chapter 12

[1] Pal Kolsto, "Ethnicity and Subregional Relations: The Role of Russian Diasporas," in Renata Dwan and Oleksandr Pavliuk, eds., *Building Security in the New States of Eurasia: Subregional Cooperation in the Former Soviet Space* (Armonk, NY: M.E. Sharpe, 2000), note 38, 225.

[2] Albert O. Hirschman, *Exit, Voice, and Loyalty: Responses to Decline in Firms, Organizations, and States* (Cambridge: Harvard University Press, 1970).

[3] Cited in S. I. Kuznetsova, *Russkie v Tsentral'noi Azii* (Moscow: Izdatel'stvo "Gumanitarii," 2002), p. 29.

[4] Lowell W. Barrington, Erik S. Herron, and Brian D. Silver, "The Motherland is Calling: Views of Homeland among Russians in the Near Abroad," *World Politics* 55 (January 2003), 290-313.

[5] Kolsto, 219.

[6] The KRO was formed in 1933 and has the goal of rebuilding Russia in its historical borders. Its leader, Dmitrii Rogozin, served as Chairman of the Duma International Relations Committee and has been a vocal advocate of the rights of Russians abroad. Rogozin is currently leader of the Rodina fraction in the Duma. For more information on KRO, see Alan Ingram, "'A Nation Split into Fragments': The Congress of Russian Communities and Russian Nationalist Ideology," *Europe-Asia Studies* 51 (1999), 687-704.

[7] Organizatsii sootechestvennikov za rubezhom (http://www.ln.mid.ru/ns-dgpch.nsf/org). Not all of the organizations are purely Slavic. In Kyrgyzstan, for example, there is the Chechen Culture Center "Bart" and the Association of People's of Dagestan "Sadara."

[8] A. Ponamarev, "10 let 'Lad,'" *Lad* no. 9 (November 2002).

[9] U.S. Department of State Human Rights Report—Kazakhstan 2003 (http://www.state.gov/g/drl/rls/hrrpt/2003/27845.htm).

[10] Vitaly V. Naumkin, "Russian Policy Toward Kazakhstan," in Robert Legvold, ed., *Thinking Strategically: The Major Powers, Kazakhstan, and the Central Asian Nexus* (Cambridge: MIT Press, 2003).

[11] AP (4 March 2004), BBC Monitoring Central Asia Unit (2 April 2004).

[12] *Financial Times* (19 February 2004); Global News Wire - Asia Africa Intelligence Wire (29 February 2004).

[13] Obshchestvenno-pravovaia ezhenedel'naia gazeta 'Delo #' (http://delo.to.kg/2004/25/01.shtml).

[14] Sergei Blagov, "Russian 'separatists' highlight ethnic tensions," Asia Times Online (16 January 2000, http://www.atimes.com/c-asia/BF16Ag01.html); Liz Fuller, "Trial of 'Separatists' Highlights Plight of Kazakhstan's Russians," RFE-RL Analysis, in Eurasianet.org (http://www.eurasianet.org/resource/kazakhstan/hypermail/200005/0013.html).

[15] Oleg Popov, "Na puti k konsolidatsii Rossiiskoi nastii (razmushleniia s Kongressa sooteches tvennikov)," *Materik* (15 June 2002), http://www.materik.ru/index.php?section = analitics & bulid =14&bulsectionid=918

[16] Kolsto, 209.

[17] Sally Cummings, "Eurasian Bridge or Murky Waters Between East and West: Ideas: Identity and

Output in Kazakhstan's Foreign Policy," *Journal of Communist Studies and Transition Politics* 19 (September 2003), 142.

[18] Paul Goble, "Compounding a Demographic Disaster," RFE/RL (20 November 2000).

[19] Zharmukhamed Zardykhan, "Russians in Kazakhstan and Demographic Change: Imperial Legacy and the Kazakh Ways of Nation Building," *Asian Ethnicity* 5 (February 2004), 70-72.

[20] UN Office for the Coordination of Humanitarian Affairs, IRIN (19 June 2003), http://www.irinnews.org/print.asp?ReportID=34862;

[21] U.S. State Department Human Rights Report—Turkmenistan, 2003; and BBC News (9 July 2003).

[22] See Farangis Najibullah, "Russia/Turkmenistan: Are Tensions Growing Between Moscow and Ashgabat?" RFE/RL (30 May 2003), http://www.globalsecurity.org/military/library/news/2003/05/mil-030530-rfel-160000.htm

[23] Sergei Blagov, "Russia Acts Aggressively to Enhance Energy Position in Turkmenistan," Eurasianet.org (26 February 2004), http://www.eurasianet.org/departments/business/articles/eav022604.shtml

[24] "Osnovnye napravleniia podderzhki sootechestvennikov," Russian Federation Ministry of Foreign Affairs website, http://www.ln.mid.ru/ns-dgpch.nsf/podd

[25] ITAR-TASS (25 September 2003).

[26] This foreign policy strategy is patterned after that of Aleksandr Gorchakov, Aleksandr II's foreign minister who directed a skillful diplomacy after Russian had been weakened by the Crimean War and was trying to retain its great power status in a tumultuous reform period. See Igor S. Ivanov, *The New Russian Diplomacy* (Washington, D.C.: Brookings, 2002), 26-28.

[27] The foreign policy aspect of Russian ethnicity has been least important in Uzbekistan, given Karimov's stubborn resistance to Russian encroachment and the small proportion of Russians in that country.

Index

N

O

P